Illinois Hiking and Backpacking Trails

Revised Edition

**Walter G. Zyznieuski and
George S. Zyznieuski**

Southern Illinois University Press
Carbondale and Edwardsville

This book is dedicated to our children, Nicholas and Elisha, to our nieces and nephews (Angela, Markus, Tiffany, Lindsey, Wills, Tegan, and in memory of Kenneth Francis, Jr.), as well as to our cousins' children, both here in Illinois and around the world. We hope that in this highly urbanized and mechanized society our children and their children will always be able to hike and explore the trails found in this book and other hiking trails throughout the world.

We would especially like to dedicate this book to our wives, Deb and Laura, who lovingly bore with us while we traveled, compiled, and wrote this revised edition.

Copyright © 1993 by Walter G. Zyznieuski and
    George S. Zyznieuski
All rights reserved
Printed in the United States of America
Designed by Kathleen Giencke
Production supervised by New Leaf Studio

96 95 94 93   4 3 2 1

Library of Congress Cataloging-in-Publication Data

Zyznieuski, Walter.
    Illinois hiking and backpacking trails / Walter G. Zyznieuski and George S. Zyznieuski. — Rev. ed.
        p.   cm.
    Includes bibliographical references.
    1. Hiking—Illinois—Guidebooks.   2. Backpacking—Illinois—Guidebooks.   3. Trails—Illinois—Guidebooks.
4. Illinois—Guidebooks.   I. Zyznieuski, George, 1961–   .
II. Title.
GV199.42.I3Z98   1993
917.7304'43—dc20   92-34532
ISBN 0-8093-1752-4   CIP

The paper used in this publication meets the minimum requirements of American National Standard for Information Sciences—Permanence of Paper for Printed Library Materials, ANSI Z39.48-1984. ♾

Contents

Appendixes

Illustrations

Preface

We are amazed at some of the remarks that we continue to hear from friends and acquaintances when we inform them of the existence of our book on Illinois hiking trails. Questions we repeatedly are asked include: (1) Are there really many hiking trails in Illinois? (2) Are there any trails with any distance to them? (3) Are the hiking trails challenging? and (4) Are they really that scenic? Well, the answer to all of these questions is yes!

Here, in the revised edition of *Illinois Hiking and Backpacking Trails*, we have completely updated our book. We describe in detail sixty-nine hiking trails that are 4 miles in length or longer. These trails total over 809 miles. In addition to the detailed trail descriptions, we have also identified other trails located throughout the state that for one reason or another were not included in our book.

Since the first edition was published, many changes have occurred either along the trails or at the parks or forests where the trails were located. To update our book we contacted the headquarters of each park and forest to obtain detailed and up-to-date information. We also revisited all of the trails that required remapping, and of course we hiked all new trails completely.

An important milestone was reached in Illinois when Congress passed an act in 1990 which created seven Wilderness Areas in the Shawnee National Forest totaling over 26,000 acres. These areas are protected forever, with no development or motorized vehicles permitted. A few of the trails described in our book go through these Wilderness Areas. Appendixes in this guide provide additional information on these places, while more specific information may be obtained by writing to the Shawnee National Forest headquarters in Harrisburg, Illinois.

We would like to point out a few items that are significant and that the hiker should prepare for or be aware of before venturing out on a trail.

First, many of the trails are located in floodplains or low-lying areas. We caution the hiker to: (1) be prepared for emergencies during inclement weather conditions; and (2) to call ahead to find out what the trail conditions are. Many times we have traveled to a trail only to find out that the trail was inundated or too muddy to hike.

Second, during the winter months, some parks, facilities, or even parts of a trail itself may be closed. Always check with the park or trail staff for trail conditions.

Third, believe it or not, some of the trails are along steep bluffs or in canyons. Be prepared for slippery trail conditions and stay away from the edges of cliffs. In addition, be aware of the possibilities of flash floods occurring in canyons.

Fourth, we've noticed that trail markers, trailboards, and park facilities tend to change periodically. We have attempted to provide you with the most up-to-date information we could obtain, but due to circumstances beyond our control, additional changes may have occurred.

Fifth, even though we have provided drawings of a given trail layout, many times the park also has trail maps that the hiker may want to obtain.

Sixth, some state parks in Illinois offer the "Rent-A-Camp" program. This program provides the user with the basic camping supplies such as tent, cot, grill, light, fire extinguisher, and broom and pan. Rent-A-Camp fees are just a small additional amount more than the camping fees. For more information on which state parks offer this program, contact the Illinois Department of Conservation.

Seventh, hikers should be aware that some trail areas may be open to different kinds of hunting activities during certain times of the year. Please contact the site superintendent for hunting information. For good reason, hikers may want to avoid certain areas during various hunting seasons.

And lastly, a fairly new disease is being transmitted that can cause significant illness to hikers and outdoor enthusiasts—Lyme disease. This illness is transmitted to individuals by the bite of the deer tick. Although not yet widespread in Illinois, this disease has been reported here. Hikers should take appropriate action when out in the woods including tucking pants into socks, wearing long-sleeve shirts, and wearing hats. Also conduct a complete and thorough check of yourself after hiking. You may contact your local health department or the Illinois Department of Public Health for further information on Lyme disease.

We hope that you get a chance to hike and explore the many trails described in our book. These trails can be hiked by the entire family or, for the more hardy soul, extended backpacking trips can be planned. We hope you enjoy Illinois' hiking and backpacking trails as much as we have!

Walter G. Zyznieuski
George S. Zyznieuski

Acknowledgments

Without the help of many individuals and organizations, this revised edition could not have come into being.

We would like to thank Thomas J. Campbell for providing us with legal services and advice.

Thanks to Mike Aherin, Danny Barker, and Gary Bensema for hiking several trails with us, as well as providing comments and suggestions concerning our text. Thanks also to Wills Nixon for hiking with us and providing trail information.

Thanks to Tom Skelly and Bill Martz for pointing out revisions needed for this new edition and for recommending additional information needed for the hiker.

Many thanks to Michelle Bodamer and Kathy Barker for editing and reviewing our text, Evan Kurrasch, former state coordinator, and Mike Ulm, present state coordinator, of Rails-to-Trails Conservancy of Illinois, for trail information, and Arlyn Sherwood for reviewing our text and providing us with accurate map-ordering information. Special thanks to Gloria Jarvis for her typing assistance.

Special thanks to Allan Greene, who is with the Shawnee National Forest, for meeting with us and providing valuable information on hiking trails and the Wilderness Areas in the Shawnee National Forest. Thanks to Joe Jobst, director of Humiston Woods Nature Center, for providing us trail information on the center as well as hiking some trails with us. Additional thanks to Jeffrey Tish, chief naturalist of Rock Springs Center, for providing us with trail and park information, and for taking time to meet with us.

In addition to these individuals, we wish to thank all of the other park site superintendents and administrators who have reviewed our original trail descriptions and have provided us with up-to-date information for their parks or trails. Without their help, this revised edition could have not been accurate and up-to-date.

And lastly, we would like to thank Southern Illinois University Press for believing in our work and publishing the original edition as well as this new version of *Illinois Hiking and Backpacking Trails*.

Introduction

Hiking is one of the fastest growing, most popular, and healthiest recreational activities in America today. Increasingly, various federal, state, and local departments, organizations, and groups have been promoting hiking outings or developing new trails for the public to enjoy.

There are many reasons why the general public has gained a new interest in hiking. First, hiking offers a person the chance to get away from worries, other people, noise, and pollution, as well as a chance to relax and enjoy the solitude that may be found along the trail. Many times we've hiked all day and not seen another person on the trail. (This may also be explained partly by the public not knowing that the trail exists in the first place!)

Second, people today want to keep in shape and stay healthy. Hiking—especially long distance hikes or extended backpacking trips—is an excellent way to stay fit and to exercise the cardiovascular system. Third, many people want a chance to travel and explore the lands, historical areas, and unique geological formations. Illinois has many fine archaeological, historical, and forested and wild areas that are not frequently visited. By getting out in the woods on a trail, the hiker has the chance to explore, discover, and enjoy these beautiful sites that never will be seen from inside cars. Fourth, hiking is usually free; therefore, it is a cheap form of recreation. And finally, hiking is a sport that may be enjoyed by all age groups. Several times we've seen both scout troops and retired couples out hiking for exercise.

Some of our experiences, including many bad ones, led us to write a guidebook for hiking trails in Illinois. There were many reasons why we saw a need for this book. These include the need for the public to know where the hiking trails are located in the state, how to get there, how long the trails are, if trail maps are available, what trail rules and regulations are in effect, and where

they may write or call to request additional trail information.

Since there are numerous groups and federal, state,
and local organizations which manage or own hiking
trails in the state, the information on these trails is
located in a variety of sources; the material was not
organized into one single guide. *Illinois Hiking and
Backpacking Trails* was written specifically to fill this
gap and to provide appropriate and up-to-date trail
information to interested parties.

This book includes information about sixty-nine
trails. For our purposes these trails had to be at least
4 miles in length or connected with another trail to total
4 miles. The trails also had to be marked either with
paint blazes or posts along the trail, or with a trail
marker, or with a trailboard at the trailhead.

The trails are located at state parks, conservation
areas and nature preserves, Shawnee National Forest,
county and municipal parks, forest preserves, conservation districts, not-for-profit organizations, Corps of Engineers property, and along utility and railroad rights-
of-way. The authors did not hike any Boy Scout trails
(unless they were part of an existing trail), because they
were usually located at their scout camps where restrictions are put on public access or the trails were actually
roads for their entire length. In addition, many times the
scout trails are part of a trail that has another name (e.g.,
the Red Caboose Trail is really the Illinois Prairie Path).
Horse trails, bike trails, or fire lanes were not hiked
either unless the organization or park noted that the trail
was for hiking also. This does not prohibit the outdoor
enthusiasts from hiking there.

The state was divided into three regions to catego-
rize the trails—northern, central, and southern Illinois—
and the book is arranged according to those divisions.
Each of the trails described has the trail length, location,
county, highway map coordinates, appropriate topographical map, history, trail description, facilities, permits needed, trail rules and regulations, mailing address
for additional information, and a trail map which we
have drawn for each trail (see "Map Information"). We
have also included some general directions by which you

can locate the parks and trails; in some instances there may be additional access routes to the park or trail.

In addition, a bibliography lists additional books related to the subject.

The Illinois Highway Map Coordinates listed under each trail description are those that are seen on the State of Illinois Highway Map issued by the Illinois Department of Transportation. Should the hiker have another map of Illinois that was not issued by the state, the map coordinates may not necessarily match. All of the trail histories were taken directly from the appropriate park booklet or pamphlet that was issued for that particular trail.

Additionally, we have listed the various park permits required under "Permits Required" in the trail description. Most state parks and some other areas require a camping permit; however, you do not need to reserve or purchase these permits in advance. In most instances, after you have chosen a campsite, a park employee will come to your site to collect the appropriate fees and issue you your camping permit.

In order for the hiker to enjoy the hike comfortably, Part 1 recommends what the hiker needs to bring along on the trail and where the hiker can obtain additional information. Part 2 lists trails in northern Illinois; Part 3 lists trails in central Illinois; and Part 4 lists trails in southern Illinois.

By following the information presented in this book and by taking our advice, you should be able to arrive at the trail properly. We hope that you enjoy some of the beautiful hiking trails in Illinois as much as we did. Get out and enjoy Illinois' hiking trails!

PART I

General Information

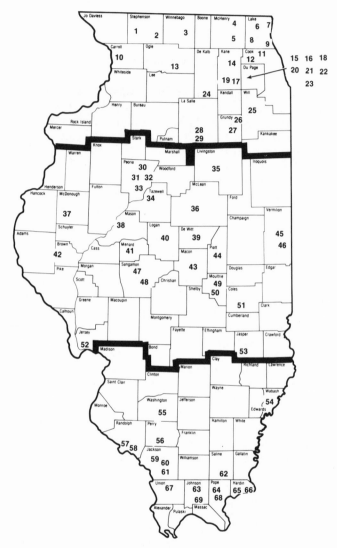

Figure 1. Hiking trails in Illinois

Trail Locations

Illinois is a large state encompassing 55,947 square miles. The state is 385 miles long from north to south and about 218 miles wide. Although Illinois is not noted for its large tracts of forested lands, there are some unique and beautiful areas that would astonish many people. The Illinois Department of Conservation (IDOC) and the U.S. Forest Service both own and administer large acreages of land that offer many trails for recreation. The IDOC owns and administers 120 recreation sites in the state totaling over 155,000 acres in size. These include both state parks and conservation areas. The U.S. Forest Service owns and administers recreation sites in the Shawnee National Forest in southern Illinois. The Shawnee National Forest covers over 260,000 acres. In addition to offering hiking trails, these recreation areas offer facilities such as campgrounds, picnic areas, and playground equipment; many areas also allow swimming, fishing and boating, and hunting.

The hiking trails in Illinois are scattered throughout the state and vary in length from short nature trails to unmarked trails that measure 80 miles. These trails vary in difficulty from very easy to extremely difficult. Figure 1 shows the location by counties of trails described in this book and how the state is divided into three regions. The numbers on the map in Figure 1 correspond to the total number of trails described in this book (69) and are arranged in descending order of location, from 1 in the northwest tip of Illinois to 69 in the southeast part of southern Illinois.

Three other figures, located at the beginning of each section, show the locations of the trails in that division. (Please note that in cases where a trail covers two or more counties, the map indicates only the county in which the trail begins.)

For convenience, the state was divided into three regions: northern, central, and southern. The boundaries for these regions do not correspond to any specific regional boundary, but were arbitrarily determined by the authors. There are twenty-nine trails located in northern Illinois; twenty-four trails in central Illinois; and sixteen trails in southern Illinois.

The majority of the trails throughout the state are located at state parks, recreation areas, forests, and historic sites administered by various state agencies. Thirty-five of sixty-nine trails are located at state-run facilities. While this may be said for the state as a whole, it is not necessarily true for specific regions in the state.

In northern Illinois, most of the trails are located at forest preserves, conservation districts, and park districts. Fifteen of the twenty-nine trails are located at these facilities.

In central Illinois, the majority of the hiking trails are located at state parks, forests, or conservation areas. Fourteen of the twenty-four trails are located at these areas.

In southern Illinois, nine of the sixteen hiking trails are located at state parks or forests. The remaining trails are located within the Shawnee National Forest boundaries. In fact, perhaps the most challenging and difficult trail described in this book, the River-to-River Trail, is located in the Shawnee National Forest.

In addition, numerous hiking trails in the state are located at municipal parks, parks owned by not-for-profit organizations, nature preserves, boy and girl scout camps, other park district lands, and county parks. Appendix J lists other trails that may be found in northern, central, and southern Illinois, their lengths, and who owns/administers these trails. The list in Appendix J includes trails that are less than 4 miles, unmarked trails, horse trails, bike trails, and scout trails.

Since most of the trails are located in state parks or recreation areas or in the Shawnee National Forest, it would be appropriate to list the rules and regulations that are in effect for these areas. Appendix A lists the rules and regulations that must be followed while at state parks or conservation areas. Appendix C lists the rules and regulations for recreation sites in the Shawnee National Forest. Some of the trails lie within state nature preserves. These areas are protected by law; therefore, the hiker needs to know the appropriate rules and regulations which are in effect for these areas. Appendix B lists the regulations that must be followed at nature preserves. Appendix E lists the uses and prohibitions in Wilderness Areas.

In addition, the appropriate rules and regulations for the other hiking trails included in the book are listed under the trails section titled "Park Rules and Regulations."

Trail Signs and Markers

The hiking trails listed in this book were included because they were all identified with a trail sign or some other sort of trail marking. Numerous other hiking trails also exist in Illinois but may be unmarked, or the markings may change periodically and may confuse the hiker. Generally, these types of trails are not maintained and are undeveloped.

The trails described here are marked either with trailboards, which may be found at the trailhead, along the trail, or at a trail intersection, or with trail markers, such as paint blazes on trees and rocks, or wooden or metal markers displaying some appropriate symbol.

Our reasons for describing only marked, established hiking trails were that: (1) additional information is usually available for the marked hiking trails; (2) many times the unmarked trail may be obscure, overgrown with vegetation, or joined with other unmarked trails; and (3) most important, the public needs information about the location of existing, developed trails. Trail signs and markers are the hiker's "road signs" in the woods.

While each trail may have a trail sign or marker, not all of them are marked the same. Even the state park and conservation areas differ on the type of trail markers used. Some parks or areas administered by the same agency may have the same marking system. For instance, the trails in the Shawnee National Forest are usually all marked with white paint blazes along the trail and usually have a hiker sign identifying the hiking trail location.

Some trailboards provide very detailed trail descriptions; others may show just a layout of the trail and the trail name. Trailboards typically include some of the following information: (1) trail name; (2) trail length; (3) park boundaries or layout; (4) facilities available on the trail; (5) rules in effect on the trail; (6) the organizational name; and (7) trail difficulty.

Most trail markers are wooden or metal posts, usually three feet high; they are found at various locations on the trail and will usually have a symbol of a hiker, biker, horseback rider, or cross-country skier on them. This symbol may be made out of wood, metal, or plastic.

One problem with these markers is that many times they may be missing or may have been vandalized. On several occasions the authors noted missing posts or symbols. If this situation occurs along the trail, you should report it to the organization in charge of the trail. Each trail description has the address for the agency in charge of the trail. The agency should be informed if there are any problems on or along the trail.

As an alternative to symbols, paint blazes are used along some trails. These blazes may be either painted on the trees or on other objects, such as large rocks or

High Point trailboard, Mississippi Palisades State Park

Trail marker, Mississippi Palisades State Park

bluffs. The paint blaze will usually be in the shape of a diamond. Paint blazes stand out better on the trail, especially if they are properly marked. Typical paint blaze colors marking the trail include white, orange, and blue.

It should be pointed out that not every trail has a trailboard. Many times there might be just a metal hiker sign or a wooden post marking the trail's beginning. In addition, the trail blazes along the trails may not be uniform along the entire length of the trail. Many times the authors discovered missing trail blazes or blazes that were marked on the wrong trail. Any trails which were marked incorrectly or sparingly are identified as such in the trail description.

In order to keep from getting lost while hiking, either due to improper trail marking or other reasons, the hiker should always carry a trail map and compass (more on maps in the next section). A compass is critical, and the hiker should carry one at all times. In some situations the hiker may have strayed off the trail or started hiking down the wrong trail spur. By using a compass, the hiker should be able to realize that he is straying off course. Some of the longer trails, such as the ones found in the Shawnee National Forest, may be easy to get lost on because some areas of the trail may not be marked correctly or the trail signs may not exist.

The bibliography lists some books that discuss the correct ways to mark trails and how to use a map and compass. In addition, local or university orienteering clubs often sponsor classes for basic map reading or sponsor orienteering meets; both are excellent ways to learn how to use a compass and a topographic map.

Map Information

Every trail described in this book has a trail map. The maps were redrawn from the United States Geological Survey's (U.S.G.S.) topographic quadrangle maps and the U.S. Forest Service Quadrangle Maps. Some trail maps were modified from park maps that were provided, and this will be indicated on the bottom of those maps accordingly. Additional information was added to each of these maps to identify pertinent areas for the hiker.

While trail maps were available for most of the trails and parks hiked by the authors, these maps usually were not marked or drawn correctly. For instance, many times the trail layouts seen on park brochures are outdated, contain errors, or simply do not list the trail or new trails.

One of the reasons this book was written was to provide the hiker with an accurate and detailed map which would show the trail layout and length correctly. In order to check map accuracy, the authors hiked each trail. We then used a topographic map measurer to measure the trail mileage for each map. The trail mileage we have listed under the trail description is what we measured. All of the trail maps were then drawn in a similar style. This makes reading the maps a little easier and more convenient for the hiker.

Each trail description lists the name of the topo-graphical (or "topo") map on which the trail is located. These maps are issued by the U.S.G.S. and have the contour lines, streams, lakes, roads, and buildings that may be found in that area. Appendix G lists agencies from which one may order topographic maps. The U.S.G.S. published an index for topographic and other maps for Illinois, as well as a catalog of topographic maps. The

U.S.G.S. also has a pamphlet which explains the symbols for topographic maps. The index shows the location of the topographic map and name. The index and the pamphlet are both free and may be ordered from the U.S.G.S. at the address listed in Appendix G.

Appendix G also lists agencies from which one may order other maps for Illinois, including county maps, township maps, and general statewide maps. Some maps, such as the county road maps, may prove to be useful for locating a particular road which may lead to the park or trail junction.

If the hiker does not want to order the topographic map for the trail, various libraries throughout the state have Illinois topographic maps in their map sections for the public to view or borrow. Appendix H lists some libraries in Illinois which have Illinois topographic maps.

The U.S. Forest Service issues Quadrangle Maps for the Shawnee National Forest. These maps are the same scale as the topographic maps (1:24,000). The Forest Service Quadrangle Maps have contour lines, roads, lakes, rivers, and buildings; Forest Service areas and private property are differentiated. These maps also have the locations of wildlife openings and ponds with their corresponding numbers. This proves to be very useful to the hiker because the wildlife openings and ponds are all marked on wooden posts next to the respective areas. When a hiker sees one of these posts next to a wildlife opening or pond, he may refer to the corresponding number on the map and then know his location.

All of the trails described for the Shawnee National Forest have the correct Quadrangle Map listed for that trail.

These maps may be obtained from the district Forest Service office that is listed at the end of the particular trail description. These maps will have to be purchased for a small fee. All U.S. Forest district offices for the Shawnee National Forest are listed in Appendix G.

In some instances, a trail in the Shawnee National Forest may cross the boundaries of two different Forest Service district offices. When this occurs one will have to order the appropriate Shawnee Maps from both offices. For instance, the River-to-River Trail crosses two Forest

Service district boundaries. In this situation the hiker will have to request maps from two different district offices (Vienna and Elizabethtown).

While the maps in this book are accurate, they do not have any contour lines drawn on them. These maps were drawn as a general guide for the hiker. To supplement the maps in this book, the appropriate topographic map or Quadrangle Map should be used to identify the elevations on the trail.

Weather Patterns in Illinois

Illinois lies midway between the Continental Divide and the Atlantic Ocean, some 500 miles north of the Gulf of Mexico. The climate is continental, with cold winters, warm summers, and frequent fluctuations of temperature, humidity, cloudiness, and wind.

During the spring and summer months, storm systems are frequent, with precipitation averaging about 38 inches a year. The amounts of precipitation vary across the state and may fluctuate from year to year. Northern Illinois typically receives about 34 inches a year and southern Illinois about 46 inches a year.

During the fall, winter, and spring, precipitation tends to fall uniformly over large regions in the state. During the summer, precipitation occurs principally as brief thunderstorms, affecting relatively small areas.

Illinois is about 385 miles long from north to south and about 218 miles wide. Temperature variations between northern and southern Illinois exist because of latitude difference. Winter temperatures may show a contrast of approximately 14 degrees Fahrenheit between the northern and southern sections of the state. During July, the range of mean temperatures across the state is about 6 degrees as both temperature and sunshine are more uniform. Northern Illinois averages about twenty days a year when the temperature is over 90 degrees, while the west-central and southern portions of the state average about fifty days of this temperature.

The length of the state causes the northern part of the state to average cooler and drier than the south. Annual precipitation is greater in the extreme south than further north, with most of the excess precipitation occurring during winter and early spring.

Snowfall also varies across Illinois, ranging from 9 inches in the south to more than 33 inches in the northern part of the state. Snowfalls of 1 inch or more occur on an average of ten to twelve days per year in the extreme north to three to four days in the southern part of the state.

Following are the average statewide temperatures in degrees Fahrenheit:

January—27.5	July—76.0
February—31.1	August—74.9
March—40.2	September—67.1
April—53.5	October—56.7
May—63.3	November—42.4
June—72.6	December—31.0

Hikers should be concerned with and always aware of the current weather conditions. Many major metropolitan areas in the state have local phone numbers available for the current or extended weather conditions for that area. Appendix I lists telephone numbers for some of these areas in the state. The hiker may call any of these numbers to find out what the weather conditions may be for that area that day.

By closely observing the weather and developing weather patterns, the hiker can be prepared to keep warm and dry. The last thing the hiker needs to experience is hypothermia or heat exhaustion. If you get wet, try to get into dry clothes as quickly as possible; if you get overheated, stop hiking, rest, and cool down your body temperature.

When in doubt, always carry spare clothes in case the weather conditions change. Always be prepared for the worst! The next section outlines the clothing articles the hiker needs to take along while hiking.

Books listed in the bibliography discuss first-aid and outdoor survival skills.

Recommendations for Hiking

Many of the trails described in this book may be hiked in one day, some within two hours. Of course, trails such as the River-to-River, at 57 miles in length, will take a few days to hike.

Not every trail or park in Illinois has the same facilities available along the trail. Common sense tells us that restrooms will not be found every two miles along a trail; for that matter, neither will water pumps. Some of the trails described in this book have facilities available along the trail at strategic locations while other trails have no facilities at all.

The trail descriptions list what will be found along each trail, at the trailhead, and within the park itself. Whether the hiker is out on the trail for a few hours or a few days, he will need to carry some essential items or supplies. This section identifies what the hiker needs to carry.

We have relied on our own years of hiking experience to compile the list of recommended items to carry when hiking. We believe the list provides the minimum items which the hiker should bring on every trail. We tried to structure the list so that the items listed would usually be on hand and would provide the hiker with a safe and comfortable outing.

In addition, we also will list optional equipment which the hiker may choose to carry, depending on the situation, trail, and season. We also realize that this list is not mandatory; the hiker should feel free to carry additional items to suit his own personal needs.

The list that follows is geared toward the day-hiker, or the hiker who is not planning to camp overnight on the trail. Although there are trails in Illinois which are sufficiently long for backpacking purposes, the majority are used by day-hikers, or those who complete the trails that same day. Also, numerous books cover the topic of equipment needs for backpackers, and a few are listed in the bibliography.

The following list is divided into two categories: items which the hiker should carry at all times (essential items) and optional items.

Essential Items: The first essential item which the hiker will need to have will be something in which to put all of his supplies. This usually will be a rucksack or daypack. Most daypacks are made of lightweight material and are inexpensive. Almost every sporting goods store or department store sporting goods section carries daypacks.

Proper footwear and clothing are also important items for the hiker to consider. Sometimes the shoe which the hiker wears while hiking may make the difference between a fabulous hiking experience and a disaster. A sturdy, lightweight boot is recommended for hiking, especially for any extended outings. Hiking boots available today are especially lightweight and extremely durable. And while it is difficult to list all the pieces of clothing the hiker should wear (depending on the season), we offer a few pointers. One of the most important things to remember when choosing the proper clothing is to wear clothing in layers: that is, wear loose clothing in a layering system. Should you become warm while hiking, you may shed a piece of your clothing.

An essential item of clothing that needs to be packed is a rain jacket or poncho. This piece of clothing is critical to have on the trail at all times, especially on long-distance hikes. Many times we have started hiking on a beautiful sunny morning only to be caught in a thunderstorm later that afternoon. Rain gear which is light, waterproof, and breathable may be purchased.

Other items that the hiker should bring along include: identification, toilet paper, small shovel, sunglasses, hat (wide brim for the summer and wool for the winter), map(s), compass, lip balm, knife, matches (preferably waterproof) or butane lighters, flashlight, pencil, paper, water bottle, water purifier tablets, first-aid kit (aspirin, moleskin for blisters, antiseptic, tweezers, adhesive bandage strips, medicines for allergies, etc.), and whistle (should you become lost or in trouble).

Optional Items: Optional items include items or supplies that may be needed in a particular season of the year, or items the hiker may find important but which are not critical to carry on each and every trail. Optional items include: camera, binoculars, additional clothing, swimsuit, gloves, guidebooks (flowers, trees, animals, geology), fishing gear, cup, sunburn lotion, snacks, space blanket, garbage bag, sewing kit (scissors, needle and thread, safety pins), and mosquito repellent.

PART II

Hiking Trails in Northern Illinois

NORTHERN ILLINOIS

1. Lake Le-Aqua-Na State Park
2. Pecatonica Prairie Path
3. Rock Cut State Park
4. Glacial Park and Nippersink Trail
5. Moraine Hills State Park
6. Des Plaines River Trail (Lake County)
7. Illinois Beach State Park
8. Lakewood Forest Preserve
9. Edward L. Ryerson Conservation Area
10. Mississippi Palisades State Park
11. Des Plaines River Trail (Cook County)
12. Palatine Trail
13. Castle Rock State Park
14. The Great Western Trail
15. The Illinois Prairie Path
16. West Du Page Woods Forest Preserve
17. Virgil L. Gilman Nature Trail
18. Blackwell Forest Preserve
19. Fox River Bike Trail
20. Herrick Lake Forest Preserve
21. The Morton Arboretum
22. Greene Valley Forest Preserve
23. Waterfall Glen Forest Preserve
24. Shabbona Lake State Park
25. Pilcher Park
26. Illinois and Michigan Canal Trail
27. Goose Lake Prairie State Natural Area
28. Starved Rock State Park
29. Matthiessen State Park

Figure 2. Hiking trails in northern Illinois

1. Lake Le-Aqua-Na State Park

Trail Length: 4.2 miles (6.7 kilometers)

Location: Lake Le-Aqua-Na State Park is located three miles north of Lena and fifteen miles northwest of Freeport. To reach the park, take State Route 20 west out of Freeport to Route 73. Proceed north on Route 73 through the city of Lena and turn left on Lena Street. Proceed on Lena Street for five blocks to Lake Road. Turn right (north) and go on Lake Road for two miles to the park entrance.

County: Stephenson

Illinois Highway Map Coordinates: A-5

U.S.G.S. Topographical Map Name and Scale: Lena, 1:24,000

Hours Open: The park is open every day of the year except Christmas Day and New Year's Day. At certain times of the year, due to freezing and thawing, the park may be closed, and access to the park is by foot only. The shower building at Hickory Hill Campground is open from May 1 to October 31.

History and Trail Description: The name, Le-Aqua-Na, is derived from the nearby town of Lena and "aqua," the Latin word for water. The Stephenson County Sportsman's Club, one of the various groups sponsoring the park, conducted the contest that resulted in the naming of the park.

The State of Illinois initially acquired 614 acres of land here in 1949. In the years since then the state has acquired more land to bring the total figure to 715 acres. Lake Le-Aqua-Na was started in 1955 and was completed in 1956. The lake is 43 acres in size, ranges from 450 to 650 feet in width, and drains over 2,000 acres. The maximum depth is 26 feet with a mile of shoreline.

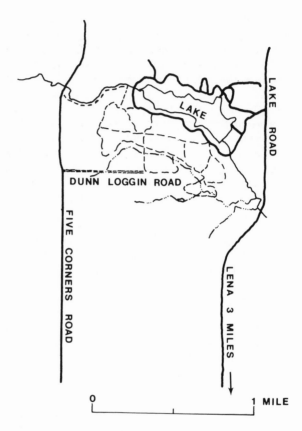

N

LAKE

LAKE ROAD

DUNN LOGGIN ROAD

FIVE CORNERS ROAD

LENA 3 MILES

0   1 MILE

KEY

ROAD ——————

TRAIL — — — —

INTERMITTENT STREAM — ··· —

4.2 MILES OF TRAILS

1. Lake Le-Aqua-Na State Park

The park has 6.8 miles of trails available to the hiker, cross-country skier, and horseback rider. The High Point Trail may be found north of the lake and measures 2.6 miles. The Sweet Gum Trail is located on the south side of the lake and measures 4.2 miles. The Sweet Gum Trail is the trail that will be discussed here.

The Sweet Gum Trail may be found by entering the park and heading west, passing the park dam. After ascending the hill you will find a parking area on the left side of the road. A large trailboard marked with the words "Sweet Gum Trail" can be seen from the parking lot. The trail starts at this point. Hikers, horseback riders, and skiers are allowed to use the multipurpose trail. The trail is really four loop trails that are interconnected for a total of 4.2 miles. The trail is generally about twelve feet wide, mowed and well kept. The trail should be followed in the direction outlined by the park trail map.

The trail is marked with wooden posts which have metal signs displaying either a skier, a backpacker, or a horseback rider on them. When a sign is covered with a red slash, it means that the specified trail activity is prohibited on that portion of the trail. When they are extremely wet and soft, the trails may be closed to equestrian activities. Consult park staff for trail conditions before riding.

The trail goes south from the trailhead, passing through a pine stand and then coming to a trail junction. The trail goes east at this point following the perimeter of the pine trees. The trail then starts heading west and comes to another trail junction. This is the second loop of the trail.

Turn left and go over a small bridge that crosses a creek. The trail then goes up a small hill and around an open field. Continuing east, the trail goes down a hill and soon parallels a small creek. The trail crosses another culvert and heads west toward the trail junction again. Turn right and follow the trail as it parallels the creek again.

You will cross two unmarked trails that lead back to the trailhead. You may take these trails or continue following the main trail.

The main trail connects with a third loop. At this point you may follow this loop, which goes over the creek and parallels a pine stand for a short distance, or you may continue straight ahead. By following the loop, the hiker will come to Dunn Loggin Road and may then turn north to the equestrian area and the trail junction passed earlier.

The trail continues west through a small valley, paralleling the small creek. The trail then turns north and crosses the main trail again. The hiker can take the main trail back to the trailhead or hike the last loop trail.

The last loop trail is fairly short and joins another trail which goes down to the parking area and feeder creek for the lake. Continuing on the loop trail, the hiker will pass a pine stand. Turn right at the pine stand and follow this trail to a large open field, the equestrian area. There are tables, a water pump, restrooms, and a shelter at this site. Here the hiker will meet the main trail which heads directly east back to the trailhead.

Facilities: Several picnic sites with shelters, restrooms, tables, and water are scattered throughout the park. Campsites are available for recreation vehicles, primitive campers, and for equestrian enthusiasts. A utility building with flush toilets and showers and a trailer dumping station are located at Hickory Hill Campground.

The equestrian area is accessible only by county roads bordering the park. Fishing and boating are allowed on the lake. A fishing pier for the handicapped is available here. All Illinois fishing rules and regulations are in effect. A concession stand is located on the lake and offers refreshments and boat rentals. A park office located on the grounds provides additional information.

Park Rules and Regulations: Fires are restricted to fire pads. Electric motors only are allowed on the lake. There is a small beach, and swimming is allowed from Memorial Day through Labor Day. The park is closed from 10:00 p.m. until 6:00 a.m. A maximum of four persons or a family per campsite is allowed. See Appendix A.

Mailing Address and Phone Number: Site Superintendent, Lake Le-Aqua-Na State Park, 8542 North Lake Road, Lena, Illinois 61048; 815/369-4282

2. Pecatonica Prairie Path

Trail Length: 17 miles (27.2 kilometers)

Location: The Pecatonica Prairie Path is located in north-western Illinois between Rockford and Freeport. The trail passes through Winnebago, Pecatonica, and Ridott and ends (or begins) at the eastern edge of Freeport. At the eastern edge of Freeport, just east of the U.S. 20 Bypass, is the westernmost point of the trail, which is at the junction of Hillcrest Road and East River Road. This trailhead is somewhat awkward and inconvenient since there is no parking, no trail sign, and traffic on East River Road is high speed. Roadways leading to this westernmost point outside of Freeport include north-south Route 26 to Freeport, east-west Route 20, and the Route 20 Bypass.

The second trailhead is located at the easternmost point in Winnebago, Illinois. Winnebago is located just south of Route 20, about seven miles west of Rockford. From Winnebago Road go west on McNair Street to N. Swift Street, then south to the trailhead (three blocks). Limited parking is available at the trailhead; however, parking is allowed at the Winnebago High School parking lot at the intersection of Winnebago Road and McNair Street.

A third access is located in Pecatonica at Sumner Park. Traveling north or south on Pecatonica Road, turn west on First Street (the first east-west street south of the Pecatonica River). This access point is very convenient because it divides the trail into two approximately equal lengths, and also there is adequate parking along with water and restrooms at Sumner Park.

Route 51 is a major north-south route leading to Rockford, and from the east the major roadway is North-west Tollroad Route 90. From Rockford follow Route 90 to Route 20 west to either of the three access points mentioned. The trail may be accessed from several other north-south roads; however, none provide any facilities other than the parking lot located at Farwell Bridge Road.

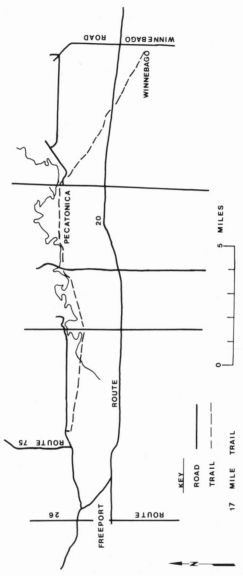

2. Pecatonica Prairie Path. Redrawn from Illinois Department of Transportation county highway maps.

Counties: Stephenson, Winnebago

Illinois Highway Map Coordinates: B-6

U.S.G.S. Topographical Map Names and Scale: Winnebago, Ridott, Pecatonica, and Freeport East, all 1:24,000

Hours Open: The Prairie Path is open to the public year-round. For safety reasons use the trail during daylight hours only.

History and Trail Description: The Pecatonica Prairie Path follows the old right-of-way of the Chicago and Northwestern Railroad, presently owned by Commonwealth Edison Company. The path is leased to the Pecatonica Prairie Path, Inc., a nonprofit organization formed to develop and manage the Path for public use.

The Pecatonica Prairie Path passes through forests and villages, over rivers and creeks, past farms, and across highways. Caution is necessary when crossing Route 20 since this is a four-lane major highway. Other hazardous crossings include Pecatonica Road in Pecatonica and Rock City Road in Ridott.

Most of the trail is gravel and dirt and is very level; it is about ten feet wide. The only indicators or markers are trailboards located at major crossings.

The undisturbed land along the undeveloped sections of the path provides an excellent refuge for a variety of Illinois wildlife. Over sixty species of birds have been recorded. Also, deer, badger, fox, and raccoon are often seen.

The path parallels the Pecatonica River in an east-west direction, although the river is visible from only a few spots. Except at Ridott and Pecatonica, water or restrooms are not available along the path. There are, however, four shelters along trailside between Pecatonica Road and Hillcrest Road. These shelters offer a picnic table with a roof for a sunscreen. Additional land leases offer three additional miles east of Winnebago; however, at this time the new section is not completed.

Facilities: No camping or restroom facilities are available on the path. Parking is available at Ridott, in Sumner

Park, at the Winnebago High School parking lot, at the Farwell Bridge crossing, and along county roads. Water is available at Sumner Park. Restroom facilities are available at Sumner Park and in Ridott.

Park Rules and Regulations: No motorized vehicles are allowed. Bicycles must have bells to warn hikers and other riders. No firearms. No bows and arrows. No kite flying. No model airplane flying. No horseback riding. Dogs must be on a leash. No alcoholic beverages. No fires.

Mailing Address and Phone Number: Pecatonica Prairie Path, 248 W. Homer, Freeport, Illinois 61032; 815/233-0814

3. Rock Cut State Park

Trail Length: 11.75 miles (18.8 kilometers)

Location: Rock Cut State Park is located seven miles northeast of Rockford, Illinois. The park can be reached from the south via Route 51 north to Rockford 251. Take Route 251 to Illinois Route 173, turn east and follow the road signs to the park. From western Illinois, the park is reached by Route 251 north from Rockford, again to Illinois 173 east. From eastern Illinois, the park is easily reached via Illinois 90, the Northwest Tollway, to the Riverside Exit.

County: Winnebago

Illinois Highway Map Coordinates: B-7

U.S.G.S. Topographical Map Name and Scale: Caledonia, 1:24,000

Hours Open: The park is open every day of the year except on Christmas Day and New Year's Day. At certain times of the year, due to freezing and thawing periods, the roads may be closed, and access to the park is by foot only.

History and Trail Description: Rock Cut State Park was first developed in 1957 when the Illinois Department of Conservation obtained over 13 acres. Pierce Lake, named after Representative William Pierce of the Illinois Legislative 10th District, was developed in 1962 when construction of a dam across Willow Creek was completed. The lake covers an area of slightly over 162 acres and has a four-mile shoreline. Total acreage in the park today is 3,092 acres.

Rock Cut State Park reportedly was named for the abandoned rock quarrying operations from more than 100 years ago. Evidence of old quarry pits are visible at the northeast shore of Pierce Lake. These pits are now

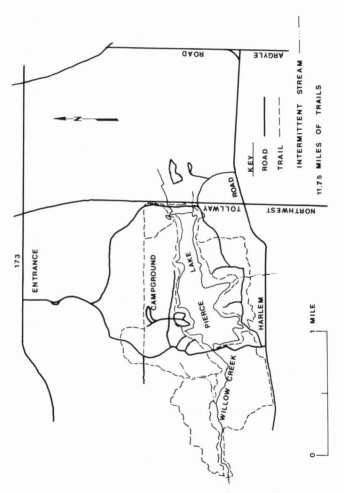

3. Rock Cut State Park

filled with water and are rearing ponds for migratory birds and local wildlife.

Good park maintenance is evident as all the trails are mowed in the grassy areas and kept clear-cut through the more dense areas. Footbridges cross different water-ways in the park. All of the hiking trails are also cross-country ski trails; these trails have symbols (brown background with figure of a hiker, and white background with a blue skier) located on all the trails in the park. Although most of the trail markers face north or east, the trails can be hiked in either direction from any access point. Additionally, the park has nature and inter-pretive trails (refer to the maps available at the park).

The campgrounds are a convenient place to start hiking. If day hiking is desired without camping, conve-nient parking locations include the three separate park-ing lanes south of Hickory Hills Campground and the parking area located directly north of the dam. The loop trail that circles the lake measures 3.5 miles; a good view of Pierce Lake can be had from most points along this trail. On the southeast side of Pierce Lake, and one-eighth mile west of the handicapped fishing pier, a rela-tively new trail is located. The new trail goes south and west along the park boundary. One mile from the trail junction, near the handicapped fishing pier, this trail crosses a paved road in the park. At the point where the trail meets the road, you can travel back northeast along the southern shore of the lake, shorten the trail by hiking a half mile north along the western shore and back to the dam and parking area, or continue the trail along the southern boundary of the park.

The trail along the southern boundary of the park is somewhat difficult and hazardous to hike. For example, beyond the first paved road the trail crosses a second paved road where there are no trail markers. You have to climb over the earthen mound created from road con-struction. Beyond the mound the trail is an abandoned asphalt road which continues for one eighth of a mile where another earthen mound is located. You must by-pass this mound and continue for nearly a half mile west along Harlem Road to the entrance to Willow Creek Picnic and Youth Group Campground.

At the entrance to the Willow Creek area, the trail system follows the asphalt road to the road's end. The trail then becomes a footpath along the creek. You will then cross a ford over the creek and will come to a junction in the trail. During the wet season the hiker can expect to get wet feet crossing Willow Creek, but the ford is a safe crossing as it is level concrete about ten feet wide and nearly twenty feet across.

On the north side of the ford two trails are available. The first meanders directly east along Willow Creek for one mile back to the parking area at the dam; the second trail passes through more dense foliage and at higher elevations. The second trail follows a ridge which over-looks a meadow, Willow Creek, and the first trail (one and one-half miles to the parking area).

From the two trails, which make a loop north of Willow Creek, another trail section is available that is one-quarter mile from the dam and connects with the trail along the ridge that begins at the ford over Willow Creek. This additional section of the trail system mean-ders along the main park road for one-quarter mile to Hart Road (gravel road going west). The trail then splits and goes for a half-mile loop where it joins the main trail again; at the gravel road it goes directly east. The trail is

Concrete ford across Willow Creek, Rock Cut State Park

clear-cut and marked as it passes by the Plum Grove Campground. The trail continues for one-quarter mile where it splits; one section borders the west boundary of the wildlife rearing ponds, and the other section continues around the north side of the rearing ponds. Both of the trail sections connect with the trail that circles Pierce Lake.

Facilities: Rock Cut State Park has five different camping areas with more than 215 class A sites. There are also five areas dedicated for picnicking only. Tables, outdoor stoves, drinking water, pit toilets, and playground equipment are available. There is a shower building in the Plum Grove Campground and shelters at the Willow Creek area. The park also has two sanitary dump stations.

The park is open for winter sports including: ice skating, ice fishing, cross-country skiing, snowmobiling, and dog sledding.

Two fishing piers are accessible for the handicapped, and outdoor privies are available at the parking lots nearby.

Pierce Lake is annually stocked, and fishing is allowed with all Illinois fishing rules and regulations in effect. Boating is allowed on the lake, with two boat launch areas available. A concession stand is located at the boat launch area.

Swimming is available at the Olson Annex at the 50-acre lake located on the extreme east side of the park (north of the Harlem Road entrance).

Permits Required: Permits are required for camping and for parking at the dog-training area.

Park Rules and Regulations: No plants or parts of any tree may be removed or damaged. The motor limit is 10 HP. All pets must be on a leash. Bicycles are not allowed on hiking trails. See Appendix A.

Mailing Address and Phone Number: Site Superintendent, Rock Cut State Park, 7318 Harlem Road, Calendonia, Illinois 61011; 815/885-3311

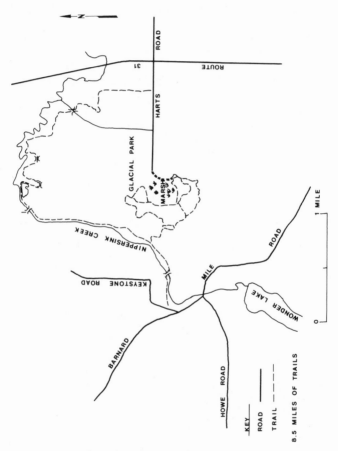

4. Glacial Park and Nippersink Trail

4. Glacial Park and Nippersink Trail

Trail Length: 8.5 miles (13.7 kilometers)

Location: Glacial Park is located in northeastern Illinois approximately sixty-five miles from Chicago. From central, southern, and eastern Illinois, Glacial Park is accessible via Illinois Tollroad 294 north to Route 120 west. In McHenry, Illinois, follow Route 31 north to the road sign for Glacial Park on Harts Road. From western Illinois, Glacial Park is accessible via Illinois Tollroad 5 east to 31 north, and from northern Illinois, via 176 to Route 31 north or 173 to 31 south.

County: McHenry

Illinois Highway Map Coordinates: A-8

U.S.G.S. Topographical Map Name and Scale: Richmond, 1:24,000

Hours Open: 8:00 a.m. until sunset

History and Trail Description: Glacial Park was started with an initial land acquisition in 1975. In 1977, an additional 115 acres were added. In 1979, in conjunction with the Corporation for Open Lands and Northern Pump Company, a 168-acre parcel encompassing the Nippersink Creek was made available to the district for trail-related activities.

All of the trails are well marked, and the trail intersections have signs with the title, length, and direction of the trail.

Within Glacial Park are two main nature trails: the Coyote Loop Trail and the Deerpath Trail. The Coyote Loop Trail is an excellent short-distance trail for students, families, and outdoor enthusiasts, as it has a wildlife observation platform, a windbreak demonstration plot, and examples of a songbird planting and northern wildlife plantings. In addition, the grassy path passes along a natural marsh and bog. Also visible along this .75-mile loop trail are old pastures and forests. There are also good examples of controlled prairie burns throughout the park.

The second loop trail, Deerpath Trail, measures two and a third miles. This trail also passes along the bog and marsh area and through more wooded areas, as well as through glacial ridges and the prairie management area. A .25-mile loop trail known as Broken Ski Extension allows the hiker to see controlled prairie burn remains, to hike up a glacial ridge, and to obtain a magnificent view from the trail junction on top of the ridge.

The Deerpath Trail has another scenic vista atop a ridge north of the prairie management area. Following this trail south, it connects with a half-mile loop trail along the base and on top of the glacial kame. The ridge of the kame provides excellent viewing.

From the Deerpath Trail, at the kame, there is a connecting trail from Glacial Park to Nippersink Trail, which goes around Glacial Park. By following the trail southeast and crossing the creek, the hiker ends the half-mile hike at the parking area and canoe landing; the northern branch of the trail meanders for four and one-half miles. Hikers must be cautious on this trail because more than half the length is also used by horseback riders, cross-country skiers, and snowmobilers.

About three-quarters of a mile north of the connecting trail to Glacial Park is a water pump located on top of a grassy sand kame. At the water pump there is a private road named Valley Road. North of Valley Road the trail becomes a gravel road several feet above the water level of Nippersink Creek. There is a shelter nearly one mile north of Valley Road, and pit toilets are accessible via a bridge and short connecting trail.

Beyond the shelter, Nippersink Trail meanders east away from the crop fields and passes a large pond. Many types of birds are visible along this northern tip of the trail. Southeast of the pond the trail meanders through a mostly marsh environment. For more than two miles past the pond, to the point where the trail parallels the railroad tracks, the trail may be impassable during the wet season, as this is mostly wetland. If the hiker wears proper footgear, this two-mile wetlands section can be very enjoyable as it offers the view of many plants and wildlife species common to wetland environments. Just before the railroad tracks, another water pump is available along the trail.

The trail ends at the parking lot along Harts Road. By taking Harts Road three-quarters of a mile west, the hiker will reach the main parking area at Glacial Park.

Facilities: Glacial Park has picnic facilities with fire grates, water, and restrooms at the parking area. Nippersink Trail has a parking lot on Harts Road and at Keystone Road. Barnard Mill Road intersection has sanitary facilities and a canoe landing. The McHenry County Conservation District Headquarters is located at Glacial Park. Information, maps, and books are available at the headquarters.

Permits Required: Permits are required for groups of twenty-five or more people.

Park Rules and Regulations: Camping is not allowed in Glacial Park or along Nippersink Creek. Fishing is allowed in Nippersink Creek with all Illinois fishing rules and regulations in effect.

Mailing Address and Phone Number: McHenry County Conservation District, 6512 Harts Road, Ringwood, Illinois 60072; 815/338-1405

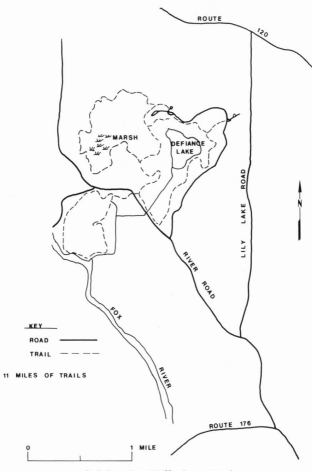

5. Moraine Hills State Park

5. Moraine Hills State Park

Trail Length: 11 miles (17 kilometers)

Location: Moraine Hills State Park is located in north-eastern Illinois just south of McHenry. The park boundaries are centered between north-south Routes 31 and 12 and east-west Routes 120 and 176. Traveling on Route 176, turn north on River Road, and go two miles to the entrance; from McHenry and Route 120, turn south on River Road and go three miles to the entrance.

Other north-south roads which are nearby Moraine Hills State Park include Illinois Tollroad 94, Route 45, and Route 47.

County: McHenry

Illinois Highway Map Coordinates: B-8

U.S.G.S. Topographical Map Name and Scale: Wauconda, 1:24,000

Hours Open: The park is open year-round except on Christmas Day. At certain times, due to freezing and thawing periods, the park is closed.

History and Trail Description: Moraine Hills State Park has 1,740 acres of upland and wetland environments. The rivers, lakes, marshes, prairies, and woodlands here are the result of the most recent glacial advance, the Wisconsin Glacier. At one time this area was occupied by several Indian tribes, including the Potawatomi, Sauk, and Fox. Construction of the McHenry Dam on the Fox River began in 1934 after several land acquisitions in the area.

Major land acquisition of the Lake Defiance area began in 1971. After a resource study and completion of a master plan, construction of the park facilities began in the spring of 1975.

The 11-mile trail system at Moraine Hills State Park consists of three main loops and includes the Lake Defiance Self-Guided Interpretive Trail as well as the Pike Marsh Interpretive Trail and connecting trails to several day-use areas. The trail system is designed to be hiked one way only and is very easy to follow. From the Northern Lakes Day Use Area, the Leather Leaf Bog Trail is located behind the comfort station, and the direction of travel is west (counterclockwise as you refer to the map).

Trailboards having maps and park rules and regulations are located at all day use areas (parking lots). Trail signs are located at all trail junctions indicating the name of the trail, direction of travel, and mileage.

The Leather Leaf Bog Trail measures 3.5 miles and represents an excellent example of kettlemoraine topography and supports very diverse plant communities. Plant species include marsh fern, marsh marigold, and several species of willow.

The Lake Defiance Trail which surrounds the 48-acre lake measures 4 miles. This trail connects the Northern Day Use Area with the Lake Defiance Day Use Area and the park office. Also, along the Lake Defiance Trail is the concession and interpretive center. As the trail meanders southward, paralleling the park road, connecting trails allow access from the Hickory Ridge Day Use Area, Pine Hills Day Use Area, Kettle Woods Day Use Area, and the Pike Marsh Day Use Area. At the southwesternmost point of this trail, there is a connecting trail going west under River Road. The connecting trail is for the Fox River Loop which also is designed for travel in one direction only.

This Fox River Trail passes through prairie areas adjacent to wetlands. A short trail leads to the parking area at McHenry Dam and to the concession area. The southern portion of this trail parallels the Fox River and the water drainage channel from Lake Defiance. The total length of this loop is 2.5 miles.

Additional trails in the park are the Lake Defiance Self-Guided Interpretive Trail, which measures nearly 0.5 miles, and the Pike Marsh Interpretive Trail.

The Lake Defiance Self-Guided Interpretive Trail is accessed from the Northern Lakes parking lot and from the Lake Defiance parking lot to the park office where the numbered posts begin.

The trail at Pike Marsh is accessed from the parking lot at Pike Marsh Day Use Area. Approximate length is 0.6 miles.

The diverse landscape in this area of McHenry County provides habitat for numerous forms of wildlife. Over 100 species of birds have been identified. The area is heavily used by mallard, teal, wood duck, Canada geese, and other migratory waterfowl.

Various mammals including red fox, eastern cotton-tail, mink, opossum, raccoon, and white-tail deer can be seen in the upland timber of oak, hickory, ash, cherry, dogwood, and hawthorn.

Facilities: Moraine Hills State Park has several parking areas. Picnic tables are available in all day use areas, along with water and comfort stations. Picnic shelters are available at the Pine Hills and Pike Marsh Day Use Areas. Also, there are flush toilets at the McHenry Dam concession building and at the Park Office.

Playground equipment is available at the McHenry Dam area and at the Whitetail Prairie and Pike Marsh Day Use Areas. Boats are available for public use on Lake Defiance.

In addition to the concession at McHenry Dam area there is a concession at the park office. An interpretive center is also located at the park office.

Permits Required: Groups of twenty-five persons or more require permission from the site superintendent.

Park Rules and Regulations: Groups of minors must have adequate supervision and at least one adult for every fifteen minors. All pets must be on a leash. There are no camping facilities available at Moraine Hills State Park. See Appendix A.

Mailing Address and Phone Number: Site Superintendent, Moraine Hills State Park, 914 S. River Road, McHenry, Illinois 60050; 815/385-1624

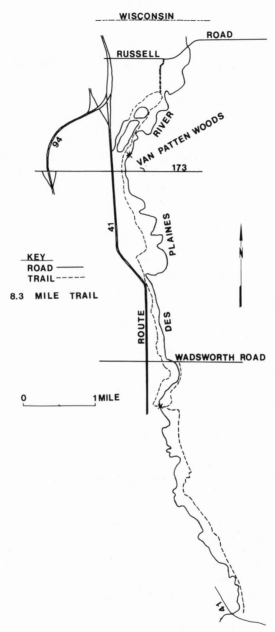

6. Des Plaines River Trail (Lake County)

6. Des Plaines River Trail (Lake County)

Trail Length: 8.3 miles (13.3 kilometers)

Location: The Des Plaines River Trail is located in north-eastern Illinois along Route 41, just south of the Wisconsin border. The main trailhead at Sterling Lake is accessible from Route 41, one eighth of a mile north of Route 173. A sharp right onto a paved road will lead to the parking area. The entrance to this parking lot may be closed at certain times of the year, depending upon the weather. However, additional access points to the trail are available.

A second access point may be reached north of the main entrance off of Route 41. Follow Route 41 north to Russell Road. Turn east on Russell Road, go a quarter mile, and turn south to the north entrance of Sterling Lake.

County: Lake

Illinois Highway Map Coordinates: A-9

U.S.G.S. Topographical Map Name and Scale: Wadsworth, 1:24,000

Hours Open: 8:00 a.m. to sunset

History and Trail Description: The trail and surrounding property are located along the floodplain of the Des Plaines River. The Lake County Forest Preserve District purchased the property in the area with the intention of developing a 40-mile recreation corridor.

Although the trailhead may be accessed from two areas from the north, probably the easiest place to begin the trail is at Van Patten Woods Forest Preserve. Van Patten Woods is located a half mile east of Route 41 off State Route 173. Van Patten Woods divides the trail into two shorter sections: 6.3 miles to the south and 2 miles to the north.

A parking lot is available at Van Patten Woods. From the parking lot the hiker may go to the picnic area and to shelter A. From here a trail will be seen which goes to a 200-foot bridge over the Des Plaines River. Once the hiker crosses the bridge he may go north to the trailheads and Sterling Lake or south toward Route 173.

The trail north of 173 is ten to twelve feet wide and is a dirt lane. This area all the way to the trailhead and around Sterling Lake may be extremely muddy during wet weather.

The section of trail south of Route 173 is surfaced with crushed stone and is generally about twelve feet wide. This portion of the trail is well maintained and is suitable for hiking, biking, horseback riding, cross-country skiing, and snowmobiling. The trail goes by open fields, prairie grass stands, and river floodplains. The trail also goes by some farm fields.

At about one and one-half miles south of Route 173 you will come across a water pump that can be used for drinking water. From the pump to Wadsworth Road, you will be on a section of trail that is a prime viewing area for observing migratory birds such as long-neck geese.

South of Wadsworth Road the trail meanders through an area of relatively significant and new importance—a 450-acre Wetlands Demonstration Project. The Wetlands Project is a restoration of the Des Plaines River and marsh areas for flood control. The return of the marsh is expected to bring back waterfowl, fish, and other wildlife that can thrive in a wetlands environment. The restoration proj-ect is most notable along the west side of the river.

South of Wadsworth Road, the trail passes through more dense woodlands than those of the northern part of the trail. The southernmost portion of the trail can be divided into two sections: one is U-shaped around the Des Plaines River from the west side of the river at Wadsworth Road, south to a ninety-foot bridge, crossing over the river, then back north along the east side of the river and ending at the Wadsworth Canoe Launch—Des Plaines River Trail Access. The second southern section of trail begins at a trail junction on the east side of the ninety-foot bridge crossing over the river. This section meanders south paralleling the active railroad tracks and the river through dense woodland and marsh areas. Periodically, there are green and white trail markers indicating the path as a snowmobile route, as this portion of the trail is a multiuse section.

From the trail junction on the east side of the ninety-foot bridge, the trail goes two miles south to a point about 500 feet short of Route 41. The southern end of the trail is effectively just beyond where a new bridge has been placed for further access to the trail along the Des Plaines River and marshlands. A wide variety of flora and fauna is visible along this section. The Des Plaines River Trail is expected to continue south and cross over Route 41 and continue along the Des Plaines River, but funding for construction is not available at this time.

To return to the northern sections of trail, you must retrace your steps since this is not a loop trail.

Facilities: Water pumps, pit toilets, and car parking are located at the trailhead, at Van Patten Woods Forest Preserve, and at Wadsworth Canoe Launch. A canoe launch, fishing dock, observation platform, car and trailer parking, drinking water, and pit toilets are available at the Wadsworth Canoe Launch area. Van Patten Woods also has picnic grounds, shelters and playgrounds, first-aid stations, and public telephones. Fishing is allowed in the Des Plaines River and Sterling Lake with all Illinois fishing rules and regulations in effect.

Permits Required: Permits are required for horseback riding and snowmobiles and may be obtained at the general offices of the Lake County Forest Preserve District. Permits are also required for groups of twenty-five or more people. The shelters and playgrounds may be reserved at the district office.

Trail Rules and Regulations: No hunting, swimming, fires, or littering. Pets must be on a leash. No amplified music allowed. Parking in designated areas only. No consumption of alcoholic beverages in or within immediate vicinity of parking areas.

Mailing Address and Phone Number: Lake County Forest Preserve District, 2000 North Milwaukee Avenue, Libertyville, Illinois 60048; 708/367-6640

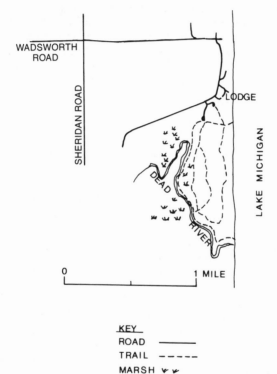

7. Illinois Beach State Park

7. Illinois Beach State Park

Trail Length: 5 miles (8.0 kilometers)

Location: The Southern Unit of Illinois Beach State Park is about 10 miles south of the Wisconsin-Illinois state line along the shores of Lake Michigan. The main entrance for the Southern Unit is Wadsworth Road east from Sheridan Road.

County: Lake

Illinois Highway Map Coordinates: A-9

U.S.G.S. Topographical Map Name and Scale: Zion, 1:24,000

Hours Open: The State Park is open year-round; the Southern Unit is open from sunrise to 8:00 p.m.

History and Trail Description: This area has been recognized for its complex geological structure, unique flora, and spectacular beauty, and is truly a dunes topography. Originally inhabited by Indians, the area became part of Lake County after a treaty with settlers was made in 1836. Illinois Beach State Park has 4,160 acres. The park consists of sand dunes, marshes, forests, and grassy areas, and is inhabited by numerous wildlife. More than 650 species of plants have been recorded, including dozens of types of colorful wildflowers. The prairies in the area have a variety of grasses and sedges.

Illinois Beach State Park has a Northern Unit and a Southern Unit area. Various recreation facilities are found at both areas. The trails described in this volume include the hiking trails found in the Southern Unit.

The trails in the Southern Unit of the Park are in an Illinois Nature Preserve. The Nature Preserve is comprised of 829 acres. The trailheads for the hiking trails are located at the southern part of the parking lot at the interpretive center.

The Dead River Trail is the westernmost trail which offers magnificent views of wildlife along the Dead River and the surrounding marsh and prairie. The trail reaches the beach along Lake Michigan where one can hike back about .5 mile to the connecting loop trail or enjoy a scenic hike along the sandy shores north to the Beach Trail which goes back to the trailhead and parking lot. When combined, the Dead River Trail, lakefront hike, and the Beach Trail will make a 2.5-mile loop starting and ending at the parking lot.

The Loop Trail is the second longest loop offering a closer look at the black oak forest and different pine trees as well as sandy ridges and a variety of wildflowers. Total length is 2 miles. There is also a shorter cut-off loop trail of 1 mile in length. This shorter loop actually is referred to as the Black Oak Trail, and it goes through the center of the dunes area and Nature Preserve.

Currently, the brochure published by the Illinois Department of Conservation has trail names printed that differ from the actual trail markers. Be sure to check for updated information when you arrive. Currently the trails are marked with brown and white markers on brown posts.

Facilities: Illinois Beach State Park has all classes of camping available, as well as a sanitary dump station, picnic areas, concessions, drinking water, toilets, fishing, boat rentals, hiking, nature preserve, swimming, and interpretive programs. The park also has a 96-room lodge and conference center. All appropriate fishing rules and regulations are in effect.

Permits Required: Permits are required for camping. Reservations can be made for camping at this site.

Park Rules and Regulations: Groups of twenty-five or more are required to register in advance. At least one responsible adult must accompany each group of fifteen minors. Pets must be kept on a leash at all times. See Appendixes A and B.

Mailing Address and Phone Number: Illinois Beach State Park, Lake Front, Zion, Illinois 60099; 708/662-4811

8. Lakewood Forest Preserve

Trail Length: 6 miles (9.6 kilometers)

Location: Lakewood Forest Preserve is located east of Wauconda, Illinois, on State Route 176. To get to the forest preserve, north and south traffic may take State Route 12 and exit onto Route 176 going east. Proceed for a few miles until just before intersecting Fairfield Road. Before Fairfield Road there will be a sign. Turn right (south) into the preserve.

County: Lake

Illinois Highway Map Coordinates: B-9

U.S.G.S. Topographical Map Names and Scale: Lake Zurich and Grayslake, 1:24,000

Hours Open: The preserve is open from 8:00 a.m. to sunset. The museum is open every day from 1:00 p.m. to 4:00 p.m.

History and Trail Description: Lakewood Forest Preserve, an area rich in history, attracted settlers from the earliest times, with weathered stone foundations as symbols of those farmsteads. The preserve contains over 1,400 acres of rolling countryside dotted with woods, small lakes, meadows, and wetlands.

The trail system consists of a combination hiking/horseback trail that meanders through the south side of the park and covers over 6 miles.

The trailhead may be reached by proceeding into the park and going past the museum and ranger station to a T junction in the road. This is Ivanhoe Road. Turn left (east) and go for a half block to a metal sign with a symbol of a hiker on it. Turn right on this road and drive down to the small parking lot that is available. During the winter season this road may be closed; if so, continue down Ivanhoe Road to a larger parking lot on the north side of the road.

ROUTE 176

FAIRFIELD ROAD

IVANHOE ROAD

TRAIL-HEAD

MILTON ROAD

ROUTE 12

N

0   1 MILE

KEY

ROAD ————

TRAIL — — — —

INTERMITTENT STREAM —··—

6 MILES OF TRAILS

8. Lakewood Forest Preserve

At the parking lot, you will find restrooms, water, and a small lake where fishing is permitted. In addition, restrooms are available for the hiker about a mile from the trailhead. The trail starts just south of the parking lot. You will have to go around a gate that is set up to prevent motorized vehicles from entering the trails. Trailboards are set up at different locations on the trail. The trailboards have a map of the trail showing the hiker's exact location at the time. You may hike the trails in any direction and may hike the entire trail length or just a few loop trails.

The trail is very wide and is an old gravel/dirt road. The trail goes by and through open fields, around three small lakes, through the woods, and onto the backside of a neighboring subdivision. At some spots the trail goes up and down some rolling hills and offers some good views of the surrounding area. The easternmost part of the trail goes by a horse stable. At this point the trail markers on the trail show that the trail ends. The gravel road actually keeps winding south of the horse stable area, and you could continue hiking. There is also access for the public on this trail off of Milton Road. The easternmost edge of the park borders a subdivision, and there is a small opening where the public may follow a trail that connects with the trail system in the park.

Facilities: The preserve has recently expanded a museum and a ranger station. There are many picnic areas in the park that have tables, restrooms, water, and shelters. The preserve also has a winter recreation area on the east side of Fairfield Road. There is also a snowmobile trail and a physical fitness trail in the park. Skiers are free to ski any of the trails in the park. There is also a tent camping area for organized youth groups of fewer than 100 persons. Fishing is allowed in the lakes with all Illinois fishing rules and regulations applying.

Permits Required: A permit is required for groups of twenty-five or more persons and for reserved shelters. In addition, snowmobile and horseback permits are required. Permits may be obtained in person at the main office in Libertyville. A permit is also required for camping.

Park Rules and Regulations: No dogs are allowed on the horse trail. No swimming in the lakes or motorcycles on the trails. No hunting or ice fishing allowed.

Mailing Address and Phone Number: Lake County Forest Preserve District, 2000 North Milwaukee Avenue, Libertyville, Illinois 60048; 708/367-6640

9. Edward L. Ryerson Conservation Area

Trail Length: 6 miles (9.6 kilometers)

Location: Ryerson Conservation Area is located northwest of Deerfield, Illinois. To reach the park, northbound traffic may take Interstate 94 and exit at Deerfield Road. Go west on Deerfield Road for a few blocks to Riverwoods Road. Turn right on Riverwoods Road (north) and proceed for two miles to the park entrance. Turn left onto the park road and follow the signs to the Visitors Center parking lot. Interstate 94 southbound traffic may exit onto State Route 22 and go west to Riverwoods. Turn left (south) and proceed one and a half miles to the park entrance.

County: Lake

Illinois Highway Map Coordinates: B-9

U.S.G.S. Topographical Map Name and Scale: Wheeling, 1:24,000

Hours Open: 8:30 a.m. to 5:00 p.m. daily

History and Trail Description: The Edward L. Ryerson Conservation Area, a part of the Illinois Nature Preserves system, is known for its wildflowers, virgin forests, and animal life. The park borders the Des Plaines River on the east.

The trail system consists of many interconnecting trails that total 6 miles. The trails may be started in the parking lot near the Visitors Center. The Visitors Center has a naturalist on duty where you can request maps and other information. The trail system has trail signs set up throughout the park that show your exact location. You may hike the trails in any direction and for any length. Some trails may be closed at times to protect the animals in the park.

The trails go through open fields, along the Des Plaines River, along a farm field, and by the farm itself.

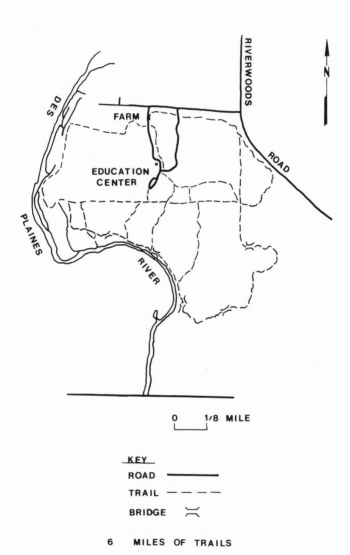

RIVERWOODS ROAD

DES PLAINES

FARM

EDUCATION CENTER

RIVER

N

0   1/8 MILE

KEY

ROAD —————

TRAIL — — —

BRIDGE ⊐⊏

6   MILES OF TRAILS

9. Edward L. Ryerson Conservation Area. Redrawn from park map.

As you hike the trail along the Des Plaines River, you will observe a few cabins. One cabin has exhibits in it dealing with the natural history of the Des Plaines River. There are some small bridges that you must cross, and the trail also crosses the park road two times. At one point along the river the hiker will see a small dam. A vacant cabin is located by the dam and provides a nice resting area.

The trail by the farm may be confusing, and you should be cautious in this area. You will walk through the center of the farm and see a trailboard set up close to the fence. You must follow this fence eastward all the way to the river. Once you reach the river, the trail turns south and parallels the river for a short distance.

All of the trails are fairly flat and are excellent for cross-country skiing.

Facilities: A Visitors Center located on the grounds provides the hiker with information, trail maps, and other materials. The Visitors Center offers a variety of school and adult group programs throughout the year. An exhibit cabin is located at the north end of the park. Exhibits on the seasons and what changes occur in the park are shown here. Many special winter programs, including animal tracking, skiing, and using a compass, are also offered at the park. A newsletter is also distributed by the Ryerson Conservation Area and may be of value to the hiker. A small farm is also located on the grounds. Water and restrooms are available at the Visitors Center and at the farm.

Permits Required: Permits are required for all groups of ten or more persons and may be obtained at the Visitors Center.

Park Rules and Regulations: No collecting of any animals or plants in the park. Walk only on the trails. No releasing of animals. Fishing, swimming, pets, and boat access are not allowed. Vehicles and bicycles are not permitted on the trails. No picnics allowed. No alcohol, taped music, ball playing, or frisbee. See Appendix C.

Mailing Addresses and Phone Numbers: Lake County Forest Preserve District, 2000 N. Milwaukee Avenue, Libertyville, Illinois 60048; 708/367-6640; or Edward L. Ryerson Conservation Area, Lake County Forest Preserve District, 21950 Riverwoods Road, Deerfield, Illinois 60015; 708/948-7750

10. Mississippi Palisades State Park

Trail Length: 11 miles (17.7 kilometers)

Location: Mississippi Palisades State Park is located three miles north of Savanna on State Route 84. The traveler may enter the park from the north or south entrance. The park office is located at the north park entrance, so the hiker may want to go there to find out the trail conditions or to request more information.

County: Carroll

Illinois Highway Map Coordinates: B-4

U.S.G.S. Topographical Map Names and Scale: Blackhawk and Savanna, both 1:24,000

Hours Open: The park is open year-round except on Christmas Day and New Year's Day. At certain times of the year, due to freezing and thawing, the park may close, and access to the park is by foot only.

History and Trail Description: The area known as Mississippi Palisades State Park was once inhabited by a considerable Indian population which left remnants of its culture upon the landscape. Numerous burial mounds are located within the park boundary. These mounds are easily accessible via well-marked hiking trails.

The park is located near the confluence of the Apple and Mississippi rivers. The name Palisades was given to the steep limestone bluffs along the Mississippi River because of their resemblance to similar geological formations on the Hudson River.

In 1929, the State of Illinois acquired 376 acres of land here to preserve the natural beauty and historic sites. The park now has over 2,550 acres.

The trail system consists of over 11 miles of hiking trails located at both the northern and southern ends of the park. The trailheads of the major trails are well

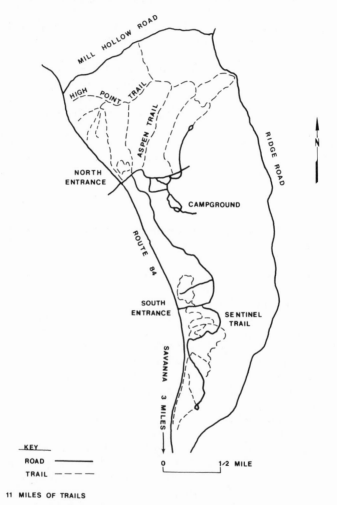

KEY

ROAD ——————

TRAIL — — — —

11 MILES OF TRAILS

10. Mississippi Palisades State Park. Redrawn from park trail map.

marked by trailboards; likewise, all trail junctions are marked by metal trail signs. The trail signs display the trail layout which is marked by a red dot showing your exact location. The trailboards show only the trail that you are hiking. All of the trails are color-coded on the trail signs.

There are six major trails located at the north area and four major trails at the south end of the park. Over 7 miles of trails wind their way through the hills at the north end of the park and over 4 miles at the south end.

The trails at the north end of the park may be started north of the park office. Vehicles may be left at the parking area by the park camping area. The Rocktop Trail, High Point Trail, and the Aspen Trail are accessible from the parking lot.

The Rocktop Trail is a short loop trail that makes its way around the top of the bluffs, offering beautiful views of the Mississippi River and its valley. There is an overlook along the trail where one may view the river. A trailboard is set up at the head of this trail, which measures 0.6 miles. The end of this trail connects with the High Point Trail.

The High Point Trail starts out as an old paved road that slowly turns to a dirt lane. The trail is about twelve feet wide and is very easy to follow once the hiker reaches the top of the ridge. The trail immediately starts climbing uphill, following the ridge line. At the top of the hill the trail continues to follow the major ridges. You will soon reach a trail intersection marked by a sign for the Goldenrod Trail. From here you may go east and follow the Goldenrod Trail, or go west and continue following the High Point Trail.

West from the Goldenrod Trail intersection, the High Point Trail continues to follow the ridge lines and intersects another trail. The trail to the north leads to a shelter overlook offering a beautiful view of the river valley below. The trail to the south leads to four sections of the High Point Trail. There is a trail sign at this point to help you determine your exact location.

The trail to the extreme right goes to the bluffs. The next trail to the right follows the valley floor to the road below. The third trail goes to the top of the hill, and the trail to the extreme left goes down through the valley, coming out near the trailhead. From here, you can follow the road to the head of the Aspen Trail.

The Aspen Trail follows the ridgetops of the hills in the area. The Aspen Trail connects with the Goldenrod Trail and also with the Deer and Bittersweet Trails. The Goldenrod Trail has a branch that leads down to Mill Hollow Road, while the second branch goes to the High Point Trail.

One primitive campsite is found on each of the Goldenrod, Bittersweet, and Aspen Trails. A marker along the trail will point to the camping area.

From the Aspen Trail you can follow the Deer Trail or the Bittersweet Trail or continue following the Aspen Trail to the end. The Deer Trail is a loop trail that branches off to areas of the Aspen Trail, goes by Ridge Road, and follows an open field for a short distance. The end of the Aspen Trail is at the end of the park road. Picnic and camping areas are available. The Bittersweet Trail takes you along the ridge top and then down to the camping area; the road will lead you back to the trailhead.

After hiking the trails at the north end, you can drive on the park road to the south end where the other trails are located.

The trails at the south end offer more spectacular views of the river valley than the trails at the north end of the park. In addition, many rock formations and 200-foot cliffs are seen along some of the trails here.

The trails at the south end of the park may be started in a few areas along the park road or along State Route 84.

The Sunset Trail is a short loop trail that may be started off the south park entrance road. The trail ascends a ridge line, follows the ridges in a loop going over another road, and passes lookout point. From the lookout point the trail goes south again to the trailhead. From here you may walk along the park road or reach the parking area by the shelter close to Route 84. The Sentinel Trail starts here.

The Sentinel Trail begins climbing the slope of the hill right away. The trail divides into two sections. The branch to the west leads to the bluffs. From here, you will see more spectacular views of rock formations and the river valley. The trail then meets again, crosses the road, and connects with the Pine Trail.

The Pine Trail ascends and descends through some beautiful valleys. You will cross a bridge, climb hills, and come to another overlook. Two large vertical rock formations are seen at the overlook area. These rock formations are referred to as Twin Sisters' Rocks. The trail crosses the park road again and joins with Upton's Trail. Upton's Trail goes past some of the largest bluffs in the park and passes by Indian Head Rock.

Upton's Trail parallels Route 84, following the base of the bluffs the entire length. The Mississippi River is visible along the entire hike. The trail passes by Upton's Cave, which can be seen from the trail itself. You can go inside this cave for a short distance. From here the hiker can retrace his footsteps along the trails to the trail start, or he can follow Route 84 back to the starting point.

Extreme caution must be used while hiking the trails in the park. Many of the trails pass by and may follow the bluffs' edge and may descend steep rock ledges.

The trails at the north end of the park are also used for cross-country skiing in the winter. Some of the trails may not be skied and are marked accordingly. The trails at the south end of the park are extremely steep, rocky, and narrow and are unsafe for skiing.

Facilities: Numerous picnic tables, water faucets, and restrooms are located throughout the park. Shelter houses and playground equipment are located at the main entrance and camping areas. Tent and trailer facilities, including three camp shower buildings and flush toilets, are available. Electric hook-ups and a sanitary dump station are provided for contained areas. There are free launching ramps for boats. Boat rentals are available from a private concessionaire, and there are no motor size limits. A park office on the grounds offers additional information. Limited horse trails are located in the park; horse rentals are available sometimes.

Permits Required: A camping permit is required.

Upton's Cave, Mississippi Palisades State Park

Park Rules and Regulations: Park closes at sundown. Quiet hours from 10:00 p.m. until 7:00 a.m. No chain saws are permitted in the park and loud mufflers are prohibited. See Appendix A.

Mailing Address and Phone Number: Site Superintendent, Mississippi Palisades State Park, 4577 Route 84 North, Savanna, Illinois 61074; 815/273-2731

11. Des Plaines River Trail (Cook County)

Trail Length: 27 miles (43.4 kilometers)

Location: The Des Plaines River Trail is located in northeastern Illinois along the eastern bank of the Des Plaines River. From Madison Street in Forest Park the trail passes through many suburbs of Chicago north to the Lake—Cook County border, Lake Cook Road.

Major access points include the Potawatomi Woods and Dam No. 1 Woods off of Dundee Road, Allison Woods and the River Trail Nature Center off of Milwaukee Avenue at Winkelman Road, Camp Pine Woods off of Euclid Avenue, Big Bend Lake off of East River Road and Golf Road in Des Plaines, Illinois. All of the aforementioned areas are considered part of the Des Plaines Division of the Forest Preserve District of Cook County.

Major access points between Touhy Avenue in Park Ridge and Madison Street in Forest Park include: Axehead Lake off of Touhy Avenue, Dam No. 4 east off of Dee Road or Devon Avenue, Robinson Woods South off of Lawrence Avenue, Schiller Woods North off of East River Road—Montrose Avenue or Irving Park Road in Schiller Park, Evans Field off of Thatcher Avenue, and Thatcher Woods and Thatcher Woods Glen off of Chicago Avenue in River Forest. All of these areas are considered part of the Indian Boundary Division of the Forest Preserve District of Cook County.

County: Cook

U.S.G.S. Topographical Map Names and Scale: Wheeling, Arlington Heights, Park Ridge, and River Forest, all 1:24,000

Hours Open: For safety reasons, use the trail during daylight hours only. The Forest Preserve District picnic grounds and parking areas close at sunset.

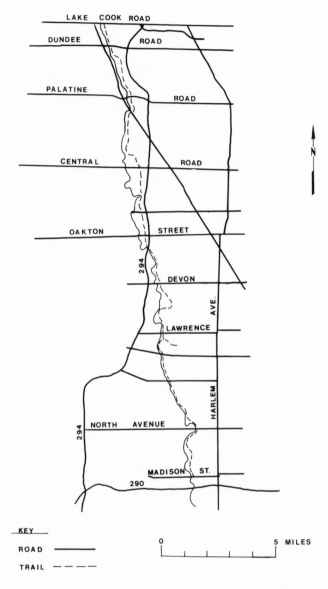

11. Des Plaines River Trail (Cook County). Redrawn from Illinois Department of Transportation Cook County highway map.

History and Trail Description: The Des Plaines River Trail passes through the narrow band of native landscape along the eastern bank of the Des Plaines River in Cook County. The area is rich with the history of the many Indians who once settled here.

Evans Field is the site of an Indian village; east of Evans Field, five mounds were built by prehistoric Indians. The Indian Boundary Line, which crosses the trail just east of Grand Avenue in River Grove, is the north line of a strip of land twenty miles wide from Lake Michigan to Ottawa ceded to the whites by the Potawatomi in 1816. Big Bend Lake is the site of an old Indian village; Camp Pine Woods is the site of a pioneer cabin.

The Des Plaines River Trail (Cook County) is the longest of two trails established along the Des Plaines River which are part of a proposal to make a 40-mile recreation corridor from the trailhead at Sterling Lake, which is south of Russell Road in Lake County, to the River Trail in Cook County. A third section, the newest, is still under construction and is not desirable for use at this time (refer to phone number at the end of this description for an update on the trail completion).

The majority of the trail is a gravel and dirt path. Native trees and wildflowers are seen all along the trail. There are many species of birds visible in this area, including many migratory birds. Many deer and rabbit can be seen at different times of the year as the Des Plaines River and surrounding preserve are an excellent refuge for all forms of wildlife.

The Des Plaines River Trail is part of two different divisions of ten divisions in Cook County. The Cook County Forest Preserve District has some 150 miles of multipurpose trails available for hikers, bikers, horseback riders, and cross-country skiers. The two divisions of this trail are the Indian Boundary Division from Touhy Avenue in Park Ridge to Madison Street in Forest Park, and the Des Plaines Division from Touhy Avenue north to the Lake—Cook County border.

Because the majority of trails in Cook County are maintained but are not appropriately marked, we have excluded them from our trail descriptions; however, these other trails are listed in trail maps available from the Forest Preserve General Headquarters (address listed under the heading "Mailing Address and Phone Number").

The Des Plaines River Trail is marked only by symbols of horses attached to posts at major road crossings (white figure on a brown background). The north end of the trail ends at Lake Cook Road, which is a four-lane road. The south end stops at Madison Street. You will see a cemetery and cannot continue south of Madison Street.

Horses are allowed on this multipurpose trail; however, the majority of horseback riders are seen between Golf Road and Lake Cook Road. One section of the trail that is a bit confusing is at the Allison Woods section. From the east, finish the gravel path at Allison Woods parking area and follow the entrance to Milwaukee Avenue. Cross Milwaukee Avenue and follow the blacktop road (Winkelman Road) beside the Holiday Inn for one eighth of a mile. The trail then goes west (left). Opposite directions are appropriate if you are traveling from west to east.

Another confusing section of the trail is between Rand Road and the crossing at Algonquin Road. Going north, cross Algonquin Road, go north on Campground Road past the Banner Day-Care Center and then the Methodist Camp. Continuing on this road you will pass the Northwestern Woods. This part of the road is known as Joseph Schwab Road. Follow the Joseph Schwab Road under the viaduct to Northwest Highway. Turn right (east), follow the sidewalk crossing the Busse Highway Intersection, and then continue for two blocks to Garland Place. Turn left (north) onto Garland Place and follow for one block to Rand Road. The trail is very visible directly across Rand Road. Be cautious as you cross the street because Rand Road is a hazardous crossing.

South of Lawrence Avenue the trail becomes narrower, almost a footpath in parts, and is much closer to the bank of the river. In fact, much of the trail between Lawrence Avenue and North Avenue is the floodplain of the Des Plaines River. During wet seasons these sections may be impassable; one section that is difficult almost year-round is between Grand Avenue and Belmont. This section is very low and is often flooded. A good alternate route is to go west from either Grand or Belmont Avenue to Des Plaines River Road. Then go north or south to your desired intersection, east again over the river, and continue the trail.

From the north crossing Belmont Avenue, the trail is hard to locate. Crossing Belmont, you will notice a cemetery. Continue south behind the guardrail and follow the iron fence toward the river. Upon reaching the last fencepost follow the narrow path around it, and continue the trail south along the fence and cemetery property.

Another difficult section is near Fullerton Woods East. The main trail goes left (east), while the connecting trail goes along the river, past a dam and a bridge, finally crossing the river. Follow the main trail to the left for about one-quarter mile where another trail junction is reached. Again, follow the left trail, and you will find yourself at the water pump at Evans Field.

If you missed the turnoff for the main trail and do not desire to cross over the river (the trail would then end at First Avenue), there is a trail on the east side of the river at the foot of the bridge. This trail meanders through some floodplains and meets with the main trail to form the aforementioned junction. Follow the right trail, and again, you will find yourself at the water pump at Evans Field.

From Evans Field follow the entrance out to Thatcher Avenue and continue south on Thatcher Avenue. Cross North Avenue and continue south about 100 yards where a section of guardrail is separated (about four feet wide). A new shelter should be visible just yards behind the guardrail. The trail continues past the shelter and along the river.

The remainder of the trail is but a footpath which passes through some densely wooded areas. At Chicago Avenue the trail becomes an asphalt path for a short distance past a lagoon and behind the Trailside Museum.

The Trailside Museum is an excellent place to stop and view a variety of birds and mammals native to this area. Many of the wildlife on display are reestablishing themselves at this wildlife shelter; staff members are available for assistance.

South of the Trailside Museum the trail divides into two sections which meet again and form a loop. The shorter route follows Thatcher Avenue south again just beyond the Chicago and Northwestern Railroad where it turns into the woods and goes west. The longer route goes west through the woods, follows the bank of the river beyond the railroad tracks, and then moves east again to where the trails meet and form a loop just beside a trail shelter.

Facilities: There are many trail shelters located along this trail; however, many have been destroyed or are being eliminated and others are being replaced with new ones. Contact the Forest Preserve to find the exact locations of those available for use.

Water and restrooms are available at most of the forest preserve lands that have picnic areas; also, shelters and parking areas may be found at these forest preserves. A youth group campground is available at Camp Baden Powell on Des Plaines River Road south of the headquarters on Foundry Road in Mount Prospect.

Permits Required: Permits are required for the youth group campground. Horseback riders must have a license. Each group of twenty-five people or more must obtain permits for picnicking at any of the established areas. For picnic permits, you may contact the following in person: Permit Clerk, Forest Preserve District Office, Daley Center, 50 W. Washington, Room 406, Chicago.

Park Rules and Regulations: Use receptacles for garbage and trash. Report any fires. No alcoholic beverages allowed.

Mailing Address and Phone Numbers: For additional facilities maps and maps of the ten divisions of forest preserve districts in Cook County contact: Forest Preserve General Headquarters, 536 North Harlem Avenue, River Forest, Illinois 60305; 708/261-8400 (city), 708/366-9420 (suburban); Des Plaines Division Headquarters, River Road at Foundry Road, Mount Prospect, Illinois 60056; 708/824-1900 or 824-1883

12. Palatine Trail

Trail Length: 4 miles (6.4 kilometers)

Location: The Palatine Trail is located in Palatine. The trail may be reached by north- and southbound traffic by taking State Route 53 and exiting west onto Palatine Road. Go on Palatine Road for eight blocks until Winston Drive. Turn right (north) on Winston Drive and proceed for about four blocks to Maple Park. The trailhead is found at Maple Park.

County: Cook

Illinois Highway Map Coordinates: B-9

U.S.G.S. Topographical Map Names and Scale: Lake Zurich and Palatine, both 1:24,000

Hours Open: The trail is open year-round.

History and Trail Description: The idea for the construction of a multipurpose hiking, biking, and nature trail was initially presented to the Board of Commissioners of the Palatine Park District in 1963 during the preparation of a Master Plan for Parks and Recreation for Palatine. A portion of an abandoned railroad right-of-way was acquired in 1966. Funds for the construction of the trail were provided by the sale of general obligation bonds as approved in a referendum in 1972.

The Palatine Trail system is a paved asphalt trail which extends through an open corridor, going by numerous parks, schools, and residential neighborhoods.

The trail is indicated with metal posts marked Palatine Trail. These signs are seen at the intersections of several roads that must be crossed.

The trail may be started across the street from Maple Park, on the north side of Anderson Drive. The trailhead at Maple Park goes northward, passing by a small creek, Doug Lindberg Park, and Lake Louise School.

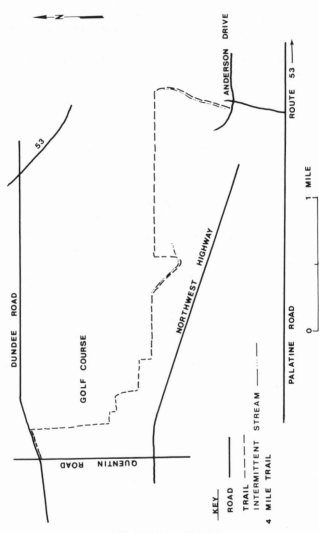

12. Palatine Trail

The trail then turns west and follows the power lines. Jane Adams School and Sycamore Park can be seen while hiking this section, where a few roads are also crossed.

As soon as you come to Hicks Highway, continue south to a small creek. The trail goes underneath the road at this point and comes up on the west side of Hicks Highway. The trail then crosses three small wooden bridges, goes by a large apartment complex, and then parallels the power lines again. You will pass Salt Creek Nature Study Area, Ashwood Park, and a water retention area.

You will cross Smith Road, following the trail behind some housing units. The trail borders the south side of Palatine Hills Golf Course and Recreation Area. From here, the trail follows the road that goes into the golf course, and then continues west through another gate and into a stretch of forest. The trail goes north at this point, passing through the woods all the way to Dundee Road. The trail then goes west on the sidewalk for a quarter mile to Quentin Road where the trail ends. Hikers can cross Dundee Road to Deer Grove Forest Preserve and hike along the Deer Grove Bicycle Trail, if they so choose.

Facilities: Various recreation facilities may be found at the parks along the route of the trail.

Mailing Address and Phone Number: Palatine Park District, 250 East Wood Street, Palatine, Illinois 60067; 708/991-0333

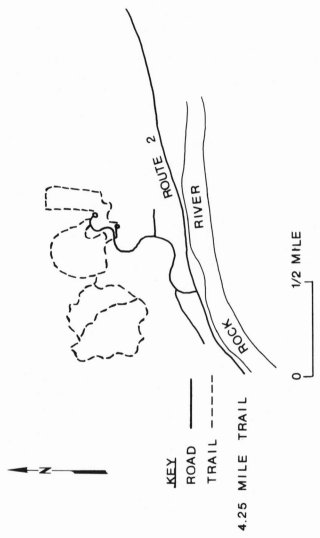

KEY

ROAD

TRAIL - - - -

4.25 MILE TRAIL

ROUTE 2

RIVER

ROCK

N

0   1/2 MILE

13. Castle Rock State Park

13. Castle Rock State Park

Trail Length: 4.25 miles (6.8 kilometers)

Location: Castle Rock State Park is located 3 miles south of Oregon, Illinois, on Route 2, and about 15 miles north of Dixon, on Route 2.

County: Ogle

Illinois Highway Map Coordinates: C-6

U.S.G.S. Topographical Map Name and Scale: Daysville, 1:24,000

Hours Open: The park is open year-round except on Christmas Day and New Year's Day.

History and Trail Description: Located along the west bank of the Rock River, the park and area have spectacular rock formations and deep ravines. A sandstone butte adjacent to the river has given the park its name.

Originally the area was inhabited by Indians. After various battles the natives were eventually forced out, and the Castle Rock vicinity was settled by New Englanders early in the nineteenth century. Proposed as a state park in 1921 by the Friends of Our Native Landscape, it was so dedicated on August 29, 1978. Now Castle Rock consists of approximately 2,000 acres, 710 of which are designated as an Illinois Nature Preserve.

The park has two trail systems, northeast of the Nature Preserve, reached from the Valley View Picnic Area and the Aspen Ridge Picnic Area (north trails, which are described in this volume), and shorter trails south of the Nature Preserve (south trails).

The north trails have four short interconnected loops which when combined total 4.25 miles. These are the Wildlife Viewing, Heather Valley, Timber Edge, and Forest Ridge trails. Each of these has a very accurate trailboard with map and directions at the trailhead, and

markers at trail junctions with trail names and direction-
al arrows.

The Wildlife Viewing and Heather Valley trails are
part of a self-guided nature trail. A separate park brochure is available for this, and it highlights 28 different
features of the area. Unique natural resources can be
observed from all the trails. These features include open
fields, hillside prairies, steep sloping bluffs and ravines,
and sandstone outcroppings.

Trailheads for Wildlife Viewing, Heather Valley, and
Timber Edge trails are at the north side of the Valley View
Picnic Area parking. Also, these trails can be reached
across the park road from the Aspen Ridge Picnic Area.

The Forest Ridge Trail is easily reached from the
extreme northeast part of the Valley View Picnic Area or
the east end of the Aspen Ridge Picnic Area. All of the
trails are well maintained as either mowed grass or
sandy/grassy.

Facilities: At this time Castle Rock State Park offers picnicking, drinking water, toilets, fishing, boating, launching
ramp, and hunting. A nature preserve is also located
within the park. All Illinois fishing rules and regulations
are in effect.

Permits Required: A hunting permit is required.

Park Rules and Regulations: No camping is allowed. See
Appendixes A and B.

Mailing Address and Phone Number: Site Superintendent, Castle Rock State Park, R. R. 2, Oregon, Illinois
61061; 815/732-7329

14. The Great Western Trail

Trail Length: 17 miles (27 kilometers)

Location: The Great Western Trail is located in north-eastern Illinois two miles west of St. Charles. The east trailhead is located on the south side of Dean Street opposite the entrance for LeRoy Oakes Forest Preserve. Traveling east or west on State Route 64, signs for LeRoy Oakes Forest Preserve can be seen. From Route 64 follow Randall Road north to Dean Street. Go west on Dean Street for one-half mile and turn south, across from the entrance for LeRoy Oakes Forest Preserve.

The west trailhead is located in Sycamore at the intersection of Route 64, Old State Road, and Airport Road. Sycamore is located at the intersection of Route 23 and Route 64, five miles north of De Kalb.

Counties: De Kalb and Kane

Illinois Highway Map Coordinates: C-8

U.S.G.S. Topographical Map Names and Scale: Geneva, Elburn, Maple Park, and Sycamore, all 1:24,000

Hours Open: The preserve is open from 8:00 a.m. to 9:00 p.m. Monday through Friday and from 7:00 a.m. to 9:00 p.m. Saturdays and Sundays. Trail users are urged to complete their journeys by sundown.

History and Trail Description: The Great Western Trail is a crushed stone path about ten feet wide which parallels the north side of Route 64 for seventeen miles. Previously, the trail was a railroad bed, and evidence of the old railroad ties and markers are seen.

The right-of-way of the Great Western Trail was developed into a railroad in 1887 by the Minnesota and Northwestern Railroad. Later that same year the Chicago, St. Paul, and Kansas Railway purchased all property of the Minnesota and Northwestern Railroad. At its

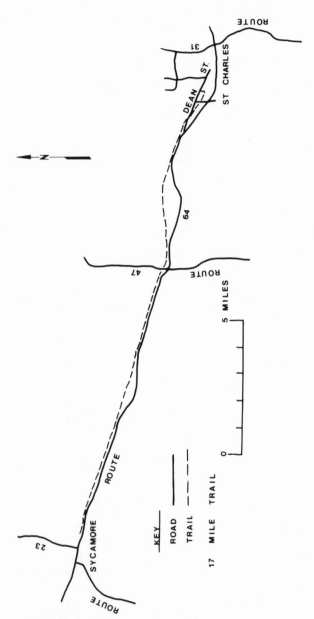

14. The Great Western Trail. Redrawn from Illinois
Department of Transportation county highway
map.

peak, the Chicago Great Western operated fifteen hundred miles of track connecting Illinois, Iowa, Kansas, Minnesota, Missouri, and Nebraska.

Along the 17-mile path are several prairie sites, marshes, wetlands resembling bogs, and several short, densely wooded areas. The trail also passes along several active farms and through the small communities of Wasco, Lily Lake, Virgil, Richardson, and Sycamore.

At several points along the trail adjoining woodlands have been developed into subdivisions. Mile markers are located on either side of the trail; these markers are wooden posts about one foot high, with red numbers on them, and are located one to two feet off the crushed stone path.

Additionally, the trail has stop signs at all road crossings, and there is a stop signal at Burlington Road, a hazardous crossing.

Wildlife in the area includes deer, racoon, opossum, beaver, fox, skunk, rabbit, and woodchucks. Also, a great variety of birds can be seen, including ducks, coot, and the great blue heron.

Primary users of the trail are bicyclists, mostly because of the trail length and because there are no camping facilities along the trail. The trail is also popular for cross-country skiers. Although LeRoy Oakes Forest Preserve and the Sycamore Community Park are the only established parking areas on the trail, there are many intersecting roads from which shuttles can be arranged for hikers if they wish to complete shorter lengths of the trail.

The Great Western Trail is a National Recreation Trail. See Appendix F.

Facilities: Restrooms are available at the trailhead (LeRoy Oakes Forest Preserve), at the Wasco Crossing, and at Sycamore Community Park. Water is available at LeRoy Oakes Forest Preserve, Wasco, Virgil, and Sycamore Community Park.

Three picnic tables and two shelters are located along the trail. Picnic tables are located between LeRoy Oakes and Wasco, one mile west of Route 47, just west of County Line Road, and at both trailheads. Shelters are available at Virgil, Lily Lake, and the trailhead opposite LeRoy Oakes Forest Preserve.

Trail Rules and Regulations: No horseback riding and no motorized vehicles. Hunting is not allowed, and pets must be on a leash.

Mailing Address and Phone Number: Kane County Forest Preserve District, 719 Batavia Avenue, Geneva, Illinois 60134; 708/232-1242

15. The Illinois Prairie Path

Trail Length: 58 miles (93.23 kilometers)

Location: The Illinois Prairie Path is located in north-eastern Illinois. The trail has five main branches: from Wheaton one branch goes northwest to Elgin; a second branch goes from Wheaton past the West Chicago Prairie to the Fox River and auxiliary trails; the third branch from Wheaton goes southwest to East-West Tollway 88 and then goes west and northwest to the Fox River and Batavia; the fourth branch from Wheaton goes south-west (same as the third branch) but then goes further southwest of the East-West Tollway to Aurora; and the fifth branch from Wheaton goes east to Bellwood.

The great length and number of main branch trails make access and desired distances very accommodating since the trail goes through many communities including Bellwood, Berkeley, Elmhurst, Villa Park, Lombard, Glen Ellyn, Wheaton, Warrenville, Aurora, Winfield, Batavia, Geneva, West Chicago, South Elgin, and Elgin.

All the main branches of the Illinois Prairie Path join at Carlton Avenue and Liberty Street in Wheaton. The midpoint is from Elmer J. Hoffman Park in Wheaton, which is on Prospect Road (north-south), off Hill Avenue, just one-half block east of where Hill Avenue crosses the railroad tracks. (See "Facilities" for other trail access points and parking locations.)

Illinois roadways to the trail include north-south Routes 25, 31, 53, 59, 83, and Tollroads 294 and 355. The east-west roads for access to surrounding communities of the Prairie Path include Tollroad 90 to Elgin, Routes 20 and 64 (North Avenue), Route 38 (Roosevelt Road), Route 56 (Butterfield Road), and East-West Tollway 88.

Counties: Kane, Du Page, Cook

Illinois Highway Map Coordinates: C-8 and C-9

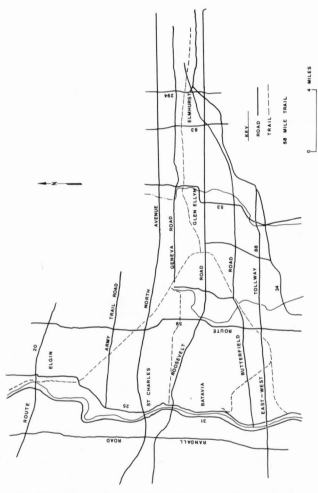

15. The Illinois Prairie Path. Redrawn from Illinois
Prairie Path map.

U.S.G.S. Topographical Map Names and Scale: Elm-hurst, Lombard, Wheaton, Naperville, West Chicago, Geneva, Aurora, and Elgin, all 1:24,000

Hours Open: The area is open year-round. No restricted hours, but daylight hours are standard for safety reasons.

History and Trail Description: The Illinois Prairie Path is a multipurpose trail available for hiking, biking, and horseback riding. The Prairie Path follows the route of the former Chicago, Aurora, and Elgin Railway.

The Illinois Prairie Path was the idea of Mrs. May Theilgoord Watts, distinguished naturalist, teacher, and author. In addition, local responses and the cooperation of utility companies and civic leaders along with state, county, and municipal officials played a vital role in the path development. In 1966, the path, a not-for-profit corporation, was formally established under a lease grant-ed by Du Page County, owner of the rights-of-way.

On June 2, 1971, a major portion of the path was designated a Recreation Trail of the National Trails Sys-tem, becoming the first trail in Illinois to be so desig-nated. (See Appendix F.) In 1972, the Illinois Department of Conservation purchased the Kane County segments of the rights-of-way and leased the property to the Forest Preserve District for use as part of the path. In 1979, the state acquired four and a half miles of right-of-way in Cook County to First Avenue in Maywood.

From the Historic Bridge over the Chicago and Northwestern Railway in Wheaton, the branch to Elgin passes through wooded areas, such as the Lincoln Marsh (one mile from the bridge) and the Timber Ridge Pre-serve. The Lincoln Marsh has a connecting trail to the short nature trail in the wetland ecosystem. Further northwest, the trail passes through residential and rural communities, many times bordering farm fields. This section is generally about six feet wide and comprised of crushed limestone. In Elgin, at Raymond Street and Purify Drive, the Prairie Path is linked to the Fox River Trail.

Wooden posts with yellow numbers are the mile markers along the trail. Most crossings have the name of the road and show the Prairie Path emblem, a green oval with three railroad spikes forming an inverted Y. Also, within the oval are the symbols for footprints, a horseshoe, and a bicycle wheel. At Kenyan Road, where the Model Railroad Club is housed, is the Clintonville Station of the Chicago, Aurora, and Elgin.

The branch of the Prairie Path from Wheaton east to Bellwood may be the most popular trail section, because it passes through many developed areas. From Wheaton going east, the Path passes through Glen Ellyn, Lombard, Villa Park, Elmhurst, Berkeley, and Bellwood. An extension to First Avenue in Maywood is being developed. Many of the communities have taken advantage of the railroad rights-of-way by developing parks along the path. These parks often have benches and water available. Some points of interest along this branch of the Prairie Path include the Villa Avenue CA & E Station, the Elmer J. Hoffman Park in Wheaton, and Wheaton College.

The trail sections from Wheaton to Batavia and Aurora are similar in construction to the other branches; that is, crushed limestone. From the Historic Bridge in Wheaton the path runs parallel to Carlton Avenue two blocks south to Roosevelt Road. Just south of Roosevelt Road is the Prairie Path Park owned by Wheaton Park District (another Prairie Path Park is in Glen Ellyn).

The newest section of the Prairie Path connects to the Fox River Trail at Bennett Park in Geneva by traveling east on Dodson Street to Eastside Drive and Water Tower Road. At this intersection the Prairie Path goes east four miles to Read-Keppler Park in West Chicago. The section of rail from Read-Keppler Park to the trail junction at the Timber Preserve is not fully developed at the time of this writing; however, this three-mile section can be easily bypassed and other parts of the trail can be picked up.

This trail section passes by Blackwell Forest Preserve. A parking area and camping facilities are available at this preserve. See Trail 18 for a description of the paths found here. This preserve is reached from Batavia Road in Warrenville; proceed east one-eighth mile on Butterfield Road to the entrance.

Just north of East-West Tollway 88 along Eola Road is another trail junction referred to as the Batavia Junction Detour. This trail junction can make a convenient connecting trail if a shorter hike and loop trail is desired; for example, hiking from Aurora northeast to the Batavia and then back south with the Fox River Trail can make a 15-mile loop section if desired. To complete this loop, go northwest from Eola Road and the East-West Tollway to the Fox River in Batavia and cross over to the west side of the river via Wilson Road. Then follow the Fox River Trail south to Illinois Avenue in Aurora; go east and access the Prairie Path again.

Facilities: Water fountains are located in various parks along the trail. Restaurants, gas stations, and other businesses are located in almost all the communities through which the path travels. For camping areas contact the Du Page and Kane County Forest Preserves listed below. Free parking is available at the following sites: in Elmhurst—east of York Road between Vallette Street and the Path and west of Spring Road north of the Path; in Villa Park—west of Villa Avenue on Central Boulevard; in Lombard—west of Westmore Avenue; in Glen Ellyn—Hill Avenue between Glen Ellyn and Lombard; in Wheaton—at the County Courthouse parking lot; near Elgin—at County Farm and Geneva Roads; in Aurora—at McCullough Park, Illinois Avenue; and in Geneva—Bennett Park, Illinois Route 25.

Permits Required: None listed; however, it is recommended that one check with authorities listed under "Mailing Addresses and Phone Numbers."

Park Rules and Regulations: No motorized vehicles, alcoholic beverages, or firearms. No kite or model airplane flying allowed. No camping or cookouts allowed.

Mailing Addresses and Phone Numbers: Illinois Prairie Path, P.O. Box 1086, 616 Delles Road, Wheaton, Illinois 60189; or Forest Preserve District of Du Page County, 185 Spring Avenue, Glen Ellyn, Illinois 60137; 708/790-4900; or Kane County Forest Preserve District, 719 Batavia Avenue, Geneva, Illinois 60134; 708/232-1242

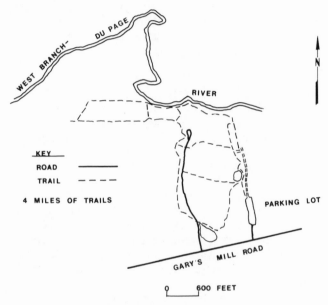

16. West Du Page Woods Forest Preserve. Redrawn from park trail map.

16. West Du Page Woods Forest Preserve

Trail Length: 4 miles (6.4 kilometers)

Location: West Du Page Woods is located in Winfield. The preserve may be reached by east- and westbound traffic by taking Roosevelt Road (Route 38). One mile west of the intersection of Roosevelt Road and Winfield Road is Gary's Mill Road. Turn east onto Gary's Mill Road and proceed for about five blocks to the parking area. This is the Elsen's Hill area.

County: Du Page

Illinois Highway Map Coordinates: C-9

U.S.G.S. Topographical Map Name and Scale: Naperville, 1:24,000

Hours Open: The preserve is open every day of the year. The preserve opens one hour after sunrise and closes one hour after sunset.

History and Trail Description: West Du Page Woods was acquired in 1919 and is one of the oldest of the Forest Preserve District of Du Page County's forty-three preserves. West Du Page Woods has 470 acres of upland woods and has one of the few fens in Du Page County.

West Du Page Woods has two areas to hike. The first as described here is at the Elsen's Hill area on Gary's Mill Road. The second location is at the west entrance off of Route 59.

The trail system at the Elsen's Hill area consists of four interconnecting loops that total 4 miles. The trail system may be started north of the parking area by the small pond. An information board which contains a trail map is set up at the north end of the parking lot.

Here the trails are marked with brown fiberglass posts which have different symbols on them such as circles, which signify the loops. These trails may be hiked in any direction and are used by hikers, horseback riders, and skiers.

Most of the trails go through upland forest, passing residential homes on the west side of the park and paralleling the west branch of the Du Page River on the north. The trail also goes by a small pond and around Elsen's Hill.

Future plans call for having the Regional Trail extend from Blackwell Forest Preserve through here and then hook up with a spur of the Illinois Prairie Path.

Facilities: West Du Page Woods has an information board, water, restrooms, picnic tables, and a site superintendent's home.

Park Rules and Regulations: Pets must be on a leash. Alcoholic beverages are prohibited.

Mailing Address and Phone Number: Forest Preserve District of Du Page County, P.O. Box 2339, Glen Ellyn, Illinois 60138; 708/790-4900

17. Virgil L. Gilman Nature Trail

Trail Length: 9.7 miles (15.5 kilometers)

Location: The Virgil L. Gilman Nature Trail is located in northeastern Illinois, beginning south of Aurora in Montgomery. From Chicago and the east, the trailhead is reached via Illinois Tollway 88 to State Route 31 south. Follow 31 south through Aurora into Montgomery to Montgomery Road.

Go one and three-tenths of a mile east on Montgomery Road to Ohio Street (some maps show this as Hill Avenue) and turn south for seven-tenths of a mile to the trailhead. The trailhead is on the west side of Ohio Street and has a small parking area and trail information board. The trail can also be reached from Bliss Woods Forest Preserve. Bliss Woods Forest Preserve is on Bliss Road about half a mile east of Route 47 (north of Route 56 and south of Waubonsee Community College).

County: Kane

Illinois Highway Map Coordinates: C-8

U.S.G.S. Topographical Map Names and Scale: Aurora South, Sugar Grove, and Aurora North, all 1:24,000

Hours Open: Sunrise to sunset

History and Trail Description: The Virgil L. Gilman Nature Trail follows the railroad rights-of-way of the Elgin, Joliet, and Eastern Railroad, and the Chicago, Milwaukee, St. Paul, and Pacific Railroad.

The Virgil L. Gilman Nature Trail is a smooth, crushed limestone path about six feet wide in many sections, while other sections are asphalt paved as this is also a very popular bike route.

Most of the path is easy to follow from any access point; however, one section in Aurora is somewhat difficult to follow. Between Terry Avenue and Lake Street

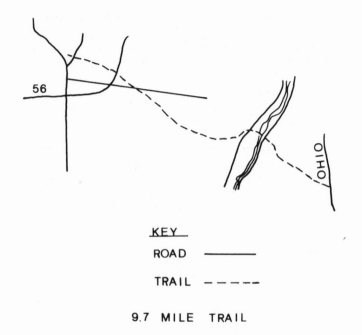

56

KEY

ROAD ————

TRAIL — — — —

9.7 MILE TRAIL

0   5 MILES

17. Virgil L. Gilman Nature Trail. Redrawn from
    Illinois Department of Transportation county
    highway map.

(Route 31) the trail actually becomes the sidewalks winding through this residential and industrial neighbor-
hood. There are signs (white arrows on a brown background) indicating travel direction for the path, but only
a few are scattered along this six-block section.

Traveling east, the path at Terry Avenue goes one-
quarter block north to the first intersection then east to
Elmwood Drive. Go north on Elmwood Drive for one
block, then east for one block. At the stop sign, turn right
(south) one block to the parking lot where the trail is
located. The opposite directions are appropriate for
going westbound.

The trail passes through rural, suburban, and urban
areas. Some sections offer a view of farmlands; other
sections pass through residential areas as well as some
commercial/industrial areas. One section near Waubausee
Creek has a marsh adjacent to the trail.

Native plants and wildlife of Illinois can be seen
along most sections of the trail. Some of the trees that can
be seen include cottonwoods, white poplars, sycamores,
and oak. Birds seen along the trail include duck, heron,
redwing blackbirds, woodpeckers, cardinals, and blue-
jays.

Probably the most interesting section of the trail is
west of Terry Avenue where the trail passes through its
most densely wooded section. Another interesting section is the crossing of the truss bridge spanning the Fox
River.

The newest section of trail crosses Galena Boulevard
and continues half a mile to Route 56 where one can
cross over Route 56 or follow the safer alternative of
using the tunnel. West of Route 56 the trail parallels
Blackberry Creek as it meanders two more miles across
Bliss Road to Bliss Woods Forest Preserve. This section of
trail offers good views of native plants and wildlife, as
well as of rural and residential areas of Illinois.

The Virgil L. Gilman Nature Trail is considered a
National Recreation Trail. See Appendix F.

Facilities: Numerous parking and access points are available for the Virgil L. Gilman Nature Trail at the Bliss
Woods Forest Preserve, at Galena Boulevard east of

Gordon Road, Barnes Road near the Blackberry Histori-
cal Village, Orchard Road, Jericho Road at Edgelawn
Drive (Copley No. 1 Park) Route 31, Route 25, Ashland
Avenue, Montgomery Road, and Ohio Street.

Restrooms and shelters are available at Lebanon
Park on Douglas Avenue, at Copley No. 1 Park, along the
trail just east of Orchard Road, and at Bliss Woods Forest
Preserve. Picnic areas are also available at several of the
access points and parking areas in Aurora, also at the
Galena Boulevard parking area and at Bliss Woods Forest
Preserve. Limited camping is available at Bliss Woods
Forest Preserve.

Trail Rules and Regulations: No camping, fires, dumping, or littering, and no hunting.

Mailing Addresses and Phone Numbers: Fox Valley Park
District, 712 South River Street, Aurora, Illinois 60506;
708/897-0516; Kane County Forest Preserve District,
719 Batavia Avenue, Geneva, Illinois 60134; 708/232-
1242

18. Blackwell Forest Preserve

Trail Length: 5.8 miles (9.3 kilometers)

Location: The Blackwell Forest Preserve is located in Warrenville, Illinois. South Blackwell Forest Preserve borders Butterfield Road and Winfield Road, with the main park entrance off Butterfield Road. To reach the trailhead at North Blackwell, travelers may take Winfield Road to Mack Road. Turn west on Mack Road, go 1 mile, and turn into a parking lot on the north side of the road. A sign there states Blackwell North Area. A trailboard is located at this trailhead.

County: Du Page

Illinois Highway Map Coordinates: C-9

U.S.G.S. Topographical Map Name and Scale: Naperville, 1:24,000

Hours Open: The Preserve is open every day of the year. The Preserve is open one hour after sunrise and is closed one hour after sunset.

History and Trail Description: Early in 1960 the Forest Preserve District of Du Page County purchased a worked-out gravel pit as their land reclamation program. The district believed that the gravel pit had excellent potential as a multiple-use recreation area. The gravel pit could be transformed into a large recreational lake and serve as a major rainwater retention basin. In order for this idea to come true, the gravel pit needed to be deeper and larger.

At the same time that the lakes were being excavated, the county leaders were concerned about the growing problem of solid waste disposal in Du Page County. The district developed a plan that would solve the problems of waste disposal and clay disposal from the construction of the lake.

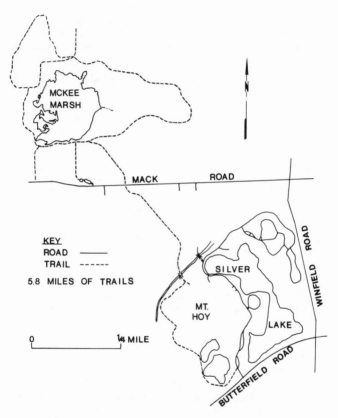

18. Blackwell Forest Preserve. Redrawn from park
map.

A hill constructed of garbage and refuse was built next to the lake. Clay removed from the lake was used to cover the refuse, which was deposited every day. When the hill was completed, it was transformed into a winter sports area. This hill, now known as Mt. Hoy, rises more than 150 feet above its surroundings, making it the highest point in Du Page County.

The district purchased adjacent forest and meadow-land to increase the size of the preserve to more than 1,300 acres. The preserve is named in honor of a former board president, Roy C. Blackwell.

Blackwell Preserve consists of two tracts: North Blackwell and South Blackwell. South Blackwell encompasses the recreation facilities, while North Blackwell remains virtually undeveloped.

The trail system at Blackwell Forest Preserve may be started or ended at North or South Blackwell areas. North Blackwell contains 5.2 miles of trails while South Blackwell contains 3.6 miles of trails.

The main trail at South Blackwell is the Regional Trail (1.7 miles). This trailhead is found near the first parking spot off Butterfield Road. Directly across from the parking area, the hiker will see a sign that states Regional Trail. The Regional Trail is an eight-foot-wide pebbled trail. The trail winds its way on the south side of a small pond, past the small lake, and then past a parking area. The hiker will notice that the beach is closed and all fenced in now. The lake is being monitored for pollutants which have leached out of a landfill (Mt. Hoy).

Mt. Hoy, the main landmark in South Blackwell, is seen constantly by the hiker as he or she hikes this trail segment. A trail makes its way up the north side of Mt. Hoy. From here you have a good view of the park and the surrounding area. A tubing run is set up here for winter enthusiasts.

Once past the parking lot near Mt. Hoy, the trail goes into a wooded section and will shortly come to Springbrook Creek. Here the hiker will cross over a small steel bridge and then start hiking through an open field. This trail segment heads northwest toward Mack Road. A trail sign will be seen near the road. The hiker then crosses this road and proceeds hiking at North

Blackwell. The trails at North Blackwell consist of a large loop trail (Circle Trail), a segment of the Regional Trail which terminates at Gary's Mill Road, and a few short trail cutbacks, one which leads to the parking area and trailhead.

The Circle Trail is a 3-mile trail which does a large loop around McKee Marsh. The trail is both crushed rock as well as dirt. The trail basically goes through open fields and some low-lying areas. Many bird species will be observed while hiking along this trail.

On the north side of McKee Marsh, the trail joins the Regional Trail, which takes the hiker to Gary's Mill Road, or the hiker can hike a little trail loop, or hike back toward the trailhead. The east side of McKee Marsh is wooded and pretty. The hiker will get some good views of the marsh here.

Cross-country skiing is allowed on any of the trails in the park.

Facilities: Blackwell Forest Preserve has campgrounds, a boat launch, a tubing run, and numerous picnic sites which have picnic tables, restrooms, water, and shelters. Fishing is allowed in Silver Lake contingent upon all Illinois fishing rules and regulations.

Permits Required: Permits are required for boating on Silver Lake. Annual permits may be obtained from the district headquarters, while daily passes may be obtained at the concessions stand. A camping permit is required at the family campground. Annual permits are required for horseback riding. Horse riders are not allowed in picnic and campground areas at the south end of the park.

Park Rules and Regulations: Pets must be on a leash. No boat shall be more than twenty feet in length. No gas motors are allowed, and no inflatable crafts, rafts, pontoons, or wind-surfers are allowed.

Mailing Address and Phone Number: Forest Preserve District of Du Page County, P.O. Box 2339, Glen Ellyn, Illinois 60138; 708/790-4900

19. Fox River Bike Trail

Trail Length: 20 miles (32 kilometers)

Location: The Fox River Trail is located in northeastern Illinois along the Fox River between Crystal Lake, Illinois, and Aurora, Illinois. Major north-south roads for access include Routes 25 and 31. The major east-west roadways include Illinois 14, 56, 38, 64, 20 and Toll-roads 88 and 90. The trail is accessed at any east-west road reaching the Fox River in Carpentersville, East and West Dundee, Elgin, St. Charles, Geneva, Batavia, and Aurora. Refer to "Facilities" for parking areas.

Counties: Kane, McHenry

Illinois Highway Map Coordinates: C-8

U.S.G.S. Topographical Map Names and Scale: Geneva, Aurora North, and Crystal Lake, all 1:24,000

Hours Open: Daylight hours

History and Trail Description: The Fox River Trail is part of the Fox Valley trail system which includes the Great Western Trail, Virgil L. Gilman Nature Trail, connecting trails with the Illinois Prairie Path, and numerous auxiliary trails. The trail has two parts, one in McHenry County beginning at the intersection of Pyott Road and Virginia Road in Crystal Lake and continuing south into Kane County all the way south to New York Street in Aurora. The trail is marked well at nearly all road crossings and is easily identifiable as it is asphalt paved virtually the entire length. Following the trail section between Crystal Lake and Carpentersville one will enjoy trail sections passing through residential and rural areas. There are numerous undeveloped wooded areas to enjoy north of Carpentersville and a good opportunity to spot wildlife.

In St. Charles the path passes along Langum Park, Riverside Park, Good Templar Park, Bennett Park, Island

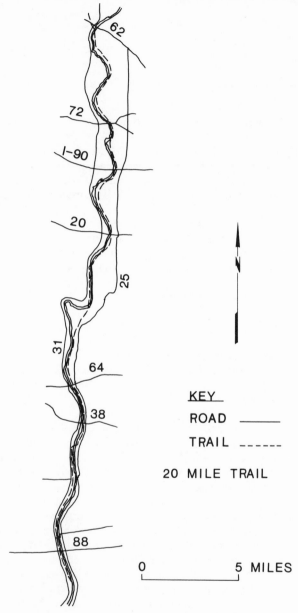

KEY

ROAD ——————

TRAIL ------

20 MILE TRAIL

0 ————— 5 MILES

19. Fox River Bike Trail. Redrawn from Illinois
Department of Transportation county highway
maps.

Park, Old Mill Park, and Fabyan Forest Preserve. In Geneva a spur trail connects with Island Park via two bridges. Either section can be hiked; take a bridge to the island or remain on the main trail along the river bank.

This section is marked primarily by symbols, such as a bicycle and an arrow, on wooden posts indicating usage and direction.

The trail south of Batavia is along the west side of the river and is marked with white symbols on a brown background and mounted on wooden posts identifying the trail system.

An auxiliary trail exists on the east side of the Fox River in Batavia. This trail is an ideal connecting trail for the Illinois Prairie Path. A trail junction north of the Fox Valley Country Club travels southeasterly toward the Kane–Du Page county line where, on the south side of Butterfield Road, is the auxiliary trail end and Illinois Prairie Path boundary.

Facilities: There are no established facilities available on the trail, but in St. Charles, Geneva, and Batavia, water, restaurants, and restrooms are available. Parking is available at parks and along most streets in these communities.

Trail Rules and Regulations: No snowmobiles, motorcycles or motorized vehicles of any type. No alcoholic beverages. Picnicking is allowed in designated sites only. Fishing is not allowed along the trail. Pedestrians and joggers have the right-of-way. Users should remain on the right hand side of the trail.

Mailing Addresses and Phone Numbers: Geneva Park District, 1250 South Street, Geneva, Illinois 60134; 708/232-4542; or Kane County Forest Preserve District, 719 Batavia Avenue-Bldg. A, Geneva, Illinois 60134; 708/232-1242; or Crystal Lake Park District; 815/459-0680

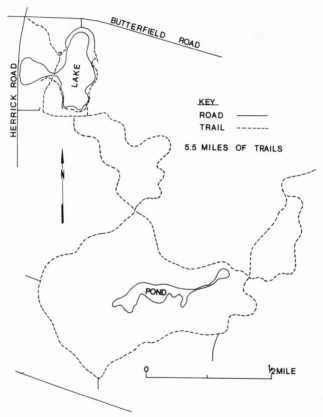

20. Herrick Lake Forest Preserve. Redrawn from park
map.

20. Herrick Lake Forest Preserve

Trail Length: 5.5 miles (8.8 kilometers)

Location: Herrick Lake Forest Preserve is located in Wheaton, Illinois. The park may be reached by east- or westbound traffic by taking Butterfield Road (Route 56). The park is two miles west of Naperville Road and one mile east of Winfield Road. The main entrance to the park is off Butterfield Road, with a second entrance to the park from Herrick Road. Herrick Road is located just west of the main entrance. Turn south on Herrick Road and proceed for a few blocks to the parking area.

County: Du Page

Illinois Highway Map Coordinates: C-9

U.S.G.S. Topographical Map Name and Scale: Naperville, 1:24,000

Hours Open: The preserve is open every day of the year. The preserve is open one hour after sunrise and is closed one hour after sunset.

History and Trail Description: Herrick Lake Forest Preserve consists of 764 acres of woodlands including a 22-acre lake. The lake is natural and was formed when the Wisconsin Glacier retreated fourteen thousand years ago.

The trail system at Herrick Lake consists of three loops which total 5.5 miles. This trail system is multipurpose; hikers, bicyclists, and horseback riders use it. The trail may be reached from the parking lots either off Butterfield Road or Herrick Road. There is an information board set up at both parking lots which show the trail layout.

If the hiker starts hiking from the parking lot off Butterfield Road he or she can pick up the trail on either side of Herrick Lake. The entire trail is surfaced with limestone screenings. The trail on the west side of Herrick Lake connects with another spur trail which goes to Herrick Road. Following Herrick Road for a short distance north, the hiker will come across the Illinois Prairie Path.

Following the trail around the lake, the hiker will go past the other parking area, or he or she can follow the trail around the lake. The trail then hooks up with the main trail and the three loops.

The first loop segment takes the hiker through some wooded areas and past the golf course. The trail is about 10 feet wide and leveled with limestone. The trail then joins the second loop in the middle of an open field.

Hikers can then choose which direction they would like to hike in. If they head east they will go through a small wooded area and a small prairie. Hikers will also go by a small pond. Shortly past the pond the hikers will reach the third loop segment.

The third loop segment goes around a small grassy area and borders recreation facilities on the east side. Also found here is the connecting trail to Danada Forest Preserve.

Hikers can then follow the trail system back to the trailhead following the second half of the three loop segments.

Facilities: Herrick Lake Forest Preserve has picnic areas with shelters, picnic tables, restrooms, and water available. On the northern shore of the lake, a concessionaire sells snacks and rents rowboats and canoes. A youth camping area is also available in the preserve. Fishing is allowed in Herrick Lake with all appropriate rules and regulations in effect.

Permits Required: A camping permit is required for youth camping. Annual permits are required for horseback riding. The two shelters and two of the picnic areas may be reserved. All permits may be obtained at district headquarters.

Park Rules and Regulations: Pets must be on a leash. Alcoholic beverages are prohibited. Private boating is prohibited, and motorized vehicles are prohibited on the grounds.

Mailing Address and Phone Number: Forest Preserve District of Du Page County, P.O. Box 2339, Glen Ellyn, Illinois 60138; 708/790-4900

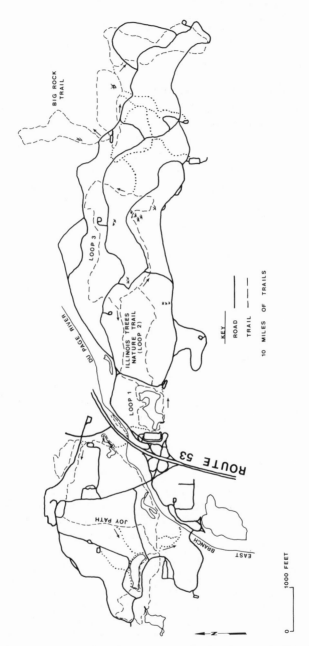

21. The Morton Arboretum. Redrawn from "Walking Trails of the Morton Arboretum."

21. The Morton Arboretum

Trail Length: 10 miles (16 kilometers)

Location: The Morton Arboretum is located just north of Lisle and the East-West Tollway (Illinois 88) and twenty-five miles west of Chicago. Exit north onto Route 53 off Illinois 88. Entrances to the Arboretum are accessible from either northbound or southbound State Route 53, which bisects the park. From Chicago and the suburbs, the Morton Arboretum is easily reached via the Eisenhower Expressway (290) to Illinois 88, or from the Tri-State Tollway (294) to Illinois 88 then west to Route 53.

County: Du Page

Illinois Highway Map Coordinates: C-9

U.S.G.S. Topographical Map Name and Scale: Wheaton, 1:24,000

Hours Open: Grounds open every day, weather permitting, Standard Time 9:00 a.m. to 5:00 p.m. and Daylight Time 9:00 a.m. to 7:00 p.m. The Visitors Center is open 9:00 a.m. to 5:00 p.m. daily.

History and Trail Description: The Morton Arboretum was established in 1922 by Jay Morton, founder of the Morton Salt Company, on the grounds of his estate near Lisle. The grounds consist of 1,500 acres devoted to cultivated plants and natural vegetation displayed outdoors for people to study and enjoy.

The Arboretum is a privately endowed, not-for-profit educational foundation administered by a board of nine trustees.

The majority of the trails are on the east side of the Arboretum. Loops 1, 2, and 3 of the Illinois Trees Nature Trail begin at the Visitors Center and main parking area. These loops are identified on trailboards as you hike northwest away from Meadow Lake and the Visitors

Center. The trails alternate from dirt to wood-chip foot-paths. East of the Illinois Trees Nature Trail are the Big Rock, Forest, and East Woods Trails.

None of the trails is marked, but all are fairly easy to follow. All secondary/connecting trails are well maintained and may or may not be as wide as the main trails.

The trails on the east side of Morton Arboretum have the greatest amount of diversity, as the trails are rugged and hilly. These trails meander through dense woodlands, around marshes and along perennial streams. The Forest and East Woods Trails can be extremely difficult during the wet seasons, especially the north section of the Forest Trail which can become very muddy in parts.

The trail around Meadow Lake (at the Visitors Center) is a crushed stone path. At the main parking area a trailboard indicates the Illinois Trees Nature Trail and the secondary trail connecting the west side trails.

North of the main parking area a connecting trail follows the Du Page River under the bridge (Route 53) to Sunfish Pond and to the trails on the west side of the Arboretum. This is the only footpath connecting the east and west sides.

The Joy Path is a rough asphalt lane starting at the Thornhill Conference Center. The Joy Path crosses Lake Road, where it becomes a dirt path. A secondary trail connects the Joy Path with Lake Marmo which then connects with the Evergreen Trail, a wood-chip path which passes through tall stands of evergreens.

Generally the west side of the Arboretum has large gardens and the east side a great variety of trees. All of the trails can be hiked in one day.

Birds represent the most abundant wildlife within the Arboretum boundaries. Many ducks and other large birds are present at Meadow Lake by the Visitors Center.

Facilities: The Visitors Center is located on the east side of the Arboretum. An information building, theater, restaurant, and book and gift shop are also located there. The administration building contains the education department, library, research laboratories, and a climate and map room.

On the west side of the park is the Thornhill Conference Center, and the Outpost, which houses the classrooms for the education department.

Parking is available at the Visitors Center and throughout the Arboretum. There are restrooms at the Visitors Center and the Outpost. A public telephone is located in the foyer of the restaurant. The parking fee is $3.00 per car and $2.00 for senior citizens; there is no fee for pedestrians.

Rules and Regulations: There are no camping or picnic grounds at the Arboretum. Collecting of specimens of any kind is prohibited. No pets, bicycles, motorcycles, snowmobiles, intoxicants, or littering allowed. No excessive noise or parking along the roads.

Mailing Address and Phone Number: The Morton Arboretum, Lisle, Illinois 60532; 708/719-2400

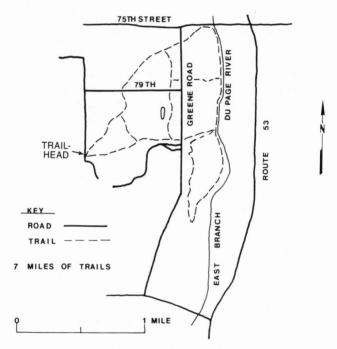

KEY

ROAD ▬▬▬▬▬▬

TRAIL ‒ ‒ ‒ ‒

7 MILES OF TRAILS

22. Greene Valley Forest Preserve

22. Greene Valley Forest Preserve

Trail Length: 7 miles (11.2 kilometers)

Location: Greene Valley Forest Preserve is located three miles west of Woodridge. To reach the park, State Route 53 may be taken by north- or southbound traffic. Turn west onto 75th Street and proceed for five blocks to Greene Road. Turn south onto Greene Road and go for another five blocks to 79th Street. Turn right (west) on 79th Street and go for a few blocks until reaching a forest preserve sign which reads "West Access Area." Turn left (south) on this road and proceed to the trailhead.

County: Du Page

Illinois Highway Map Coordinates: C-9

U.S.G.S. Topographical Map Name and Scale: Romeoville, 1:24,000

Hours Open: The preserve is open every day of the year. The preserve is open one hour after sunrise and is closed one hour after sunset.

History and Trail Description: Greene Valley Forest Preserve is named after the Greene family who settled and farmed the area. The site consists of 1,441 acres.

Greene Valley Forest Preserve's trail system consists of interconnecting loop segments which total over 7 miles in length. The trail system is multipurpose, with hiking, skiing, bicycling, and horseback riding allowed. Fourteen hundred acres of woodlands and grasslands are found at Greene Valley Preserve. An information board is found at the parking lot in the west access area. A trail map and park rules are encased in the information board.

The trails may be hiked in any direction and on any of the loops. There are a few cutbacks along the trails which can reduce the miles hiked. The trails are marked with geometric symbols on brown fiberglass posts. The trail system consists of a mowed grass path about twelve feet wide.

The main trail is designated with a white circle and starts at the trailhead. One segment of the main trail heads due east and goes by the site superintendent's home. This part of the trail goes through open fields. The trail comes to one of the cutback trails, which goes north. The trail heading north goes by a small pond, through woodlands, open fields, along power lines, and over 79th Street twice.

Trails on the east side of Greene Road parallel the east branch of the Du Page River and join with one of the cutbacks. The southern loop trail segment goes through an open field, with the landfill to the west. The trail also goes through some woods then heads back north back to the main trail segment, which the hiker can follow back west to the trailhead.

Facilities: Greene Valley Forest Preserve has an information board, restrooms, drinking water, telephone, and seventeen campsites set up for youth camping only. There is a designated area for dog sledding.

Permits Required: A camping permit is required for group camping. Annual permits are required for horseback riding. A permit is also required for dog sledders.

Park Rules and Regulations: Pets must be on a leash. No trespassing around the landfill site. Alcoholic beverages are prohibited.

Mailing Address and Phone Number: Forest Preserve District of Du Page County, P.O. Box 2339, Glen Ellyn, Illinois 60138; 708/790-4900

23. Waterfall Glen Forest Preserve

Trail Length: 8.5-mile loop trail (13.6 kilometers)

Location: Waterfall Glen Forest Preserve is located in northeastern Illinois approximately twenty-five miles southwest of Chicago. The most direct route to the parking area and trailhead is via Interstate 55 to Cass Avenue South. About one-eighth mile south of Interstate 55 one will find the entrance to the frontage road where the parking area and information building can be seen. Just beyond the information building is Northgate Road, where you turn west to the main parking area and trailhead.

Waterfall Glen Forest Preserve surrounds Argonne National Laboratory, which is centered between north-south routes 53 and 83, just south of Interstate 55.

County: Du Page

Illinois Highway Map Coordinate: C-9

U.S.G.S. Topographical Map Names and Scale: Sag Bridge and Romeoville, both 1:24,000

Hours Open: One hour after sunrise to one hour after sunset

History and Trail Description: The trail system at Waterfall Glen Forest Preserve surrounds Argonne National Laboratory. This area is a glacial till deposited by the Wisconsin Glacier.

At the trailhead an information board with a map displays the trails and identifies the other facilities available at Waterfall Glen.

The trail system is designed as a multipurpose trail and is used by hikers, horseback riders, cross-country skiers, and those interested in orienteering.

The trail system at Waterfall Glen consists of a main trail which circles Argonne National Laboratory and is

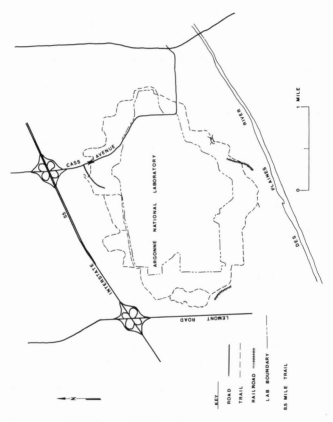

23. Waterfall Glen Forest Preserve

8.5 miles long. There are three loop trails connected to the main hiking trail which the hiker can also hike. These three loop segments are known as Tearthumb Swamp Cutback, Westgate Road Cutback, and the Kettle Hole Woods Cutback. By taking one of these loops the hiker can reduce the length of his or her hike.

Trails are marked with fiberglass posts which are brown in color and have a geometric symbol corresponding to the trail. The main hiking trail is designated by a white circle. Most of the trails are wide grassy lanes 30 feet wide. However, the main trail from the campground to Kettle Hole Woods Cutback is a combination of crushed stone paths and gravel roads.

All three loop segments pass through tall stands of evergreens, occasionally along bogs, and in several locations right through or right next to marsh. One side of the loop segment of the Tearthumb Swamp Cutback and Westgate Road Cutback follows along the fence surrounding Argonne Laboratory.

The main trail offers more variety than the shorter loop segments as it passes along marshes, bogs, prairies, and through densely wooded areas. A great variety of wildlife may be observed along the marshes of the main trail. A model airplane field also is located along this path.

On a high ridge at the southernmost point of the main trail is a scenic area which overlooks the Des Plaines River Valley. Another scenic view may be had from the iron footbridge. Here the trail crosses over the creek (there is a ford for horses) and offers a fine view of the V-shaped valley. A third attraction, probably the highlight of this trail, is the waterfall located a half mile west of the campground.

All along this trail system are footpaths, intersecting roads, and other wide lanes which intersect the main trail. The hiker must stay on the established trail since some of the surrounding property is privately owned.

A variety of wildlife can be seen at Waterfall Glen. The most frequently seen animals are the native white-tail deer and the white fallow deer imported from Asia. Also, many migratory birds can be seen.

Facilities: Restrooms, parking, and drinking water are available at the trailhead and campground. East of the blue loop, one-quarter mile south along the red loop, is a model airplane field. Orienteering courses are established along the northeast corner of Waterfall Glen.

Permits Required: Reservations are required for the model airplane field as well as for the campground; the parking area at the campground is reserved for people with camping permits. The campground is for organized youth groups. A County horse tag is required for equestrians.

Park Rules and Regulations: No alcohol is allowed on Preserve grounds. No collecting or hunting of trees, shrubs, flowers, or wildlife, except mushrooms, is permitted.

Fires must be contained in fireplaces and grills provided, or in a burner. Cutting and gathering firewood is not permitted. Pets are allowed, but must be on a leash at all times.

Mailing Address and Phone Number: Forest Preserve District of Du Page County, P.O. Box 2339, Glen Ellyn, Illinois 60138; 708/790-4900

24. Shabbona Lake State Park

Trail Length: 4.5 miles (7.2 kilometers)

Location: Shabbona Lake State Park is located one mile south of Shabbona off of State Route 30. To reach the park, State Route 30 can be taken to the town of Shabbona. In town there will be a sign pointing in the direction of the recreation area; this street is Preserve Road. Turn south on Preserve Road and proceed for one-half mile. Turn left (east) on another road and follow the sign one-half mile to the park entrance.

County: De Kalb

Illinois Highway Map Coordinates: C-7

U.S.G.S. Topographical Map Names and Scale: Shabbona Grove and Waterman, both 1:24,000

Hours Open: The park is open year-round. During the summer the park is open from 6:00 a.m. until 10:00 p.m. and in the winter from 8:00 a.m. until sundown.

History and Trail Description: Shabbona Lake State Park is a 1,550-acre recreation complex. The site development began in 1973 with a lake basin clearing program which included tree removal in selected areas, shoreline modification, and construction of earthen fishing piers. In 1974 the three-thousand-foot-long earthen dam and associated concrete spillway structure was started. The dam was completed in the fall of 1975, and the lake is now 318 acres in size. Day use area development began in 1976 and is continuing today.

   The 4.5-mile hiking trail follows the lake shore. The trail may be started at the Shabbona Grove Picnic Area or by Three Fires Picnic Area. The trail is called the Arrowhead Trail and is marked with two-foot wooden markers which have red arrowheads painted on them. At both

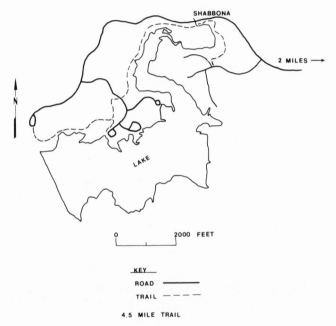

24. Shabbona Lake State Park. Redrawn from park
trail map.

starting points of the trail, trailboards have been set up showing the trail layout.

The trail is about eight feet wide and goes by wildlife food plots, up and down gently rolling hills, through open fields, and through wooded areas. The trail goes over three small wooden bridges and by many bird feeders. The trail crosses the park road once. Shortly after crossing the road you will come to a sign pointing to a wildlife viewing blind. You may go inside the blind to view the refuge area on the lake. This area is a resting area for waterfowl and allows you to see several rare species of birds. The trail then continues paralleling the lake, with a steep drop of about thirty feet down to the lake from the trail.

The northern part of the trail ends at the road to the campground. You must then retrace your path back to the starting point.

The trail is also used by cross-country skiers.

Viewing blind, Shabbona Lake State Park

Facilities: A ranger station located on the grounds offers additional information. There are also various picnic areas with tables, grills, shelters, restrooms, playground equipment, and water faucets. A new campground with 150 sites is now open, with 50 of them having electricity. The campground has a shower building, trailer dump station, and boat launching facilities for campers. Fishing is allowed in Shabbona Lake, contingent upon all Illinois fishing rules and regulations. A boat ramp and a concession stand are also available, with boats for rent. A 7-mile snowmobile trail has been constructed and may be used by the hikers. Dove hunting is allowed during the appointed hunting season. A softball diamond and horse-pits are also available.

Permits Required: A dog-training area permit is available upon request. Snowmobilers must register at the park office.

Park Rules and Regulations: Swimming and/or wading is prohibited at Shabbona Lake. There is a 10 horsepower limit on the lake. See Appendix A.

Mailing Address and Phone Number: Site Superintendent, Shabbona Lake State Park, Route 1, Box 120, Shabbona, Illinois 60550; 815/824-2106

25. Pilcher Park

Trail Length: 4 miles (6.4 kilometers)

Location: Pilcher Park may be reached from either Interstate 55 or Interstate 80. Interstate 55 travelers may exit onto Interstate 80 and go east for eight miles to Briggs Street. Turn north on Briggs Street and proceed for about one mile until the road turns into Hillcrest Road. Follow Hillcrest Road east for one-half mile to State Route 30. Turn left (west) on Route 30, proceed one block and go under the railroad tracks. Turn right onto the first street (Highland Drive) and proceed to the park entrance.

Westbound Interstate 80 traffic may exit at State Route 30 and proceed north for three miles to Highland Drive. From here, follow the same directions as described above.

County: Will

Illinois Highway Map Coordinates: D-9

U.S.G.S. Topographical Map Name and Scale: Joliet, 1:24,000

Hours Open: Pilcher Park Nature Center is open Monday through Friday from 9:00 a.m. until 4:30 p.m. and on Saturday and Sunday from 10:00 a.m. until 4:30 p.m.

History and Trail Description: During the turn of the century, Pilcher Park was a private arboretum. The park was bought by Robert Pilcher, and its 327 acres were given to the City of Joliet in 1921. The park is now operated by the Joliet Park District.

The trails at Pilcher Park consist of four interconnecting trails that total over 4 miles. All of the trails may be started at the Nature Center and at the small zoo.

The High Trail starts near the back door of the Nature Center and winds its way northward for one mile through the upland woods. The trail goes over a small

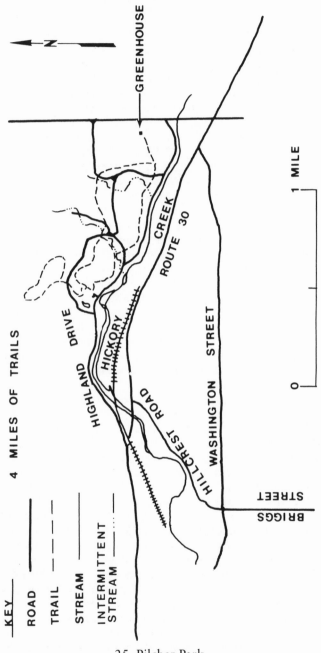

25. Pilcher Park

bridge and creek and then crosses the bicycle trail and park road. At this point you will see orange paint blazes on the trees. Do not pay attention to these markings for they were painted by a horse stable operator who used them on the horse trails in the park. Very shortly after this, the trail splits, and you may go north or east. If you go east the trail continues through a stand of large old trees, crosses the bicycle trail two more times, then parallels a steep stream valley. From here the trail turns west and will connect with the original trail again. This can be followed back to the Nature Center and to other trails.

Back at the Nature Center you can walk to the zoo which is situated directly behind the center. The zoo currently does not have any animals because the animals were killed a few years ago by some vandals. A short trail called the Walk in the Woods Trail begins at the zoo. At various points along the trail, information boards attached to wooden posts describe the animals, trees, and natural systems that can be observed in the forest.

At the halfway point the Trail of the Oaks joins the Walk in the Woods Trail. You may stay on the Walk in the Woods Trail or hike eastward on the Trail of the Oaks. There is a wooden trail marker at this point. Continuing on the Walk in the Woods Trail, you will return to the Nature Center area where you can hike the Sensory Trail which connects with the Walk in the Woods Trail.

The Sensory Trail is a short asphalt trail which goes through the woods. There is a large wooden sign at the start of the Sensory Trail. Hiking this trail you will go over a small bridge and see a trail sign that points in the direction of Trail of the Oaks. The Trail of the Oaks goes in an easterly direction, crossing the park road twice and traversing small bridges and creeks. As you go across the park road the second time, you will reach a junction in the trail and a trail marker will be visible. You can continue straight on the trail, proceeding ahead to the greenhouse, or you can turn left (north) and follow the trail as it joins the Walk in the Woods Trail.

Heading north on the trail, you will come across some horse stables and a cement water well. From here the trail crosses the park road and continues through the woods on a wooden walkway which was constructed above a low, wet area. The trail then crosses the park road again and joins another trail. At this point, you can continue on the Trail of the Oaks or follow the trail branch southward back to the southern part of the Trail of the Oaks and finally back to the Nature Center.

All of the trails are easily distinguishable and are fairly easy to follow. The park also has cross-country skiing and bicycle trails. The hiker may also hike on these trails. Horseback riding is allowed in the park on some of the bicycle trails and part of the High Trail.

Facilities: A Nature Center is located on the grounds where one may request trail maps and other general information from the ranger on hand. The Nature Center has many displays of animals and plants. Water and restrooms are located at the Nature Center and at the water well. A greenhouse is located on the grounds where flowers may be seen year-round; the greenhouse also offers seasonal flower shows. The park offers many special programs and special events, such as spring wild-flower walks, fall color walks, and instruction in gathering maple syrup. A small creek flows by the park where one may go fishing. All Illinois fishing rules and regulations are in effect.

Permits Required: No horseback riding except by permit.

Park Rules and Regulations: All dogs must be on a leash. No ice skating allowed on the creek.

Mailing Address and Phone Number: Joliet Park District, 3000 W. Jefferson, Joliet, Illinois 60435; 815/741-7277

26. Illinois and Michigan Canal Trail

Trail Length: 52 miles (83.2 kilometers)

Location: The Illinois and Michigan Canal Trail has many starting points. Some main beginning locations include Channahon State Park, Gebhard Woods State Park in La Salle, as well as in Utica, Illinois.

To reach Channahon State Park, take Interstate 55 from the north and south. Southwest of Joliet you meet State Route 6. Turn west onto Route 6 and go to the town of Channahon. Turn left onto Canal Street in Channahon and proceed a half mile until you see the park signs. Turn right and proceed one block to the entrance.

To reach Gebhard Woods State Park, take Interstate 80 or Route 6 from the west or east. The motorist may then go to the intersection of Routes 6 and 47 in Morris. Proceed west on Route 6 for five blocks to Union Street. Turn south on Union Street and follow the signs to the park entrance.

To reach the trail in La Salle follow Route 351 through La Salle. When you see Canal Street on the north side of the canal, turn west and go about 100 feet to a parking area on the south side of Canal Street.

The trailhead in Utica may be reached by taking Route 178 into Utica. South of the canal, turn west onto Johnson Street and go three blocks to Morton Street. Turn north on Morton Street and proceed to the parking area.

Counties: Will, Grundy, and La Salle

Illinois Highway Map Coordinates: D-7 and D-8

U.S.G.S. Topographical Map Names and Scale: Channahon, Minooka, Lisbon, Morris, Seneca, Marseilles, Ottawa, and La Salle, all 1:24,000

Hours Open: Gebhard Woods, Buffalo Rock, and Channahon State Parks are open year-round except on Christ-

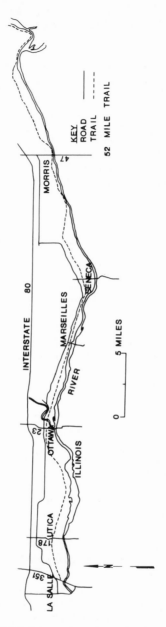

26. Illinois and Michigan Canal Trail. Redrawn from
Illinois Department of Transportation county
highway maps.

mas Day and New Year's Day. When weather conditions necessitate the closing of the roads during freezing and thawing periods, access to the park or facilities is by foot only.

History and Trail Description: The Illinois and Michigan Canal was the impetus for the settlement and development of northeastern Illinois. The canal was directly responsible for the beginning of Chicago's growth as well as the cause for the development of Lockport, Joliet, Morris, Seneca, Marseilles, Ottawa, Utica and La Salle–Peru.

The Illinois and Michigan Canal actually had its origin with the Indians at the Chicago Portage, the low divide between the waters of Lake Michigan and the Des Plaines River. The Indians used it as a carrying place long before the advent of the white man. This portage was also recorded in the annals of the French explorers Joliet and Marquette in 1673. It was also noted in 1790 by the French military engineer Victor Collot and in 1807 by U.S. Secretary of the Treasury Albert Gallatin in his report on roads and canals.

The original boundaries of Illinois were moved about fifty miles in order to give Illinois a coast on Lake Michigan and to ensure that Chicago, the point at which the canal would connect with Lake Michigan, would be in Illinois.

Construction of the canal was started by the State of Illinois in 1836 and was completed in 1848. The canal cost about $9.5 million, stretched ninety-six miles, and linked Lake Michigan with the Illinois River at La Salle, the two bodies of water from which the canal took its name. When the canal was originally built, it was 36 feet wide at the bottom, 60 feet wide at water level, and had a 15-foot wide towpath. The canal included fifteen locks, three dams, and four aqueducts. Several feeder streams, two with aqueducts, once fed the canal. Today, some of the locks and aqueducts may be seen while hiking.

On January 1, 1974, the canal was transferred to the Department of Conservation for the development of a hiking and biking trail. In addition, about twenty-eight miles of the canal are filled with water for canoeing.

In February 1984, Congress established the Illinois and Michigan Canal Heritage Corridor. The Act created a 100-mile linear historical park system with a commission to oversee that the corridor is preserved. The goals are to protect and enhance the cultural, natural, and recreational resources along the Illinois and Michigan Canal Corridor. The National Park Service plans to produce guides and will market the Corridor's resources to encourage economic development.

There are approximately 51.7 miles of marked hiking trails along the Illinois and Michigan Canal State Trail, with an additional 3.8 miles of unmarked trail heading east from Channahon Campground to Interstate 55.

Along the nearly 52 miles of trails, there are various state parks, parking lots, roads, and towns, where the hiker can get to the trail. In addition, these trail access points may serve as starting or ending points for the hiker. Since the trail is linear, the hiker would have to backtrack to his or her vehicle, or set up a vehicle or ride at the other end of the trail.

Although the hiker may hike the entire 52 miles of trails along the canal, not all segments of the canal have water in them. In fact, not even half of the canal has water anymore. Water is not found in the canal from the east side of Utica all the way to the spillway, 1.5 miles west of Gebbard Woods State Park. For nice views of the canal with water in it, we recommend doing the trail segments from Channahon State Park to the spillway west of Gebhard Woods State Park, or Utica, Illinois, to Lock 14 in LaSalle, Illinois.

The 15-mile trail segment between Channahon and Gebhard Woods State Parks may be started at either end. The trailhead at Channahon State Park is located just south of the park off of Bridge Street. Lock 7 is on the north side of Bridge Street, and a parking area is found right next to the canal. A trailboard set up at the parking area gives the trail distances for four locations: McKinley Woods—2.8 miles; Dresden Access—5.8 miles; Aux Sable Access—8.1 miles; and Gebhard Woods—14.8 miles.

The trail starts heading south with the canal on the right and the Des Plaines River appearing on the left side.

Lock tender's house and lock and dam no. 6, Channahon State Park

At McKinley Woods you will see a small wooden bridge that goes over the canal, leading to the woods. Picnic tables, car parking, and a shelter are found at McKinley Woods.

From here, the trail goes west. Prior to reaching Dresden Lock and Dam, you will see a sign for a camping and picnic area on the left side of the trail. There you will see some picnic tables, a small wooden shelter with a fireplace in it, and restrooms.

Just beyond the camping area you will pass Dresden Lock and Dam, which has a rest bench. Approximately two miles later you will arrive at Aux Sable Access. Before reaching this access point you will pass another camping area. Beyond the camping area the trail crosses a road and then comes to the access area. Another lock and dam and an aqueduct can be seen at this access. A parking lot, water pump, and restrooms are also available at this access. In addition, a small wooden bridge, which allows you to view the lock and dam system, goes over the lock and dam.

Past the Aux Sable Access Area you will cross a bridge over the canal and will follow the towpath on the south side again. In a few miles you will see many residential homes on the north side of the canal. At this point, the trail is at the outskirts of Morris.

The trail goes by William G. Stratton State Park and then crosses a bridge to the north side of the canal.

Prior to reaching Gebhard Woods State Park, you will see the Nettle Creek Aqueduct. From this point you may continue following the towpath a short distance to the park, or you may follow the trail and paint blazes away from the canal to the camping and picnic areas within the park, or head west along the trail.

Heading west past Gebhard Woods State Park, the hiker will follow the south side of the canal and after about 2.5 miles he or she will run across a spillway for the canal. Here the water from the canal goes over a small spillway and flows toward the Illinois River. Shortly past this location the canal is dry, and for the most part remains dry all the way to Utica. Although the canal has no water in it past the spillway, there are some very nice wooded stretches along the canal. Between the spillway and the outskirts of Seneca, the trail is all gravel and wooded. A good variety of birds may be seen in this section.

At the edge of Seneca the trail becomes a gravel road. In Seneca, the hiker will see an old grain elevator next to the canal. A sign here states "John Armour's warehouse erected in 1861–62. This building is the earliest grain elevator along the canal." West of Seneca, the trail follows a gravel road, goes through some wooded areas, by some farms, and then becomes a part of the road. On the east side of Marseilles, the trail goes past various industries and chemical plants. The trail goes through Marseilles where the hiker will see Locks 9 and 10 (dry), and then continues heading through town. The trail then for the most part parallels Route 51. The trail along this segment also goes through many wooded areas.

On the east side of Ottawa, the trail crosses the Fox River over the Fox River Aqueduct. A good view of the river and town is seen from the aqueduct. The trail then continues through the center of town.

In five miles the hiker will come across access to Buffalo Rock State Park. Found here at Buffalo Rock State Park are five earthenware sculptures of aquatic animals native to the area. These sculptures were created from the spoil material left as a result of coal mining operations.

The next five miles from Buffalo Rock State Park to the edge of Utica also has some nice wooded areas. At the edge of Utica, the hiker will see a spillway. This spillway drains part of the canal which now contains water all the way to Lock 14. Found here in Utica, on the north side of the canal, is the La Salle County Historical Museum. This building is an 1848 warehouse which contains artifacts of the area, as well as information on the canal.

The trail then passes through town; a little way beyond one will have good views of the Illinois River backwaters on the left side. Bluffs are seen on the right side of the canal, and one rock formation is named Split Rock. Once the hiker gets to La Salle, he or she will see Lock 14. There are some stairs on the north side of the canal which take you to a parking area. Lock 14 was restored in 1981–82. Past Lock 14, the Illinois and Michigan Canal joins the Illinois River.

Facilities: Gebhard Woods State Park has picnic facilities with tables, grills, water, restrooms, and a shelter. A baseball diamond and horseshoe pits are also available. Children may fish in the four ponds in the park. Youth camping sites are also available.

Channahon State Park has picnic tables, shelters, restrooms, water, grills, and playground equipment. Tent camping is also available. Locks 6 and 7 and the lock tender's house at lock 6 are at Channahon State Park. Fishing is allowed in the canal and in the Du Page, Illinois, and Des Plaines rivers, contingent upon all Illinois fishing rules and regulations.

Permits Required: A camping permit is required.

Park Rules and Regulations: See Appendix A.

Mailing Addresses and Phone Numbers: Site Superintendent, Gebhard Woods State Park, Box 272, Morris, Illinois 60450; 815/942-0796; Channahon State Park, Box 54, Channahon, Illinois 60410; 815/467-4271; or Buffalo Rock State Park, P.O. Box 39, Ottawa, Illinois 61350; 815/433-2220

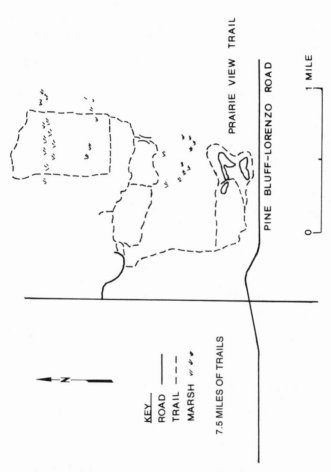

27. Goose Lake Prairie State Natural Area

27. Goose Lake Prairie State Natural Area

Trail Length: 7.5 miles (12.0 kilometers)

Location: From Morris Illinois, take Highway 47 south 0.7 miles past the Illinois River to the blacktop road which is known as Pine Bluff–Lorenzo Road, turn left (east) and go 6 miles to Jugtown Road, then turn north (park entrance). Access from Interstate 55 south is at Exit 240 onto Pine Bluff–Lorenzo Road going west approximately 7 miles to Jugtown Road, then turn north (park entrance).

County: Grundy

Illinois Highway Map Coordinates: D-8

U.S.G.S. Topographical Map Names and Scale: Coal City and Minooka, 1:24,000

Hours Open: The Area is open year-round except on Christmas Day and New Year's Day.

History and Trail Description: Goose Lake Prairie was sculpted by glaciers. The area became part of a continuous grassland that stretched from Indiana to the Rockies. Goose Lake Prairie, whose original 240 acres were purchased by the state in 1969 and which now totals 2,537 acres is the largest remnant of prairie left in Illinois.

Mound-building groups of Native Americans lived northwest of the area in what is now Morris. Tribes of the Illini Confederation intermittently inhabited the area. These and other Native Americans lived off the land and made few permanent changes. Settlers, relying on the land for their livelihoods, made drastic alterations to the area: They planted trees to serve as windbreaks and fences for their farms; in an effort to get more farmland, they completely drained the 1,000-acre Goose Lake; they removed the underlying clay, first to make pottery and jugs and later for firebricks; they mined coal beginning in the 1820s and in 1928 began strip mining the land. Presently, there are over 1,700 acres of prairie and marsh and over 1,500 acres dedicated as an Illinois Nature Preserve.

The Prairie View trailhead is at the southeast corner of the parking lot at the Visitors Center. This trail is a 3.5-mile (round trip) trail offering a moderate hike through and along prairie and farmland. The trail also offers some diversity by going through a grove of black ash and chokecherry trees.

Along the easternmost part of the Prairie View Trail is the Strip Mine Loop. In this area the visible remains of strip mines are located. One can choose to bypass the eastern loop and go south around the western portion of this strip mine area and return to the main loop and trail. This round trip segment is .66 miles shorter, and therefore the round trip from the Visitors Center is 2.84 miles.

The Tall Grass Nature Trail goes into the Goose Lake Prairie Nature Preserve, and begins about 50 yards east of the parking lot and Visitors Center. This trail system offers a diversity of topography and natural features. Round trip, this trail is 4 miles when combining the Tall Grass Nature Trail with the Marsh Loop Trail and the Sagashka Trail (also marked as SCE TAY Trail). Shorter hikes can be completed by eliminating any one of the loops or sections of the loop trails. The Tall Grass Nature Trail goes through prairie and the nature preserve allowing one to see the effects of an attempt to gain more farmland by draining Goose Lake. A very interesting site along the Marsh Loop Trail is the floating bridge across the open marsh.

Facilities: The Visitors Center offers excellent nature displays and various programs on the park and the area. There are facilities for picnicking. Drinking water and toilets are available, all with handicap access.

Permits Required: Groups of twenty-five or more require registration in advance with the site superintendent.

Park Rules and Regulations: See Appendixes A and B.

Mailing Address and Phone Number: Site Superintendent, Goose Lake Prairie State Natural Area, 5010 North Jugtown, Morris, Illinois 60450; 815/942-2899

28. Starved Rock State Park

Trail Length: 15 miles (24 kilometers)

Location: Starved Rock State Park is located in north central Illinois one mile south of Utica. Travelers coming from west, east, and north can reach the park by exiting off Interstate 80 south onto State Route 178, which leads directly to the park entrance. Starved Rock can be reached from the south by taking State Route 51. From Route 51 follow State Route 351 through Oglesby to State Route 71. Travel east on Route 71 to the park entrance.

County: La Salle

Illinois Highway Map Coordinates: D-7

U.S.G.S. Topographical Map Names and Scale: La Salle and Starved Rock, both 1:24,000

Hours Open: The park is open year-round. At certain times, due to freezing and thawing periods, the park may be closed, and access to the park is by foot only.

History and Trail Description: Indian tribes were known to live in this area, and the name Starved Rock was derived from an Indian legend which states that the Illiniwek tribe who took refuge on top of the 125-foot sandstone butte were surrounded by the Ottawa and Potawatomi tribes and eventually starved. A series of battles which led to this event occurred during the 1760s. About a hundred years earlier the French had built a chain of forts along the Illinois River. Fort St. Louis was constructed on top of Starved Rock and was used by traders, trappers, and local Indians. It was destroyed by fire in the early 1700s.

There are over 15 miles of hiking trails at Starved Rock State Park. These trails wind their way through many of the canyons, along the Illinois River bank, and on the bluffs located throughout the park. Throughout

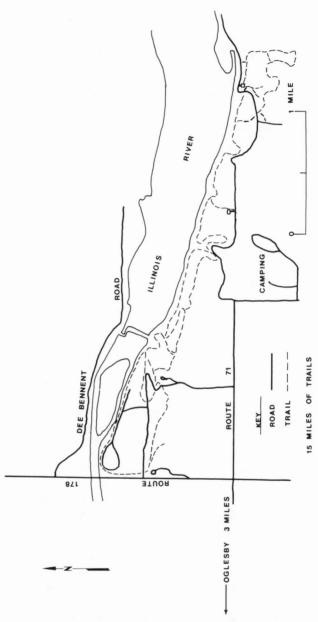

28. Starved Rock State Park. Redrawn from park map.

the park the hiker will observe the rock formations in the area. The trails are all interconnected and the hiker can vary his or her hiking distances.

The trails in the park are all marked very well with metal markers. These guides have different colored dots, such as red for the River Trail, brown for the Bluff Trail, and so forth. In addition to the main color dots, the hiker will see another dot on the marker, either white or yellow in color. The yellow dot means that the trail is going away from the lodge area, and the white dot means that trail is coming back to the lodge. In addition to these trail markers, the hiker will see steel map cases at trail access points, intersections, and other points of interest. Thirty-five of these map cases are found along the trails.

Most people start hiking from the lodge area where the main parking areas are located. In addition to the lodge parking areas, there also are small parking spots set up at the east end of the park along Route 71. From these lots, hikers can get access to the canyons at the east end of the park without having to hike the entire trail system. From the lodge area, the hiker can get to the rock formation which made this park famous, Starved Rock, and get a great view of the Illinois River and the dam. There are stairs leading up to the top of the bluffs here.

From Starved Rock the hiker may get on a connecting trail and go to the River Trail or to a bluff trail leading east toward the many canyons in the park. Some of the more popular canyons in the park include French Canyon, Wildcat Canyon, and Tonti Canyon. These canyons are especially popular to ice climbers in the winter months. St. Louis Canyon, which is west of the lodge, has a sixty-foot waterfall. In the winter it becomes a great icefall.

The interior canyon trails allow one to view the great rock formations formed by natural erosion processes. Streams, waterfalls, and pools may be seen in many of the canyons.

The River Trail allows the hiker great views of the Illinois River. Hikers who go along the Bluff Trail will be afforded spectacular views of the river valley. There are numerous overlooks found up on the bluffs and along the river.

The hiker should take caution when he or she hikes at Starved Rock State Park along the bluff tops. In addition, some of the canyons can be very muddy and wet. During the rainy season, the canyons can quickly fill with floodwaters, as some of them drain large areas. If in doubt about trail conditions, check with the ranger on duty.

Permits Required: A camping permit is required.

Park Rules and Regulations: No swimming, climbing, or rappelling anywhere in the park. All pets must be on a leash. See Appendixes A and F.

Facilities: A park office and interpretive center are located in the park. A lodge is located here and has a dining room, refreshments hall, and 72 hotel rooms and 22 cabin rooms. There are 135 campsites in the park with electricity, restrooms, two shower buildings, and water available. Near the lodge there are picnic tables, restrooms, shelters, water, and a boat landing. Fishing is allowed in the Illinois River, with all Illinois fishing rules and regulations in effect.

Mailing Address and Phone Number: Site Superintendent, Starved Rock State Park, Box 116, Utica, Illinois 61373; 815/667-4726

29. Matthiessen State Park

Trail Length: 6.25 miles (10 kilometers)

Location: Matthiessen State Park is located along the Vermilion River three miles east of Oglesby. It can be reached from State Route 51 from the north and south, and Interstate 80 from east or west. The park is just three miles from the campground at the south end of Starved Rock State Park. The northern boundary is Route 71, and the eastern boundary is Route 178.

County: La Salle

Illinois Highway Map Coordinates: D-7

U.S.G.S. Topographical Map Name and Scale: La Salle, 1:24,000

Hours Open: The park is open year-round except on Christmas Day and New Year's Day. At certain times, due to freezing and thawing periods, the park is closed, and access to the park is by foot only.

History and Trail Description: Prior to 1943 this area was known as Deer Park and was under the private ownership of Frederick William Matthiessen. In 1943 the state took over the property and renamed the park in honor of Matthiessen.

Matthiessen State Park is quite similar to Starved Rock State Park in geological features. The main canyon in the park was formed by stream erosion; it consists of two sections, the upper and lower dells. The entire area is a series of beautiful canyons and wooded bluffs carved out of sandstone.

The 6.25 miles of hiking trails are made up of six trails. In the dells area the trails loop around the canyons and bluffs, allowing the hiker to view the natural features in both the upper and lower dells.

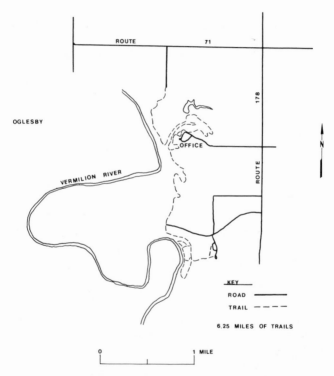

ROUTE 71

OGLESBY

ROUTE 178

OFFICE

VERMILION RIVER

ROUTE

N

KEY

ROAD ———

TRAIL ———

6.25 MILES OF TRAILS

0   1 MILE

29. Matthiessen State Park

The lower canyon trail which winds through the upper and lower dells measures a little over 1 mile. The Bluff Trail in the upper dells, which begins at the concession stand, loops around the east side and measures about 1 mile. Some sites seen while hiking the Upper Bluff Trail include the dam, 11-acre lake, Giants' Bathtub, Cascade Falls, and most of the lower canyon which includes Sandy Point.

From Cascade Falls, a bluff trail loops around the lower dells; it measures less than 1 mile. Along this trail the "Wishing Well," the "Paint Box," and "The Strawberry Rock" can be seen in the lower canyon. A connecting trail meanders northward from this trail to the archery range and eventually out of the park. The connecting trail which leads to the archery range appears to be an abandoned one-lane road. This section passes through open fields and also through dense woods. Much of this section is overgrown. As you near the parking area for the archery range, you will parallel a private drive and the road for Deer Park Country Club (golf course). Beyond the archery range you can follow the road north to Route 71, to the nature preserve, and to Starved Rock State Park on the north side of Route 71.

Another connecting trail winds southward to the section of the park known as the Vermilion River Area. This southbound trail measures approximately 2 miles. The trail goes through woods, above the bluffs, through open fields, and by a viewing platform, which is located a little over one mile from the lower dells area.

Shortly after passing the viewing platform you will cross over the park blacktop road. After crossing the blacktop road, the trail heads east as a one-way dirt road known as the Township Road. Following the road, you head south past the shelters and picnic areas. To your right (west) is a dirt path which leads down to the lower area trail along the river. As you near the river you will cross a bridge over a feeder creek; you can go north, where the trail becomes a loop and joins with the same trail near the Township Road you just left, or you can go south along the river. If you go south, you have the option of cutting the trail short and hiking the middle staircase/trail, or you can follow the river trail to the end and climb the third flight back to the bluff trail.

Within the Vermilion Area are several short connecting trails, all of which lead down to the lower canyon trail along the east bank of the river. This trail is connected to the upper bluff trails via bridges and steps.

In periods of high water, the interior canyon trails and low-lying trails are impractical to hike because of flooding. Eight miles of horseback, cross-country skiing, and snowshoe trails are also available in the park.

Facilities: The Dells Area has a concession stand, shelter, toilets, park office, parking, and picnic facilities. The Vermilion Area has shelters and restrooms.

Park Rules and Regulations: No camping, rappelling, rock or ice climbing allowed. Hiking allowed only on marked trails. All pets must be on a leash. See Appendix A.

Mailing Address and Phone Number: Site Superintendent, Matthiessen State Park, Box 381, Utica, Illinois 61373; 815/667-4868

PART III

Hiking Trails in Central Illinois

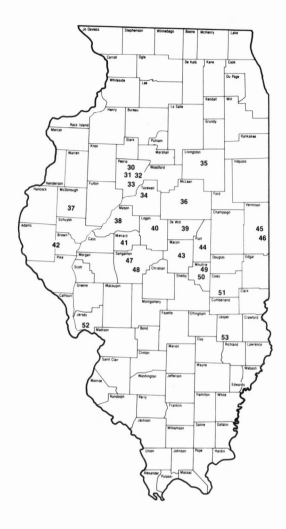

CENTRAL ILLINOIS

30. Rock Island Trail
31. Jubilee College State Park
32. Forest Park Nature Center
33. Wildlife Prairie Park
34. Dirksen and McNaughton Parks
35. Humiston Woods Nature Center
36. Constitution Trail
37. Argyle Lake State Park
38. Sand Ridge State Forest
39. Clinton Lake State Recreation Area
40. Railsplitter State Park
41. New Salem State Historic Site

42. Siloam Springs State Park
43. Rock Springs Center
44. Robert Allerton Park
45. Kickapoo State Park
46. Forest Glen Preserve
47. Carpenter Park
48. Lincoln Memorial Garden
49. Fishhook Waterfowl Area
50. Chief Illini Trail
51. Fox Ridge State Park
52. Pere Marquette State Park
53. Newton Lake Conservation Area

Figure 3. Hiking trails in central Illinois

30. Rock Island Trail

Trail Length: 26 miles (41.6 kilometers)

Location: Rock Island Trail is located northwest of Peoria, Illinois. The trail has two main trailheads, one in Alta, Illinois, and the other one on the outskirts of Toulon, Illinois. The trail may be started or finished at either of these two locations.

To reach the trailhead in Alta, travelers may take the bypass (474) to Route 6. Follow Route 6 to Allen Road (Exit 5). Proceed north on Allen Road to Alta. The main parking lot is 1 mile from Route 6 and it is located on the right side of the road. This parking area will have a trailboard that states Rock Island Parking, along with water, pit toilets, and a small picnic area.

To reach the trailhead at Toulon, travelers may continue on the road through Alta until they reach Route 91. Stay on Route 91 north for 38 miles, going through the towns of Dunlap, Princeville, Wyoming, all the way to the east side of Toulon. On the north side of the road, travelers will see another sign that says Rock Island Parking. This parking area also has water, toilets, and a small picnic area.

Counties: Peoria and Stark

Illinois Highway Map Coordinates: E-5 and F-5

U.S.G.S. Topographic Map Names and Scales: Dunlap, Edelstein, Princeville, Castelton, Wyoming, 1:24,000

Hours Open: The trail is open dawn to dusk, year-round.

History and Trail Description: In the late 1950s the Chicago, Rock Island, and Pacific Railroad ceased operation along its track running from Peoria to Toulon. In subsequent years the tracks, ties, some ballasts, drainage structures, and bridge components were salvaged and removed from the right-of-way.

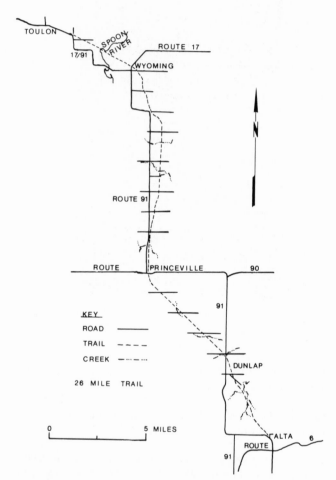

TOULON

17/91

SPOON RIVER

ROUTE 17

WYOMING

ROUTE 91

N

ROUTE   PRINCEVILLE 90

91

KEY

ROAD ————

TRAIL — — — —

CREEK —·——·——·

26 MILE TRAIL

DUNLAP

0   5 MILES

ALTA 6

ROUTE

91

30. Rock Island Trail. Redrawn from Illinois
Department of Transportation county highway
maps.

Rock Island trailboard, Rock Island Trail

In 1965 the Forest Park Foundation of Peoria obtained title to the right-of-way, and it subsequently became known as the Rock Island Forest Park Trail. In
addition, the Forest Park Foundation purchased approximately 160 acres of land adjacent to the railroad between Alta and Dunlap. Sixty acres were given to the
Illinois Youth Commission in return for a promise to
provide maintenance and development services at Jubilee
College State Park and along the right-of-way. One hundred acres known as the Mayer Tract, north of Alta, were
given to the Department of Conservation along with the
right-of-way to be developed as a wildlife refuge and
linear recreational corridor.

The Department of Conservation undertook a study
to evaluate the potential of the Rock Island Trail as a

multiple-use linear recreation corridor. It was determined that the Rock Island Trail would provide needed recreational opportunities for the region and the state. Plans called for opening over 27 miles of bicycle, hiking, and associated camping facilities along the old Rock Island Trail. Over the years many obstacles have impeded the development of the Rock Island Trail. These included adjoining landowners who objected to any development and lack of funding for the project. In 1986 the controversy concerning the trail ended when an agreement was signed among the State of Illinois, Friends of the Rock Island Trail, and landowners represented by the Rock Island Trail Property Owners Association (Fred Tetreault, "A Mighty Fine Line," *Outdoor Highlights* 17, no. 6 [Apr. 17, 1989]:13–16). The agreement allowed the state to develop the entire 26 miles of trail as well as to protect the adjacent landowners' property. The agreement called for the Department of Conservation to fence areas of the trail to reduce the potential for trespassing, replace and repair culverts to ensure proper drainage, to trim trees and brush adjacent to agricultural land, and to buy additional property for the site only when an owner was willing to sell ("Rock Island Trail: Development

Chicago, Burlington, and Quincy Railroad Depot, Wyoming

Work to Begin Soon on Trail after 17 Years of Controversy," *Outdoor Highlights* 14, no. 14 [July 21, 1986]:3).

In 1989 development of the Rock Island Trail was initiated. Trail development included trail markings, development of a campground and trail surfacing. The trail was completed at the end of 1989 and is now open to hikers, bikers, and skiers.

The Rock Island Trail is now a 26-mile one-way linear trail. Hikers who plan on walking the entire length or a partial segment of the trail will have to leave a vehicle at the other end of the trail or have someone pick them up. The trail is very well marked with trailboards as well as mile markers. The hiker also will see bridge ahead signs, stop signs by roads, and bicycle signs through the towns of Dunlap, Princeville, and Wyoming. The entire trail is also laid down with compacted limestone.

Starting in Alta, the hiker will start going through some tree-lined canopy. Within two miles he or she will see a sign for the Kickapoo Creek Recreation Area. This is an area for picnicking and primitive camping. Tables, grills, water, and toilets are found here. Shortly past this area, the hiker will cross over Kickapoo Creek and will find a beautiful view of the creek valley below. Hikers will then come to the edge of Dunlap, which they will pass through, following the bicycle signs along the road. Between Dunlap and Princeville the trail is generally uneventful, going by farms and a few small wooded tracts.

The trail then comes to the southern part of Princeville and goes through the center of town following the roads. Again, follow the bicycle signs through town. At the north end of town the hiker will see a sign which takes him or her off of the road and back onto the old railroad grade. This is mile 11 at this point.

Between Princeville and Wyoming the hiker will go by a nature preserve and a small parking lot. This is found at County Line Road OON. Past this area the hiker will cross two small creeks. These are Mud Run and Camp Run creeks. Camp Run Creek is near mile 16.

At the outskirts of Wyoming, the hiker will see the old Chicago, Burlington, and Quincy Railroad Depot. This is a nice spot to take a break. The trail then goes through town following the streets. Follow the bicycle signs again to the trailhead at the other end of town. There are a few stores in town should the hiker be interested in stopping for some refreshments.

The stretch between Wyoming and Toulon is very pretty, especially over the Spoon River. The trail goes over the wood bridge here, and it is worth the time to stop here and rest for a while to view the Spoon River Valley below. Past the Spoon River, the trail heads west, and in 3 miles it terminates at the parking lot on the outskirts of Toulon.

Facilities: The facilities along the trail include benches and the Kickapoo Creek Recreation Area facilities. In addition, as previously stated, there are a few items at the trailheads. Facilities such as restaurants, stores, and so forth are available in Dunlap, Princeville, and Wyoming, as well as in Alta and Toulon.

Permits Required: A camping permit is needed.

Park Rules and Regulations: No motorized vehicles allowed on the trail. See Appendix A.

Mailing Address and Phone Number: Site Superintendent, Rock Island Trail State Park, P.O. Box 64, Wyoming, Illinois 61491; 309/695-2228

31. Jubilee College State Park

Trail Length: 4.5 miles (7.3 kilometers)

Location: Jubilee College State Park is located in central Illinois approximately fifteen miles northwest of Peoria. The major access road is Interstate 74. Road signs both west of the park and east of the park along Route 74 indicate the proper exit ramp for access to the park.

Major access roads to Peoria include east-west Route 24 and north-south Route 121, along with Interstate 74. The park has a new entrance; approximately 3 miles west of Kickapoo, along Route 150, there is a State Park entrance sign and new road going north into the park.

County: Peoria

Illinois Highway Map Coordinates: F-5

U.S.G.S. Topographical Map Name and Scale: Oak Hill, 1:24,000

Hours Open: The park is open year-round except on Christmas Day and New Year's Day. When weather conditions necessitate the closing of roads during freezing and thawing periods, access to facilities is by foot only.

History and Trail Description: The site is known for the Jubilee College which operated from 1840 to 1862, one of Illinois' earliest educational enterprises.

The founder of Jubilee College was Bishop Philander Chase, who was called to Illinois to assume jurisdiction of the newly formed Episcopal diocese, one of his many duties. In 1933 the college and grounds consisted of 96 acres which were presented to the State of Illinois as a memorial. Today Jubilee College State Park totals more than 3,500 acres.

The trail system at Jubilee College State Park includes 4.5 miles of established hiking trails and approx-

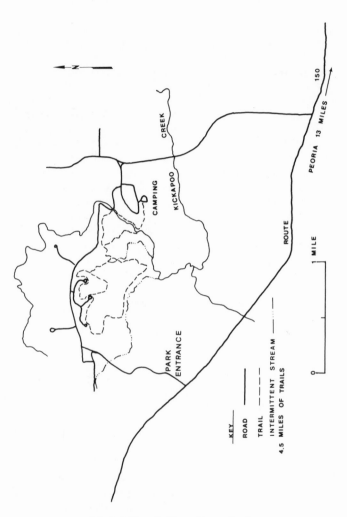

31. Jubilee College State Park

imately 35 miles of equestrian trails. Hikers are allowed to use the equestrian trails; however, these trails are not consistently marked along the entire trail nor are they maintained for use other than as equestrian trails. At road crossings the equestrian trails are marked with an orange horseshoe and diamond, with an arrow indicating trail direction. Also, there are several miles of newer trails designated as cross-country ski trails, which can be hiked. It is recommended that the hiker check with park personnel for cross-country ski trail access and conditions.

The 4.5 miles of hiking trails are marked with a combination of symbols to identify the trail. There are white figures of a skier on a blue background, white figures of a hiker on a brown background, and for those portions which follow the equestrian trail, a white horse on brown background.

A trailboard is set up at the west edge of the tent camping area, signifying the start of the trail. The first section of trail meanders southwest until it meets the Jubilee Creek. The trail formerly crossed the creek via a suspension bridge; however, a new trail is located along the eastern bank of the creek, and crossing is made farther north at the ford. There are plans to install a suspension bridge at the ford.

The trail along the eastern side of Jubilee Creek is hazardous even though it is fairly new. Water bars and steps have been placed where necessary; however, several places warrant extra caution as the trail follows the sloping shoreline.

Most of the trail system is on the west side of the ford. After crossing the ford, the trail goes west and becomes part of the equestrian trail. Less than fifty yards from the ford is a trail marked with a symbol of a skier. This trail, the alternate for hikers, travels northwesterly until it crosses the equestrian trail again. Also, before the equestrian trail there is a connecting trail that meanders in a southeasterly direction. This trail leads back to Jubilee Creek and the old suspension bridge crossing.

Upon reaching the equestrian trail again, go south to a major trail junction. At the junction, follow the connecting trail that goes northwest until you come to another junction. This trail junction has a bench and a trail sign indicating direction and travel to the other sections of the park. The trail to the right meanders northwesterly to the Bow Wood Glen Picnic Area, past the Milkweed Meadow Picnic Area, and south to the Prairie Drift Lane Picnic Area. Here, south of the Prairie Drift Lane Picnic Area, is the end of the trail that goes to the left at the junction mentioned above.

A newer trail connects the Prairie Drift Lane Picnic Area with the Cone Flower Cove Picnic Area. From the Cone Flower Cove Picnic Area, the trail goes west until it joins the equestrian trail once again. By following the equestrian trail southeast, a hiker will eventually join the same trail junction that goes west to the second trail junction already mentioned.

Wildlife is abundant; many species can be seen at Jubilee College State Park. The large acreage and waterways also support a variety of trees and vegetation as well.

Facilities: Jubilee College State Park has class A, B, C, and D camping available. An equestrian camping area is located at the north end of the park. There are several picnic areas which have tables, shelters, water, charcoal grills, restrooms, and litter receptacles.

Permits Required: Use of the equestrian area must be approved by park staff. Camping permits are also required.

Park Rules and Regulations: Groups of twenty-five persons must obtain permission from the site superintendent. Groups of minors must have adequate supervision and at least one adult for each group of fifteen minors. All pets must be on a leash. See Appendix A.

Mailing Address and Phone Number: Site Superintendent, Jubilee College State Park, R.R. 2, Box 72, Brimfield, Illinois 61517; 309/446-3758

32. Forest Park Nature Center

Trail Length: 7 miles (11.2 kilometers)

Location: Forest Park Nature Center is located off of Route 29 (Galena Road), just north of Peoria, Illinois. Travelers to Peoria can take east-west routes such as Interstate 74 to Route 29. Five miles north of Interstate 74, one will come to Gardner Lane. A sign along Route 29 states Forest Park Nature Center. Turn left on Gardner Lane and drive 1 mile to the parking lot for the museum, office, and gift shop.

County: Peoria

Illinois Highway Map Coordinates: F-5

U.S.G.S. Topographical Map Name and Scale: Spring Bay, 1:24,000

Hours Open: The park is open year-round, and one may hike the trail system from dawn to dusk. The museum and gift shop are open Monday through Saturday from 9:00 a.m. until 5:00 p.m., and on Sunday from 1:00 p.m. until 5:00 p.m.

History and Trail Description: Forest Park Nature Center is one of many parks which is operated by the Peoria Park District. The Park consists of over 530 acres, all of which are a nature preserve. According to Mike Miller in a phone conversation, November 1991, the park previously used to be a Girl Scout camp between World Wars I and II. In 1962 the present headquarters building was built, and in the early 1980s, the Youth Conservation Corp constructed many of the trails. The park is located on the west side of the Illinois River with many of the trails placed on the steep bluffs above the floodplain. There are some spectacular views of the river valley below from some strategic trail locations, especially when the leaves are off the trees.

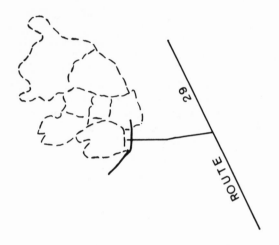

ROUTE 62

N

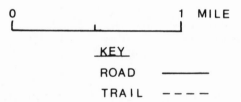

0   1   MILE

KEY

ROAD   ——————

TRAIL   - - - -

7 MILES OF TRAILS

32. Forest Park Nature Center

The trail system begins at the Interpretive Center, which consists of a museum, gift shop, and offices. The paths are all interconnected and total 7 miles in length. There are seven interconnecting trails ranging in length from .75 to 2.75 miles long. The hiker can walk all seven trails for the full 7 miles or less, depending on his or her inclination.

All of the trails are marked with wooden markers which are 3 feet high and name each trail in black lettering. Trail maps are available inside the Interpretive Center, and a larger map of the park also can be viewed inside. The trails found in the park make their way up and down the steep ridges in the park then back down into valleys, paralleling and going over some small creeks. Some of the trails can be very strenuous.

The Wilderness Trail takes the hiker up a hill to a ridge. Following the ridge, one will come to a viewing/listening point. This is an area where one can look toward the river valley and get a view of Peoria Lake as well as enjoy the tranquility. The trail eventually makes its way to the valley below where one can hike the Valley Trail.

From the Valley Trail other trails are accessible, such as the Bee Trail, where another good view of the river

Park bench along trail, Forest Park Nature Center

valley can be had. The Wake Robin Trail offers a nice hike along a ridgetop and then winds its way down into a creek valley. Wooden benches are found along the trails, and the hiker also will cross over some wooden bridges.

The Forest Park Nature Center trail system is a real gem for hikers and central Illinois outdoor enthusiasts. It can be said that this is central Illinois' version of the Smoky Mountains, with its hilly terrain. Although the hills are not quite as tall as the Smokies, nor the park all that large, the trails are challenging for the hiker.

Facilities: Forest Park Nature Center has an Interpretive Center housing a small museum and gift shop. Books, postcards, trail information, restrooms, and water are available. Year-round programs and classes also are held. The Nature Center has a 100-mile hiker club and a publication entitled *Tracks and Trails* which can be picked up here.

Permits Required: None

Park Rules and Regulations: This is an Illinois Nature Preserve. See Appendix B. No bikes or pets are allowed. Smoking, hunting, and collecting of plants are prohibited.

Mailing Address and Phone Number: Forest Park Nature Center, 5809 Forest Park Drive, Peoria Heights, Illinois 61614; 309/686-3360

33. Wildlife Prairie Park

Trail Length: 4 miles (6.4 kilometers)

Location: Wildlife Prairie Park is located ten miles west of Peoria and one mile south of Edwards. Travelers from the west and east may take Interstate 74 to Exit 82 (Edwards Road). Turn south on Edwards Road and proceed four miles to Edwards. South of Edwards, the road is known as Taylor Road; the entrance is on the east side of Taylor Road.

County: Peoria

Illinois Highway Map Coordinates: F-5

U.S.G.S. Topographical Map Name and Scale: Peoria West, 1:24,000

Hours Open: May through October: Weekdays 10:00 a.m. to 6:30 p.m. and on weekends 9:00 a.m. to 6:30 p.m. November and April: Weekdays 11:00 a.m. to 4:00 p.m. and weekends 9:00 a.m. to 4:30 p.m. December through March: Weekdays 11:00 a.m. to 4:00 p.m. and Sundays 10:00 a.m. to 4:00 p.m.

History and Trail Description: Wildlife Prairie Park was developed and opened in 1978 to provide educational, conservational, and recreational activities for the citizens of central Illinois. The park consists of over 2,000 acres of grazing land, rolling hills, lakes, floodplains, and hardwood forests. Currently, 150 acres have been developed; the remaining acres serve as natural buffers to protect the native wildlife.

The park, operated by the Forest Park Foundation, a nonprofit organization which relies on contributions, such as fees for memberships, admissions, and services, sales in the store and gift shop, and thousands of volunteer hours for its development, construction, and operation.

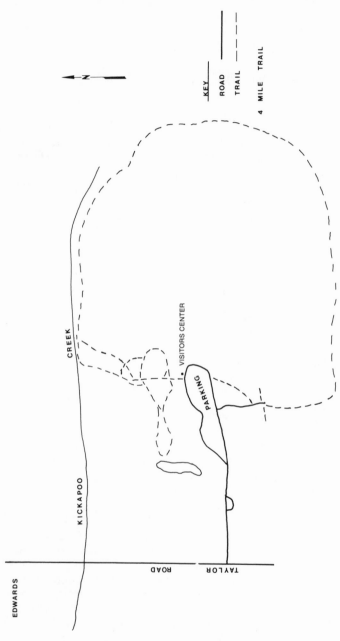

33. Wildlife Prairie Park. Map not drawn to scale.

The park is a small wildlife sanctuary and zoo. Many animals roam in their natural settings, with short hiking trails taking the hiker past all of the wildlife in the park. Some of the animals at the park include bison, elk, black bear, coyotes, bobcat, cougar, wolves, bald eagle, deer, and badgers. The animals are all fenced in, making it safe for the hiker.

The trail system at Wildlife Prairie Park consists of short trails which meander past many of the animals and waterfowl in the park. In addition, the main 4-mile hiking trail in the park takes the hiker through the floodplain of the Kickapoo Creek and around the strip mined areas of the park. Approximately one third of the park was strip mined for coal in the 1950s.

The short trails may be started at the Visitors Center. Maps of the trail are available inside the center. All of the trails are well marked with trail maps found along the trails, showing your exact location. In addition, wooden trail signs point to the direction of other trails. All of the trails are about six feet wide and are very easy to follow.

The Merrill Woods Trail passes many of the animals in the park. A black bear, puma, and wolves are some of the animals that can be seen from this trail. The Helligae Trail and Linder Trail connect with the Merril Woods Trail. The Helligae Trail takes you to the waterfowl blind, while the Linder Trail takes you to a wildlife viewing deck.

The Linder Trail goes into the Old Wagon Trail and passes by a large eagle-viewing area. From here a short trail connects with this trail and takes you to the pioneer farmstead. A small barn with animals, a restored cabin, and a school are located in this area. Close to the cabin you will access the main trail of the park.

The main trail of the park, appropriately known as the Floodplain Trail, measures about 4 miles. As part of the trail lies within a floodplain, it may at times be inundated. You may check with the Visitors Center or call the park to find out the condition of the trail. The trail varies in width, starting out as a small footpath by the cabin and becoming a large gravel road toward the end of the trail on the other side of the park. Wooden benches are also found along the trail.

At the trailhead by the cabin, you will see a trailboard identifying the trail. From here you will descend the hill and go through some forested areas eventually making your way to the floodplain of Kickapoo Creek.

The trail follows Kickapoo Creek for almost one mile. The trail then crosses a small hill, eventually following and traversing a small creek. You will then climb another small hill following a ridge, and will be in a large open field.

Soon you will come to the area in the park where strip-mining took place. You will walk on top of the strip-mined area, go by a lake that resulted from the strip-mining, and will come down to a gravel road. You will go by some other strip-mine lakes here also. Some trail markers will be seen here which state Floodplain Trail.

This gravel road leads to a service road that you passed when first entering the park. Follow the service road a short distance until the trail goes back into the woods. The trail ends near Forest Hall.

Facilities: A Visitors Center is located on the grounds and has a small gift shop, restrooms, and animal and plant displays inside. Food and drinks may be bought in the Arboretum Building. A small country store and a ranger first-aid station are also located at the park. Numerous picnic areas and playground equipment are located here. A small railroad in the park takes visitors past some of the areas in the park. In addition, many wild animals that are native to Illinois will be seen in their natural habitats. Restrooms are available in the Visitors Center, Arboretum, Prairie Hall, Train Depot, and the Pioneer Pavilion.

Park Rules and Regulations: No pets and no alcoholic beverages are allowed.

Mailing Address and Phone Number: Wildlife Prairie Park, R.R. 2, Taylor Road, Hanna City, Illinois 61536; 309/676-0998

34. Dirksen and McNaughton Parks

Trail Lengths: McNaugthton Park, 6 miles (9.6 kilometers); Dirksen Park, 4 miles (6.4 kilometers)

Location: Dirksen and McNaughton Parks are both located in Pekin. To reach the parks, take State Route 29 from the north or the south. Turn right (east) at State Route 98 and proceed two miles to the park entrance. The park road turns south into McNaughton Park. McNaughton Park is located on the south side of Route 98 and Dirksen Park on the north side. Follow this road either to the horse stables area or to the end of the road where there is a turnaround.

County: Tazewell

Illinois Highway Map Coordinates: F-5

U.S.G.S. Topographical Map Name and Scale: Marquette Heights, 1:24,000

Hours Open: 6:00 a.m. until 10:00 p.m.

History and Trail Description: McNaughton Park was named after John T. McNaughton, who once owned the *Pekin Times* newspaper. Dirksen Park was named after the late Senator Everett Dirksen, a resident of Pekin. The development of the trail in McNaughton Park was started in the summer of 1970 and was completed in the spring of 1971. The trail was completed with the help of hikers, Boy Scout Troop 194, and the Pekin Park District.

The trail in McNaughton Park, called the Potawatomi Trail, measures 6 miles, while the trail in Dirksen Park, the Running Deer Trail, measures 4 miles. Both of the trails are blazed very well with spray paint on the trees. The Potawatomi Trail is marked with red paint; the Running Deer Trail, with yellow paint.

Both trails may be started near the horse stables right off of Route 98, or you may begin at the end of the

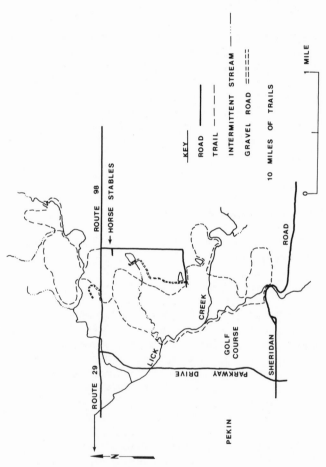

KEY

ROAD ———
TRAIL — — —
INTERMITTENT STREAM ·······
GRAVEL ROAD ======

10 MILES OF TRAILS

1 MILE

ROUTE 98

← HORSE STABLES

ROUTE 29

LICK

CREEK

GOLF COURSE

SHERIDAN ROAD

PARKWAY DRIVE

PEKIN

N

34. Dirksen and McNaughton Parks

road where there is a turnaround for vehicles. There is also a little parking area at the horse stables. The horse stables are run by a private firm, the land being leased to them by the Pekin Park District.

From the parking area, walk due west past the stables, through a few gates, and then continue onward to a small picnic area and shelter. From this spot both the Running Deer Trail and the Potawatomi Trail may be reached. A wooden trail marker behind the shelter shows the direction of the Running Deer Trail. The Potawatomi Trail is found by hiking west until red trail blazes are seen on the trees.

The Running Deer Trail slowly starts heading downhill and passes a small creek before approaching Route 98. From this point the trail crosses the road and follows it east for the short distance until it reaches the archery range. From here the trail follows the road and then branches off into the woods. Soon you will cross a creek. Follow this creek west for a short distance. The trail will start to follow another creek valley, and then it starts heading in a westerly direction, going by open fields. The trail crosses another small creek and comes out of the woods at the edge of an open field. The trail then goes around the open field and starts back into the woods again. Following the natural topography, the trail comes down to cross another creek, then climbs another small hill. From here the trail follows the edge of a cliff for a short distance before dropping off to the creek valley again, where it crosses the creek once more.

After reaching the highest point in the park (639 feet in elevation) you descend to the main creek that was crossed earlier. After crossing the creek, you head west toward private homes. The trail turns south toward Route 98 and the road that leads into the park. From here you follow the road back to the trailhead.

Passing the stables you will reach the Potawatomi Trail. You also have the option of taking the car to the turnaround area to start hiking the trail beginning north of the parking area.

The trail is clearly marked with red blazes. The trail goes downhill over a small creek and over small bridges. The trail then follows some power lines for a short distance. From here the trail heads back into the woods, paralleling the open fields. The trail bridges another creek and comes to the picnic areas just west of the stables. From here the trail heads west, goes under the power lines again, and then turns south moving down-hill. Shortly, the trail crosses Lick Creek, which may be quite high during the wet season.

From here the trail parallels the creek for a long time, going up and down the small hills in the area. The trail then passes a golf course and starts south, coming finally to Sheridan Road. Follow this road eastward for a short distance and, as soon as you pass the creek, start north into the woods. From here the trail soon skirts an open field and then heads west until it reaches the creek again. You will see a platform overlooking the creek. The trail continues paralleling the creek, going by a forty-foot eroded stream bank, and moving uphill to another open field. The trail parallels this open field for a short distance, then crosses another creek. The trail parallels this creek for a short distance, starts north and then west, passing an old house foundation. Finally it comes to some restrooms that are east of Joseph Zurcher Lake. The trail goes around the south end of the lake and up a small hill to the car turnaround area.

Facilities: There are picnic facilities with picnic tables and restrooms available by the turnaround. A small shelter and observation are also at the Joseph Zurcher Lake. Picnic facilities are also available west of the horse stables.

Permits Required: Camping is by permit only. A permit may be obtained by contacting the Pekin Park District.

Park Rules and Regulations: No alcoholic beverages, hunting, trapping, or swimming allowed. No vehicles on the grass and no one allowed on the ice.

Mailing Address and Phone Number: Pekin Park District, 1701 Court Street, Pekin, Illinois 61554; 309/347-3178

35. Humiston Woods Nature Center

Trail Length: 7 miles (11.2 kilometers)

Location: Humiston Woods Nature Center is located six miles northwest of Pontiac. To reach the center, motorists may take Interstate 55 and exit onto State Route 23 (Exit 201). Proceed north 1 mile and turn left (west) onto Rowe Road. A sign on Route 23 points to Humiston Woods. Proceed on Rowe Road for four miles to the park entrance, which is located on the north side of the road.

County: Livingston

Illinois Highway Map Coordinates: E-7

U.S.G.S. Topographical Map Name and Scale: Northwest Pontiac, 1:24,000

Hours Open: The park is open at 8:00 a.m. and closes at dusk year-round.

History and Trail Description: According to Joe Jobst, in an interview, Humiston Woods Nature Center is part of the Camp/Humiston Trust, which came into being in 1920. In 1975, the Trust started the Nature Center. Since then, the Nature Center has grown, and new trails and facilities are continually being added.

In the parking lot, the hiker will see a trailboard that shows the layouts of the seven trails in the park. Each trail is identified by an appropriate name and symbol. In addition, each trail is blazed with a different color. The beginning of each trail is also identified with wooden trail markers.

Four trails may be started at the main trailboard. At all four of these trailheads are gates which were built to keep motorized vehicles from entering the trails. You may hike the trails in any direction you want. At some trail junctions there are signs to identify the trail. Just to the northeast of the trailboard is a small pond, referred

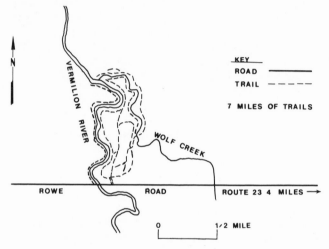

35. Humiston Woods Nature Center

Trailboard, Humiston Woods Nature Center

to as the Mikey Hoffman Pond; two of the trails go past this pond.

One trail, known as the Mushroom Trail, is on the west side of the Vermilion River. Hikers may leave their cars in the parking lot and go to the trailhead, or park their cars along the road near this trailhead.

The River Trail may be started just west of the main trailboard and basically parallels the Vermilion River. The trail starts going down toward the river where the hiker will see a canoe ramp. Shortly the hiker will reach a pavilion and picnic area that has tables and small grills, all overlooking the Vermilion River. Also a small platform offers a beautiful view of the river valley. From here the trail continues paralleling the river and soon joins another branch of the trail. At this point the trail may be followed north to the junction of the Vermilion River and Wolf Creek, or looped back to the pavilion. The junction area of the Vermilion River and Wolf Creek is in a floodplain; during periods of heavy rainfall, the trail gets inundated.

Also at the junction, the Coyote Trail joins the River Trail and heads south paralleling Wolf Creek on the west side. The Coyote Trail then meets up with the Pioneer

Trail at a rock ford. The Pioneer Trail crosses Wolf Creek
and parallels Wolf Creek on the east side all the way to
the Scout Camp. The Pioneer Trail starts near the pond.
Another trail starting near the pond is the Deer Trail. The
Deer Trail basically stays on top of a ridge, parallels Wolf
Creek for a short distance, follows the park fence, and
comes back to the east side of the parking lot and
trailboard.

All of the trails are fairly easy to hike and may be
enjoyed by the entire family. The Fox Trail is a handicap
trail and is found near the pavilion. Wildlife, including
numerous bird species, may be seen while hiking here.

Facilities: Maps are found at the main trailboard at the
parking lot. Pit toilets and a small picnic area are also
located here. A pavilion, grills, water, benches, picnic
tables, and pit toilets also may be found along the River
Trail. There also is a 15-acre restored prairie on the east
side of the preserve near Deer Trail. Fishing is allowed in
the pond, Vermilion River, and Wolf Creek. The pond is
stocked with catfish, crappie, bluegill, and largemouth
bass. All appropriate Illinois fishing rules and regulations are in effect.

Observation platform overlooking the Vermilion River, Humiston Woods Nature Center

Rock ford across Wolf Creek, Humiston Woods Nature Center

Park Rules and Regulations: No hunting. No motorized vehicles.

Mailing Address and Phone Number: Humiston Woods Nature Center, P.O. Box 73, Pontiac, Illinois 61764; 815/844-7350

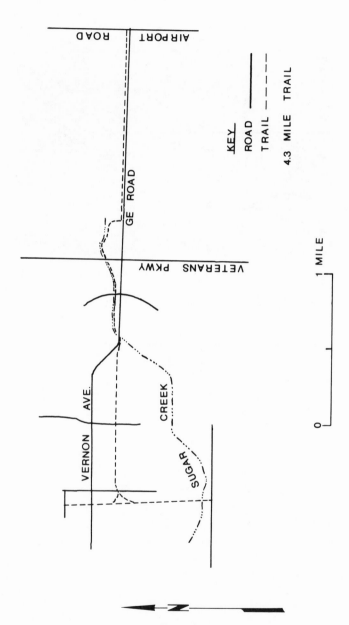

36. Constitution Trail

36. Constitution Trail

Trail Length: 4.3 miles (6.9 kilometers)

Location: The Constitution Trail is located in Bloomington and Normal, Illinois. The trail has two designated parking lots from whence one can get on the trail. There also are numerous other starting locations since the trail passes through many residential areas.

In order to reach the two designated parking areas, travelers proceeding on Interstate 55 may exit onto Veterans Parkway. Follow Veterans Parkway to Vernon Avenue/GE Road. Vernon Avenue heads west and GE Road heads east. Turn east, and along the south side of GE Road is the parking lot for General Electric Company. Hikers can park at the east end of this lot. Directly across the street the hiker will find the trail as well as a sign identifying the trail. Found here also is GE's Progress Park, a private facility for GE employees.

In order to find the second designated parking lot, head west on Vernon Avenue from Veterans Parkway. Follow Vernon Avenue for about 2 miles to Grandview Drive. Turn south on Grandview and go 2 blocks to the Colene Hoose School parking lot. The trail is visible on the south side of this lot.

County: McLean

Illinois Highway Map Coordinates: G-7

U.S.G.S. Topographical Map Names and Scale: Normal East and Bloomington East, both 1:24,000

Hours Open: The trail is open dawn to dusk.

History and Trail Description: The Constitution Trail is a joint project between the Cities of Bloomington and Normal. Roughly half of the trail is located in each town.

According to Keith Rich, in a phone conversation, November 1991, the trail concept came into reality after the Illinois Central Gulf Railroad wanted to sell its right-of-way. The two towns came together and came up with the idea for a multipurpose trail for the hiker, biker, and skier. With the aid of a development grant from the State of Illinois, the trail was opened in 1989.

The Constitution Trail is paved for its entire distance and is about 10 feet wide. It is marked with brown and white trail signs which state the trail name, the hours, and to whom it is open (hikers, bikers, and skiers). This is a highly urbanized path. Since the trail is paved, many bicyclists use it, as well as many hikers and some skiers (weather permitting). This pathway goes through Bloomington and Normal, passing by residential areas, light industries, businesses, and open fields. The trail also goes under and over a few roads and by some small creeks.

The trail is shaped like the letter T; the western end of the trail is the north/south part, with the northern end terminating at Phoenix Avenue (Normal Town Hall), while the southern end finishes at Emerson Street in Bloomington. The trail between Veterans Parkway and Airport Road (east-west segment) parallels GE Road, going by some light industries, residential areas, and open fields. The eastern end of the trail winds up at Airport Road, where a trail sign and benches are located.

Heading west past Veterans Parkway, the trail goes under the road and parallels Sugar Creek, and then shortly goes under Towanda Road. The trail crosses Vernon Avenue (watch for traffic), then goes along the sidewalk for 2 blocks where it goes by a residential area. Soon the trail goes by Colene Hoose School and then past other residential areas. A bridge takes the hiker over Linden Street where soon the trail splits going to the north and south. This is the north/south segment.

The northern section goes by apartments and shortly to the Normal City Hall. The southern part of the trail is pretty, as it is tree-lined and under a canopy. The trail goes by an old railroad signal, over Sugar Creek again, and stops at Emerson Street. Future plans call for opening another trail segment from Emerson Street south to Washington Street (roughly 1 mile), ending close to where the historic David Davis Mansion is located.

Facilities: Benches are located along the trail, and rest-rooms are found on the west side of Towanda Avenue. Restaurants and stores are found along the main roads which the trail intersects.

Permits Required: None

Park Rules and Regulations: No bike racing. Motorized vehicles prohibited. Obey all laws and regulations when crossing streets. Do not trespass on private property along the trail.

Mailing Addresses and Phone Numbers: Bloomington Parks and Recreation Department, 109 East Olive, P.O. Box 3157, Bloomington, Illinois 61702-3157; 309/828-7361; or Normal Parks and Recreation Department, 100 East Phoenix Avenue, Normal, Illinois 61761; 309/454-2444

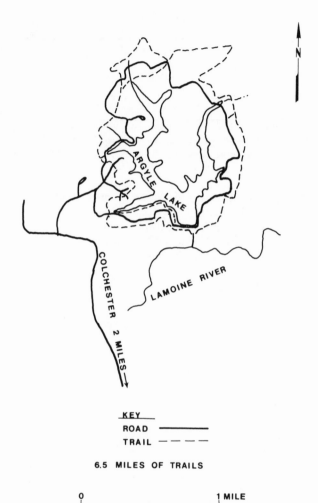

N

ARGYLE LAKE

COLCHESTER 2 MILES →

LAMOINE RIVER

KEY
ROAD ———
TRAIL — — —

6.5 MILES OF TRAILS

0   1 MILE

37. Argyle Lake State Park

37. Argyle Lake State Park

Trail Length: 6.5 miles (10.4 kilometers)

Location: Argyle Lake State Park is located seven miles west of Macomb and two miles north of Colchester. To reach the park take State Route 136 seven miles out of Macomb. In Colchester you will see a sign for Argyle Lake State Park. This road is known as Coal Street. Turn north on Coal Street and proceed two miles to the park entrance.

County: McDonough

Illinois Highway Map Coordinates: G-3

U.S.G.S. Topographical Map Name and Scale: Colchester, 1:24,000

Hours Open: The park is open year-round except on Christmas Day and New Year's Day. At certain times, due to freezing and thawing periods, the park is closed, and access to the park is by foot only.

History and Trail Description: A group of early settlers of McDonough County began the first Cumberland Presbyterian Church which met at the residence of John McCord. In 1854, the congregation moved to the Argyle Presbyterian Church near the west side of the park. The church founder, of Scottish descent, gave the community its name from Scotland's famous county of Argyle, for which the park was also named.

The initial land acquisition for Argyle Lake State Park was 1,052 acres in 1948, and soon afterwards lake construction started on a tributary of the east fork of the LaMoine River. The lake, completed in 1949, consists of 95 acres and has a drainage of approximately 3,800 acres. The park currently has over 1,750 acres.

The trail system in Argyle Lake State Park comprises many interconnecting trails which wind their way around the park's main road for over 6 miles. These trails have various names; most of them are marked at their starting points. Also seen are trail markers with a hiker symbol on them.

The trails can be started at numerous areas in the park. At certain trailheads, trailboards outline the trail layout. The trails are about six feet wide, although some parts of the trails may be the width of a one-lane road.

While hiking the trails you will see numerous signs marked Foot Trail or Horse Trail. In many cases the horse trails in the park join the hiking trail for a short distance and then branch off.

The trails are moderately rough as they go up and down along numerous small hills and some steep banks close to the lake. There are many stairs and several small creeks to cross via small wooden bridges. One section of the trail takes you past the dam and spillway. You will have to cross the spillway on the concrete apron or over rocks. During periods of high water this area may be impossible to cross by foot. The trails also have water bars to help divert the water off the trails; during the wet times of the year, the trails can become very muddy and difficult to walk.

In the future the park is planning to change all of the trail signs to one new name. The site superintendent thought that one name would be less confusing to hikers than the numerous trail names currently used.

One designated camping area along the trail may be used by the backpacker. The camping area is found on the eastern part of the trail.

Certain areas of the trail have restrooms, benches, or picnic tables.

Facilities: The park has picnic facilities, such as tables and stoves, grills, water, restrooms, playground equipment, tent and trailer camping (electricity and a shower building), and a summer interpretive program. In addition, a concession stand located on the lake offers a variety of refreshments during the summer months. Boats and pontoons may be rented at the concession stand. At the site superintendent's office located in the park, hikers may request maps and get camping permits. Fishing is also allowed on the lake, contingent upon Illinois fishing rules and regulations.

Permits Required: A camping permit is required.

Park Rules and Regulations: Motor limit is 10 HP. See Appendix A.

Mailing Address and Phone Number: Site Superintendent, Argyle Lake State Park, R.R. 1, Colchester, Illinois 62326; 309/776-3422

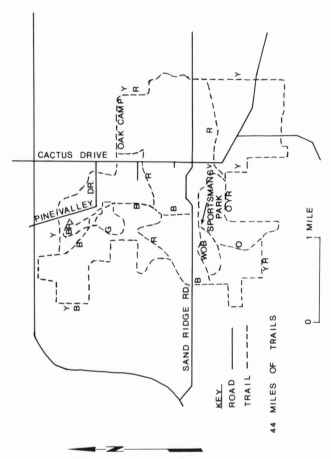

38. Sand Ridge State Forest. Redrawn from Sand Ridge
trail guide.

38. Sand Ridge State Forest

Trail Length: 44 miles (70 kilometers)

Location: Sand Ridge State Forest is located twelve miles northeast of Havana off State Route 136. To reach the park, take Route 136 east out of Havana and turn north onto a gravel road when you see the sign for Forest City and Sand Ridge State Forest. Proceed six miles on this road to the park entrance.

County: Mason

Illinois Highway Map Coordinates: G-5

Illinois Topographical Map Names and Scale: Manito and Duck Island, both 1:24,000

Hours Open: The park is open all year except Christmas Day and New Year's Day.

History and Trail Description: Sand Ridge State Forest was initially acquired by the state in 1939 when 5,504 acres were purchased. The forest at that time consisted of small lots of natural hardwood timber and abandoned farms. After the state purchased the land, the forest was managed as a total forest ecosystem. The forest, formerly called Mason State Forest, was renamed Sand Ridge State Forest in 1971. Currently the forest has over 7,180 acres.

The trail system at Sand Ridge State Forest consists of seven different trails which total over 44 miles. These trails are all connected and the hiker may choose to hike as little as 1.6 miles or the entire trail system of 44 miles.

Trails are all color-coded with a different color for each. These paths are known as the Yellow Loop Trail, Red Loop Trail, and so forth. Each of trails is marked by 3-foot wood or metal posts that have colored blazes signifying the trail. When the hiker comes to a trail junction, the post will show more than one colored blaze, and an arrow showing in which direction a particular trail heads.

There are three main trailheads in the park. The first, at Sportsman's Park, is located west of Forest Headquarters along Sand Ridge Road. Sportsman's Park is a large camping area where many horseback riders start their trail riding. Here one will find hitching rails, pit toilets, water, and a shelter. From this location, hikers can get to the White and Orange loops, as well as the Blue and Red loops. The Orange and Blue loops are the two main trails which most of the horseback riders in the park use. Since many of the horseback riders start at Sportsman's Park, some of the trails leading from this spot can be rough to hike due to the heavy horse use.

The second trailhead is at Oak Camp along Cactus Drive. Oak Camp is a group camping spot which also contains a shelter, water, and pit toilets. From here, the hikes can get to the Yellow and Red loop trails. These two trails are the only two which, during the winter, snow-mobilers are allowed to use.

The third trailhead is found along Pine Valley Drive, where there is a parking area and a trailboard. From the parking lot one can get to the Brown and Green loops and then to the Blue Loop Trail. For hikers looking for fairly short trails, and seeking a good sense of the trail system throughout the forest, the Green and Brown loops are good ones with which to start.

The entire trail system within Sand Ridge State Forest is underlain with sand, making it difficult for the individual to hike. In addition, prickly pear cactus as well as sand burs grow along all of the trails, which can make hiking miserable. Furthermore, water is not found along any parts of the trails, other than at Sportsman's Park and Oak Camp trailheads. We recommend that the hiker consider doing the trails here in the early spring when the plants and other flowers are blooming, or in the fall when the leaves are turning color. Winter sports enthusiasts may want to ski these trails.

Motorists, while driving in the park, will see Trail Crossing signs, which let them know that trails are found up ahead. In addition, the paths contain 12 backcountry campsites where hikers, once they have obtained their permits, may camp.

Prickly pear cactus, Sand Ridge State Forest

Facilities: Sand Ridge State Forest has a park office where you may request additional information. Picnic sites are scattered in the park and have water, picnic tables, and restrooms. Camping is available here with a group camping area, a family area, a horse area, and a walk-in campground available. There are twenty-four campsites at the family area and three sites for the walk-in campground. Hunting is allowed in the forest during open season and with applicable rules and regulations applying. Nature-study groups, school classes, scout groups, insect collectors, and bird watchers also use the forest.

Required Permits: A camping permit is required and may be obtained from the ranger.

Park Rules and Regulations: All motorized vehicles are prohibited from the trails and fire lanes. See Appendix A.

Mailing Address and Phone Number: Site Superintendent, Sand Ridge State Forest, P.O. Box 82, Forest City, Illinois 61532; 309/597-2212

39. Clinton Lake State Recreation Area

Trail Length: 10 miles (16 kilometers)

Location: The trail, located within Clinton Lake State Recreation Area, is approximately eight miles northeast of Clinton, thirty-five south of Bloomington, and thirty miles north of Decatur. From the east or west, Clinton Lake can be reached from Route 10. To reach the trailhead, take Route 54 east out of Clinton for five miles to Birkbeck. Turn north here and follow the signs to North Fork Access Area.

County: De Witt

Illinois Highway Map Coordinates: G-7

U.S.G.S. Topographical Map Name and Scale: De Witt, 1:24,000

Hours Open: Clinton Lake State Recreation Area is open year-round. The site office hours are 7:00 a.m. to 3:00 p.m., Monday through Friday.

History and Trail Description: The Clinton Lake State Recreation Area was developed by the Illinois Department of Conservation in conjunction with the Illinois Power Company. The site is 10,000 acres in size, and the 4,900-acre lake acts as a source of cooling water for the nuclear power plant. Various recreation facilities also are found around the lake.

The trail described here follows the perimeter of Clinton Lake between North Fork Boat Access Area and the North Fork Canoe Access Area. Hikers may also start at the northern tip of the trail by the canoe access parking lot. The trail is marked with white signs on metal posts. Due to the trail length, the path is infrequently hiked. This accounts for its being highly overgrown with vegetation, and at times difficult to locate. It is highly recommended that hikers wear trousers as the vegetation can

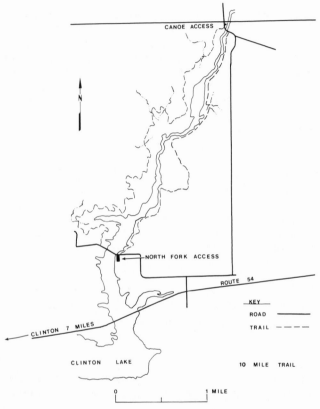

CANOE ACCESS

NORTH FORK ACCESS

ROUTE 54

KEY
ROAD
TRAIL ----

CLINTON 7 MILES

CLINTON LAKE

10 MILE TRAIL

0   1 MILE

39. Clinton Lake State Recreation Area

reach heights of three feet or more. Poison ivy and other plants which can cause skin irritations are found in abundance all along the trail.

Along this trail you will encounter steep hill grades, dense underbrush, dense woods, and open fields. Numerous habitats will be encountered such as hardwood forests, wetlands, prairies, and savanna. Many footbridges exist on the trail and allow easy access over stream crossings. Many times the trail descends to lake level, offering panoramic views of the water, and then goes back into the woods on a ridge. You should pack your own water, as sources along the trail are inadequate for drinking.

Facilities: Restrooms, water, and parking facilities are available at the North Fork Boat Access Area. A site office is located in the main park grounds on the lake (Mascoutin Area), and additional information may be obtained there. Also available are a marina, several day use areas with boat access, picnicking, swimming, water-skiing, fishing, and 135 campsites. All appropriate fishing rules and regulations are in effect.

Permits Required: Permits for camping, hunting, metal detector use, and groups of twenty-five or more persons are required.

Park Rules and Regulations: All pets must be on a leash. Swimming is allowed only at the Mascoutin beach during the posted hours. No fires on the ground are permitted. Camping and cooking fires are permitted in designated areas only. See Appendix A.

Mailing Address and Phone Number: Site Superintendent, Clinton Lake State Recreation Area, R.R. 1, Box 4, De Witt, Illinois 61735; 217/935-8722

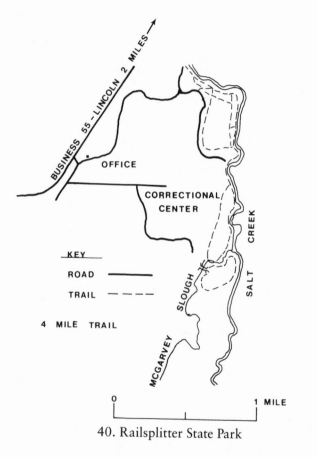

40. Railsplitter State Park

40. Railsplitter State Park

Trail Length: 4 miles (6.4 kilometers)

Location: Railsplitter State Park is located two miles south of Lincoln and borders Salt Creek. The park also surrounds the Lincoln Correctional Center. To reach the park, exit Interstate 55 at Business 55 (Exit 123) and proceed one mile to the state park sign. Turn right at the sign and go over the railroad tracks; the park is immediately to the left.

County: Logan

Illinois Highway Map Coordinates: G-6

U.S.G.S. Topographical Map Name and Scale: Broadwell, 1:24,000

Hours Open: The park is open every day of the year except Christmas Day and New Year's Day. At certain times, due to freezing and thawing periods, the park may be closed, and one must enter on foot.

History and Trail Description: The Department of Conservation initially acquired 741 acres of land from the Department of Mental Health. The following year, park development began; currently there are 751 acres of land in the park.

There are two trails in the park. The first is a short jogging trail located at the first parking facility. The other trail is a 4-mile multilooped trail. The majority of the trail goes along Salt Creek and is known as the "Salt Creek Trail."

The trail can be reached from numerous points in the park. Maps of the park trail system can be obtained at the ranger's office, and trailboards are set up to show your location and the direction of the trail.

The trail can be started by the cartop boat launch. The trail then heads south, following Salt Creek and joining two other trail segments along the way. One of these trails branches west and parallels the park road, while the other trail parallels Salt Creek; this section of the trail may be inundated during the wet season. Both trails are about ten feet wide, and during the winter months they are excellent ski trails.

The trail along Salt Creek soon branches west and parallels McGarvey Slough. The trail crosses a bridge, passes by a small picnic area, and then makes a short loop back to the bridge.

Facilities: A ranger station located in the park offers additional information. Picnic tables, grills, restrooms, drinking water, and shelters are also scattered throughout the park. A canoe/cartop boat launch is also located in the park. Salt Creek can be fished for large- and smallmouth bass, bluegill, sunfish, crappie, catfish, bullheads, and carp. All appropriate Illinois fishing rules and regulations are in effect.

Park Rules and Regulations: No hunting allowed. See Appendix A.

Mailing Address and Phone Number: Site Superintendent, Railsplitter State Park, R.R. 3, Lincoln, Illinois 62656; 217/735-2424

41. New Salem State Historic Site

Trail Length: 6-mile loop trail (10 kilometers)

Location: New Salem State Historic Site is located approximately 20 miles northwest of Springfield and 2 miles south of Petersburg, Illinois. To reach the site, take Route 125 west out of Springfield for 5 miles until it joins with Route 97. A sign at the junction of Routes 125 and 97 will indicate New Salem State Park. Turn north on Route 97 and go for approximately 11 miles until one sees the park sign. The park entrance is located on the west side of the road.

County: Menard

Illinois Highway Map Coordinates: H-5

U.S.G.S. Topographical Map Name and Scale: Salisbury, 1:24,000

Hours Open: The site is open every day of the year except for Thanksgiving, Christmas, and New Year's Day.

History and Trail Description: The New Salem State Historic Site is a reconstruction of the village where Abraham Lincoln spent his early adulthood. Abraham Lincoln spent six years in this village, beginning in 1831, where he undertook various jobs.

Beginning in the 1930s the State of Illinois began permanent improvements to the site to reconstruct the village. Twelve timber houses, the Rutledge Tavern, ten workshops, stores, mills, and a school where church services were held have been reproduced and furnished as they were in the 1830s.

The trail is a 6-mile one-way loop trail referred to as the Volksmarch Trail, and it is sanctioned by the American Volksmarch Association. The trail starts on the north end of the campground, which borders South Shore Drive. The trail also may be intersected at the park

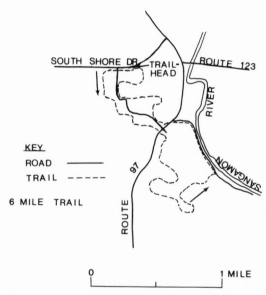

41. New Salem State Historic Site

Reconstructed pioneer village, New Salem State Historic Site

entrance, picnic areas, and also at the historic village. In fact, part of the trail goes right through the center of the settlement. The trailhead is located directly across the street from the restaurant on the north side of the campground. There is an opening in the park gate here and the hiker will see a trail marker which is a 3-foot-high blue sign which has a white backpacker symbol on it. This is the main trail marker which is seen along the entire trail.

The trail heads west through the campground. Once the hiker crosses the park road, the trail parallels the fence. On the left side will be the group camping area. Once past the group camping area, the path turns south and goes past the picnic areas, through some woods, and by the main parking area for the village.

At this point the Mentor Graham Footstep Trail joins this trail. A trailboard for this other path is seen along with the blue and white hiker sign. This combined trail now heads off into the woods and begins descending down a small hill where one will cross a few wooden bridges and a small creek. The trail will then head uphill and stay on top of the ridge for a short distance. The Mentor Graham Trail splits off before heading uphill.

On top of the hill, the hiker will run across an old pioneer cemetery with some gravestones dated back to the mid-1800s, one at 1844. Shortly the trail descends down the hill, crosses a small creek, and then comes out to Route 97.

The hiker then has to cross Route 97 (watch for traffic) and proceed up a hill on the other side of the road. Once on top of the hill, brown markers with a skier on them will be seen. The trail stays on top of this ridge and winds its way around a small valley, going to a park road. The trail will cross and parallel this road for a short distance and then head back into the woods and proceed up and down a small valley, eventually coming back to the same park road and a small picnic area.

The trail goes past the picnic area paralleling the road until a hiker sign is seen on an old dirt road. The path follows this dirt road, going by a gate, and then descends a hill. Once down the hill, a few buildings will be seen on the right side of the trail. The trail stays behind these buildings and shortly comes to Prichartville Road. The trail crosses this road and parallels it for the next half mile back to Route 97. Good views of the Sangamon River will be had from this trail section. During heavy rains the Sangamon River occasionally floods, and Prichartville Road may be inundated.

The trail will then cross Route 97, follow it briefly, go over a wooden bridge, past the old building and toward the park road. The trail follows the park road until the service road is reached. Follow the service road uphill until one is in the back part of the village. The trail then goes through the center of the village. This is an excellent chance to sit down for a break and then to tour the village, looking at the historic homes and buildings. The trail then goes by the Visitors Center, the south side of the campground, and finally makes its way to the campground road which takes the hiker right back to the trailhead.

Facilities: There are several picnic areas with water, tables, and grills. Camping is also available for tents and trailers with showers, electricity, and a sanitary station being provided. A concession stand and bookstore is available at the entrance of the pioneer village. These are open during the summer months. In addition, a new

Visitors Center is now open. The Visitors Center has an auditorium, an exhibit on the life and times of Abraham Lincoln, restrooms, and an administration wing. A replica of a steamboat provides hourly trips on the Sangamon River, provided the water level is sufficient. During the summer months plays about the life and times of Lincoln are performed in an outdoor amphitheater.

Permits Required: A camping permit is required.

Park Rules and Regulations: Food and drinks are prohibited in the Pioneer Village. See Appendix A.

Mailing Address and Phone Number: New Salem State Historic Site, R.R. 1, Box 244A, Petersburg, Illinois 62675; 217/632-7953

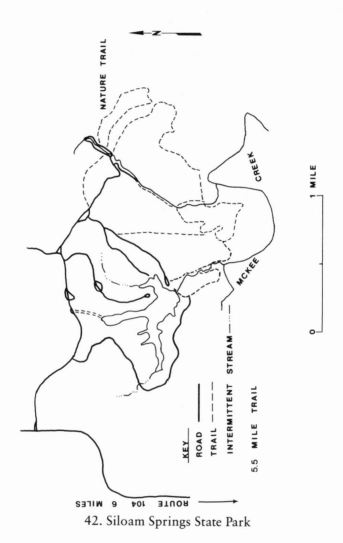

ROUTE 104 6 MILES

42. Siloam Springs State Park

42. Siloam Springs State Park

Trail Length: 5.5 miles (8.8 kilometers)

Location: Siloam Springs State Park is located twenty-five miles east of Quincy and fifty-two miles west of Jacksonville off State Route 104. A state park sign on Route 104 points in the direction of the park. Turn north off Route 104 onto an asphalt road, and the entrance to the park will be approximately six miles down the road.

Counties: Adams, Brown

Illinois Highway Map Coordinates: H-2

U.S.G.S. Topographical Map Names and Scale: Kellerville and Fishhook, both 1:24,000

Hours Open: The park is open year-round except Christmas Day and New Year's Day. At certain times, due to freezing and thawing periods, the park roads are closed, and access to the park is by foot only. The park is open 6:00 a.m. to 10:00 p.m. daily.

History and Trail Description: This area was part of the military tract of western Illinois. The land was acquired around 1852 by George Meyers, and it is thought that he claimed the land as a veteran for his service in the Black Hawk and Mexican wars. Shortly after the Civil War, the Rev. Reuben K. McCoy, a Presbyterian minister from Clayton, discovered the springs there. Quincy Burgesser, a Clayton businessman, analyzed the waters and thought that they might provide wonderful cures for all physical ailments. In 1884, Burgesser built the Siloam Forest Home Hotel, a bathing house, spring houses, and other facilities. As medical science advanced, there was a decline in the hotel business and the town. In 1935 the Siloam Springs Recreation Club purchased the site and tried to restore it to popularity. After 1940, the old hotel and bathhouses were torn down, the swimming pool was abandoned, and the springs were no longer used. Today, one can still see the sites of the hotel and springhouses while driving through the park. In 1940, the State of Illinois purchased 2,665 acres of land here. Currently there are over 3,323 acres in the park.

About 12 miles of trails are scattered throughout the park, with the main backpack trail being 4 miles. The trailhead begins at the east picnic area as soon as you go over an old steel bridge. Water bars help divert water from the trail. The trail, generally about seven feet wide, runs for about three miles on a ridge and through the woods. Backpack signposts, scattered on the trail about every quarter mile, show the distance walked. The trail crosses a stream about four times. During spring runoff, the water can be at a very high level.

At the trailhead, you will see a trailboard that states Red Oak Backpack Trail, Length 4 Miles. The trail immediately begins ascending a small hill along an old road. About two miles into the hike, an old abandoned house and foundation is seen along the trail. At 2.7 miles, you will reach the camping area. Some pit toilets, picnic tables, and 4 tent sites are seen. A camping permit must be secured from the ranger to camp here. Backpackers

Rock outcrop along trail, Siloam Springs State Park

who plan on camping at the backpack camping area must leave their vehicle at the ranger station and hike down to the trail.

Beyond the campsites, the backpack trail connects with a fire lane which goes back to the lake road, or the backpack trail splits off and leads to the trail end, or another trail, called the Crabapple Creek Trail, may be followed.

The last mile of the backpack trail goes through the woods, down a steep ridge, crosses a creek a few times before connecting with an access road. At this point the road can be followed back to the trailhead.

Crabapple Creek Trail takes the hiker past McKee Creek where some great views of the creek and some boulders are had. The trail then heads north toward the lake. Prior to reaching the lake another trail joins this trail and is referred to as the Prairie Bluff Trail. You can follow Crabapple Creek Trail to the parking area for the boat launch, or follow Prairie Bluff Trail.

Prairie Bluff Trail crosses the creek, then follows the side of a hill, goes up the hill, and then winds its way toward the earthen dam for the lake. A trail sign will be seen at the dam. Some small rock outcrops will be seen along the side of the hill, and a great view will be had from the top of the hill.

Facilities: A ranger station is located in the park to offer additional information and to issue camping permits. Shelters and playground equipment are scattered through-out the park. The park has over 230 sites available for tent, trailer, and group camping. A sanitary station for trailers is nearby. Water and toilet facilities are also available. A concession stand is open during the summer months and provides boat rentals. A launching ramp and docks are available for private boats if there is enough space. The lake is stocked with largemouth bass, bluegill, sunfish, channel catfish, and trout. All appropriate fishing laws and regulations must be followed. Twenty-three miles of equestrian trails are located in the park also.

Permits Required: A camping permit is required.

Park Rules and Regulations: No horses are allowed on the hiking trails. No swimming or wading. See Appendix A.

Mailing Address and Phone Number: Site Superintendent, Siloam Springs State Park, R.R. 1, Box 204, Clayton, Illinois 62324; 217/894-6205

43. Rock Springs Center

Trail Length: 7 miles (11.3 kilometers)

Location: Rock Springs Center is located on the south-west side of Decatur and borders the Sangamon River. The center can be reached by taking Interstate 72 to State Route 36 (Exit 30 A). Take Route 36 a few miles to Wyckles Road (County Highway 41). A sign along Route 36 states Rock Springs Center. Proceed south on Wyckles Road for about three miles and turn left at the Rock Springs Center sign. This is known as Rock Springs Road (County Road 10). Travel on this road for about one mile, then take a left and proceed to the park entrance.

County: Macon

Illinois Highway Map Coordinates: H-7

U.S.G.S. Topographical Map Name and Scale: Harris-town, 1:24,000

Hours Open: Rock Springs Center is open year-round. The hiking trails are open Monday through Sunday from 8:00 a.m. until dusk. The Visitors Center is open 9:00 a.m. to 4:30 p.m. Monday through Saturday, and 1:00 p.m. to 4:30 p.m. on Sunday.

History and Trail Description: Rock Springs Center is owned and operated by the Macon County Conservation District. It was formally opened in the mid-1970s. Prior to that time the land was held by a variety of owners, with the area being used for farming and for gravel operations. The Center has now been set aside for the preservation of plants and animals and for education and various types of recreation compatible with the area. Currently the Center comprises 1,323 acres.

The Center's hiking trails consist of seven intercon-necting trails which total about 7 miles. The longest trail, about 2.25 miles, is called the River Trail. This trail goes

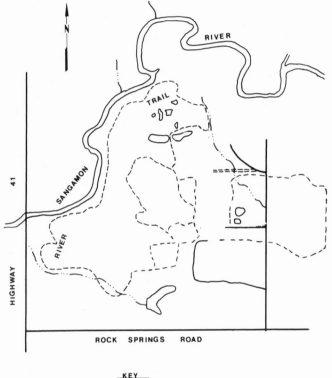

KEY

ROAD ————

TRAIL — — — —

INTERMITTENT STREAM —·—·—

7   MILES OF TRAILS

0 ————————————— 1/2MILE

43. Rock Springs Center

by the Sangamon River, a mill, a gravel pit, several ponds, and a viewing deck. At certain times of the year parts of this trail are under water. One trail, referred to as the Lookout Trail is on the east side of Brozio Lane. The Lookout Trail is the only trail where pets are allowed. This trail also has a lookout tower where one can get a nice view of the Sangamon River valley.

Each trail has a trail sign for easy identification when hiking. Maps which show the locations and distances of the trails can be picked up at the Visitors Center. The trails are all cleared and are about eight feet wide. Some areas of the trail become a single lane for a while. The trail system developed at this park can easily be walked by the whole family, although in some areas there are steep climbs. During the wet season the trails can become very muddy, so check with the Visitors Center prior to going on the trail. The trails can also be used for cross-country skiing.

Facilities: Maps, water, toilets, and information are provided at the Visitors Center. The Center has many programs throughout the year for the general public, including interpretive hikes and wagon tours, and programs such as ice fishing and star gazing.

Park Rules and Regulations: Alcoholic beverages, firearms, horses, vehicles, and fires are not allowed on the trails. All plants and animals are protected and cannot be collected. Vehicles must use only marked roads and parking areas.

Mailing Address and Phone Number: Rock Springs Center for Environmental Discovery, 1495 Brozio Lane, Decatur, Illinois 62521; 217/423-7073

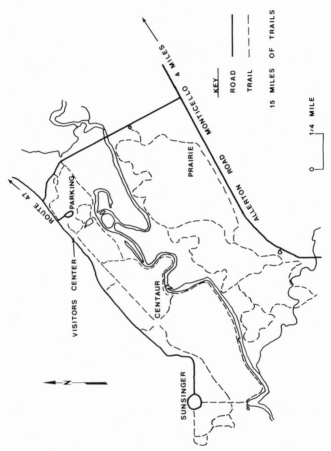

44. Robert Allerton Park. Redrawn from Robert
Allerton Park map.

44. Robert Allerton Park

Trail Length: 15 miles (24 kilometers)

Location: Robert Allerton Park is located twenty-six miles southwest of Champaign and twenty-five miles east of Decatur. To reach the park, take Interstate 57 from the north or south to Interstate 72. Turn west on Interstate 72 and proceed to Exit 61 for Monticello. At the first road (State Route 47) turn right (west) and proceed a few miles until an Allerton Park sign is seen. Turn left (south) and follow the park signs to the entrance. Travelers coming from Decatur on Interstate 72 may turn at Exit 53 and head south to State Route 47. Turn east on this road and proceed on Route 47 to the park signs. Follow the signs to the park entrance.

County: Piatt

Illinois Highway Map Coordinates: H-7

U.S.G.S. Topographical Map Names and Scale: Cerro Gordo and Weldon East, both 1:24,000

Hours Open: The park is open daily from 10 a.m. until sunset.

History and Trail Description: Robert Allerton Park is a unique feature in the central Illinois landscape. The park consists of 1,500 acres of rolling hills, with landscaped gardens, statues, and a Georgian mansion.

Robert Allerton (1873–1964) donated the park to the University of Illinois in 1946. The gift included the 1,500 acres of woodland property which form the park, a twenty-room mansion used for conferences, 250 acres for the 4-H Memorial Camp, and 3,775 acres of land in eight farms whose income supports the park.

At the time Robert Allerton inherited the farms from his father, the majority of the land was used for farming and grazing. The park as we see it today is the

Statues of Chinese musicians, Robert Allerton Park

product of over seventy years of planning and development.

The Sangamon River divides Allerton Park into two
sections. Houses, gardens, and sculptures are set in the
woodlands and meadows north of the river, while native
forests and a 50-acre restored prairie can be seen by
hiking or skiing the trails south of it.

The southern 1,000 acres of Allerton Park were
designated as a National Natural Landmark in 1971. The
floodplain forest and upland woods are excellent examples of native Illinois habitats. In this area identification
of 1,032 species of flowering plants and 154 species of
birds and mammals has been made.

The trail system at Allerton Park consists of hiking/
skiing trails that wind their way on both sides of the
Sangamon River. These trails total 15 miles, with about
7 miles of trails on the north side and 8 miles on the south
of the river. The trails do not connect between the north
and south; therefore, you would have to hike one side
and move your vehicle to another location to start hiking
the trails on the other side.

The trails are very wide, averaging about twelve
feet. The trails are all dirt and very easy to follow. Trail
maps are encased in metal cases and are found at most of

the trail junctions and trailheads. These maps have arrows on them that identify your specific location.

The trails on the north side of the park may be started at numerous locations depending on where you park your vehicle. A good area from which to start hiking is the greenhouse, which is located close to the formal gardens. The Visitors Center is inside the greenhouse. You can request trail maps and view a large trail map that is posted on the wall. In addition, you can purchase booklets on the park history and direct any questions to the person on duty.

Trails lead away from the gardens and head in many different directions. One set of trails takes the hiker by the Allerton House and eastward by some statues.

Another set of trails pass through the Formal Gardens and the Sunken Gardens. These gardens have a wide variety of beautiful flowers, bushes, and statues. The Sunken Gardens is a large concrete-walled garden dug below ground level. From here the trail continues southwest toward the Centaur statue; another trail heads south toward the Sangamon River. Both of these trails lead through the woodlands of Allerton Park.

The trail leading down to the river heads west, paralleling the river for a long distance. As it lies within the floodplain, this trail may be inundated during wet weather. This trail connects with other trail segments which take the hiker to the Centaur and the Sunsinger statues.

In addition to these trails, you may hike the many loop trails on the north side of this park. You may also park near the Sunsinger statue and start hiking from that area.

The trails on the south side of the Sangamon River may be started at two different parking areas. The first parking area is located about two miles from Allerton House and may be found by going back out the road to the park entrance. Turn right (south) onto the road, cross the Sangamon River, and you will come to a parking area that is surrounded by a fence. The other parking area may be found by continuing down this road until you come to the T, where you join Allerton Road. Turn right and proceed until you come to the parking area on the right side.

The trails on the south side of the Sangamon River offer the most seclusion for the hiker. The area consists of woodlands and prairies. The interconnecting loop trails here wind through upland woods, through a stream valley, and above the bluffs overlooking the Sangamon River. The trail passes by the second parking area and goes over a few small bridges. Numerous birds and other wildlife may be observed while hiking the trails.

Facilities: Picnic areas, public telephones, drinking water, and restrooms are located adjacent to the main parking area near Allerton House. Restrooms and drinking water and other refreshments may also be found at the Visitors Center in the greenhouse.

Park Rules and Regulations: Allerton House, other buildings in the park, and the 4-H Memorial Camp are used for conferences and camp sessions which require privacy. These facilities are not open to park visitors. Leash all dogs brought in the park. Alcoholic beverages and firearms are not allowed. Swimming is not permitted in the lakes or in Sangamon River. Do not disturb plant and animal life. Motorized vehicles are not allowed on the trails. No fishing or hunting permitted. No open fires are permitted. Horseback riding is confined to the roads and is not permitted on the trails.

Mailing Address and Phone Number: Robert Allerton Park, R.R. 2, Monticello, Illinois 61856; 217/762-2721

45. Kickapoo State Park

Trail Length: 7 miles (11.2 kilometers)

Location: Kickapoo State Park is located 6 miles west of Danville and 25 miles east of Champaign, Illinois. To reach the park, travelers heading west on Interstate 74 can take Exit 210 where a sign for Kickapoo State Park is seen. Follow this road for less than a mile and then turn left on Henning Road. Proceed on Henning Road one and a half miles to County Road 32. Follow this road two miles to the park. Travelers heading east on Interstate 74 can take Exit 206. Follow the signs along the roads for Kickapoo State Park. The park entrance is 3 miles from Exit 206.

County: Vermilion

Illinois Highway Map Coordinates: G-10

U.S.G.S. Topographical Map Names and Scale: Danville NW and Collison, both 1:24,000

Hours Open: The park opens at 8:00 a.m. and closes at 10:00 p.m., except for campers and fishermen.

History and Trail Description: Direct evidence of prehistoric man's occupation of the Kickapoo area was uncovered by an archeological excavation of a village site along the Middle Fork River a few miles north of the park. The Kickapoo had several villages just south of the park at the confluence of the Middle Fork and Salt Fork rivers near Vermilion salt salines.

The Vermilion salt salines located just southeast of the present park brought the first white settlement, called Salt Salines, to Vermilion County. An expedition led by Joseph Barron discovered the saline in 1819 and then returned to Fort Harrison. The first cabin at Salt Salines was constructed by several members of the party who remained behind to spend a miserable winter on the

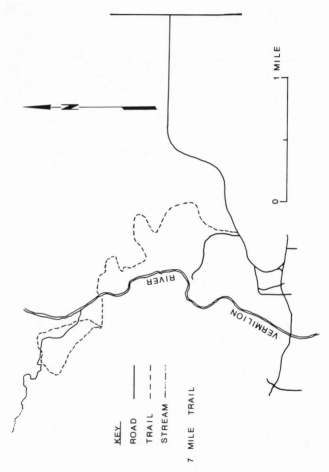

KEY

ROAD

TRAIL

STREAM

7 MILE TRAIL

1 MILE

45. Kickapoo State Park

Johnson Hill Bridge, Kickapoo State Park

Salt Fork of the Vermilion River. Wells were dug to obtain the salt brine which was then boiled in large rendering kettles to evaporate the water and obtain salt. The saltworks were operated by a variety of different operators until 1848.

Today Kickapoo is a example of nature reclaiming its territory. At the turn of the century, about one-half of what is now the park was strip mined for coal. These mining operations left the area with bare ridges of subsoil separated by deep gullies. Over the years, the ridges were partially covered with trees and other vegetation. The stagnant mine ponds were gradually transformed into fish-inhabited clear water. Today there are over 2,842 acres in the park, along with 22 ponds.

In 1986, the Middle Fork River was designated an Illinois Scenic River. In 1989, the Middle Fork was also designated as a National Scenic River by the U.S. Secretary of the Interior. The river is now protected by state and federal law because of its outstanding scenic, recreational, ecological, and historical importance.

The main hiking trail described here is referred to as the Out and Back Trail, which is 7 miles in length. The hiker goes out on this trail, does a loop around a hill, and then retraces his or her steps back to the trailhead.

To find the trailhead, hikers need to travel to the road in the park that takes them to the Inland Sea and Emerald Pond. This road is northeast of the maintenance building and office area. As soon as people turn on this road there is a small parking area. Park here. The trailhead is 50 feet from the parking area.

Hikers can also park their vehicles by the park maintenance building. Right across the road from the maintenance building, hikers will see a trailboard that states Rugged 7.6-Mile Running and Hiking Out and Back Trail, along with an arrow pointing to the trailhead down the road. Hikers parking near the maintenance building will have to go a short distance down the road to reach the trailhead.

Once at the trailhead, a gate is seen, along with a trailboard with the words Group Camp. Follow this dirt road as this is the beginning of the trail. Shortly, the hiker will see the group camp area on the right. The trail will continue past the camp and then will head into some woods. Hiker signs with arrows (white background) on metal posts will be seen along the trail. In addition, the hiker will see mile markers.

The trail then goes around an open field where some other trails will intersect this trail. Keep an eye out for the trail signs to follow. The trail then will go back into the woods.

At about two and one-half miles, the hiker will come to the Johnson Hill Bridge, which is over the Middle Fork of the Vermilion River. This is a scenic area for the hiker to rest, or even try his or her luck at fishing.

Past the bridge the trail follows the road for a short distance then turns north toward the hill. The trail goes up the hill and follows the ridge top. This hill is all wooded and very secluded. Orange paint on trees will be seen along the trail, indicating the path. A 3-mile marker will be seen on top of the hill.

The trail eventually makes its way down the hill into the stream valley, then winds its way along the base of the hill. The trail will tie in with the path at the road again where the path first started going up the hill. From here the hiker retraces his or her footsteps all the way back to the trailhead.

Facilities: There are numerous picnic areas in the park with tables, water, grills, toilets, and playground equipment. A concession stand offers refreshments as well as canoe and boat rentals. Call to check on the river conditions before coming out here to canoe. Camping is available. Boat launch ramps are provided on nine lakes. Scuba diving is allowed in Inland Sea and Sportsman's Lake, with prior registration with park staff. A fishing license is required to fish the lakes and the Vermilion River.

Permits Required: A camping permit is required.

Park Rules and Regulations: No swimming. See Appendix A.

Mailing Address and Phone Number: Site Superintendent, Kickapoo State Park, R.R. 1, Box 374, Oakwood, Illinois 61858; 217/442-4915

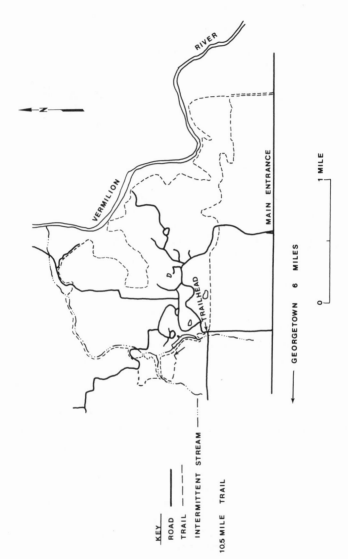

KEY
ROAD
TRAIL
INTERMITTENT STREAM
10.5 MILE TRAIL

N

VERMILION RIVER

MAIN ENTRANCE

TRAILHEAD

GEORGETOWN 6 MILES

0   1 MILE

46. Forest Glen Preserve

46. Forest Glen Preserve

Trail Length: 10.5 miles (16.8 kilometers)

Location: Forest Glen Preserve is located eleven miles south of Danville and seven miles south of Westville. The preserve borders the Vermilion River and the State of Indiana on the east. To reach the preserve, travelers may take Interstate 74 and exit south in Danville on Route 1. Proceed south for four miles to the square in Westville (second stop light). Turn left here (east) and follow this asphalt road for five miles (County Highway 5). Highway 5 turns into County Highway 27. Follow Highway 27 two miles to the Preserve entrance, which is on the left side of the road. A sign here states Forest Glen County Preserve.

County: Vermilion

Illinois Highway Map Coordinates: H-10

U.S.G.S. Topographical Map Name and Scale: Danville S.E., 1:24,000

Hours Open: The preserve is open year-round. The summer hours are 8:00 a.m. to 10:00 p.m.; spring and fall hours are 8:00 a.m. to 8:00 p.m.; and winter hours are 8:00 a.m. to 4:30 p.m. The Gannett Education Center and the Sycamore Nature Center are open to the public on Sundays from 1:00 p.m. to 5:00 p.m., Memorial Day through Labor Day.

History and Trail Description: On June 16, 1966, a referendum was passed and a governing board of five trustees was appointed for the new Vermilion County Conservation District. The board quickly moved to purchase land, and in January, 1968, the first parcel of land was acquired for Forest Glen Preserve, which was opened in October of the same year. Forest Glen Preserve encompasses 1,800 acres and is considered an Illinois Nature

Preserve. The Preserve has three miles of frontage along the Vermilion River, with countless species of plants and animals in the area.

The Preserve has twelve different hiking trails with the longest trail being the River Ridge Backpack Trail at 10.5 miles. Before hiking this trail, all hikers must register at the ranger station. The trailhead is located at the Naturalist Staff Office parking lot.

The trail, which is marked very well with orange arrows, orange plates, or orange bands around the trees, goes clockwise around the park. The trail connects with many of the other trails in the park, and the hike may be shortened at a few locations. The trail varies in width from a single lane to a cleared path of eight feet. At times, the trail goes along the park road. The trail has many stairs, bridges, and water bars that must be crossed.

Little signposts are scattered along the first three miles of the trail, describing in general terms the plants, geology, and animals in the area. The trail goes past wooded ravines, grassy meadows, a restored tall grass prairie, several ponds, an environmental center, and an old cemetery. In one and one-half miles, the trail passes through the Sycamore Hollow Campus. Water and pit toilets are located here. Located at Sycamore Hollow Campus is the Gannett Outdoor Education Center, which has various nature displays, conference rooms, and restrooms. Also seen here is the Sycamore Hollow Nature Center. The Nature Center has natural history displays, a souvenir shop, and outside caged areas which hold great horned owls and some hawks. At about the halfway point of the hike, or at the river canoe access area, one can follow a road that leads up to an observation tower. The tower is seventy-two feet high and offers a great view of the preserve and the Vermilion River Valley.

The trail past the river canoe access area, until it meets the road again, is the most scenic and difficult section to hike. One must be in very good shape to hike this stretch of the trail. The trail goes up and down many steep ravines and crisscrosses many small streams and tributaries. The trail can be extremely wet and muddy during the rainy season, and one must be prepared for this.

View of the Vermilion River Valley from the observation tower, Forest Glen Preserve

If the entire trail is hiked in one day, allow a minimum of five hours to complete the trail. Tent camping is allowed at two locations along the trail; at the group camp (mile 3.5) and at the east camp (mile 7.5). The east camp is located on top a bluff and overlooks the Vermilion River Valley. An appropriate camping permit must be secured before camping.

Facilities: Hiking, fishing, camping, and ice fishing are some of the seasonal activities available. Picnicking is available with charcoal grills at each picnic site. A family campground offers forty-two campsites (twenty-eight with electricity), a central water supply, sanitary dumping station, and restrooms. In addition, there is a tent camping area with eighteen tent sites and six group sites. Two fishing ponds are located on the grounds and have bass and channel catfish. There is an outdoor school to which fourth- and fifth-grade classes from schools around the country can come to study nature and conservation. Maps and other information can be obtained from the ranger station. Also located in the preserve is a tree research area, the Michael Reddy Arboretum, a 40-acre prairie restoration area, and a one-third mile long handicapped trail.

Permits Required: A camping permit is required.

Park Rules and Regulations: No firearms, minibikes, or unlicensed vehicles allowed in the park. No vehicles or horses on grass or hiking trails. No collecting of plant, animal, or mineral specimens. No swimming in preserve waters. Have all dogs on a leash. Park in parking lots only. The observation tower is closed at dark; fires are allowed in designated areas only, and fishing anywhere in the preserve is governed by Illinois rules and regulations. See Appendix B.

Mailing Address and Phone Number: Site Superintendent, Forest Glen Preserve, R.R. 1, Box 495A, Westville, Illinois 61833; 217/662-2142

47. Carpenter Park

Trail Length: 4.5 miles (7.2 kilometers)

Location: Carpenter Park is located three miles north of Springfield. To reach the park, travelers may take Interstate 55 and exit at the Sherman Exit (Exit 105) and head south on this road (Business 55). Go through Sherman and in two miles one will see a sign for the Rail golf course and Rail Meadows Homesites. Turn right and go one block, following the signs to the park straight ahead.

County: Sangamon

Illinois Highway Map Coordinates: H-5

U.S.G.S. Topographical Map Names and Scale: Springfield West and East, both 1:24,000

Hours Open: The park is open all year (weather permitting), and hiking is allowed until sunset.

History and Trail Description: Carpenter Park is owned and operated by the Springfield Park District. The park was purchased by the Springfield Park District in 1921 and has been relatively untouched since then. In 1979, parts of the park were dedicated as a nature preserve under the Illinois Department of Conservation's Nature Preserve System.

The park displays both upland and floodplain forest, with rock outcrops along the Sangamon River. The uplands support black oak, with red oak and white oak on slopes and ravines. The floodplain supports silver maple, sycamore, scattered bur, oak, and hackberry.

The park trails comprise ten interconnecting trails which total 4.5 miles. Most of the trails originate in the parking area. All of the trails are well marked, showing the trail name and the general direction of the trail. A trailboard is found on the north side of the parking lot. This trailboard shows the trail layout and some general

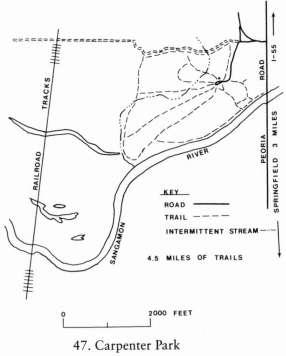

N

RAILROAD TRACKS

I-55

PEORIA ROAD

SPRINGFIELD 3 MILES

RIVER

SANGAMON

RAILROAD

KEY

ROAD ———
TRAIL – – –
INTERMITTENT STREAM —·—·—

4.5 MILES OF TRAILS

0   2000 FEET

47. Carpenter Park

Rock outcrop along the Sangamon River, Carpenter Park

information about the park. The trails go up and down the small hills in the park and over numerous small wooden bridges.

The Twisted Tree Trail starts from the parking lot, is about six feet wide, and narrows to a single lane which is hard to see. Twisted Tree Trail goes to the North Road Trail.

Canyon Trail, directly south of the parking lot, is a short trail that leads to the Sangamon River. This trail descends a canyon along a series of stairs and follows a small creek to the river. During the wet season, this trail is extremely dangerous. Canyon Trail branches with the Hi-Point Trail to the east and the Wild Flower Trail at the Sangamon River.

The Wild Flower Trail connects with the Canyon Trail and parallels the river for a short distance. Since the trail is located in the floodplain, this section may be inundated during the wet season. Do not attempt to walk this trail when the water level is rising. This trail connects with the River View Trail which can be hiked to other trails in the park. All trails in the park, except for the Canyon and Hi-Point trails, are excellent for cross-country skiing in the winter.

Facilities: A parking lot accommodates about twenty cars. There is a picnic shelter with two fireplaces. There are restrooms but no drinking water; all water must be brought in. Do not drink any water out of creeks in the park.

Park Rules and Regulations: Motorcycles, firearms, horses, weapon devices, ground fires, and camping are all prohibited in the park. It is illegal to take any plants or trees. See Appendix B.

Mailing Address and Phone Number: Springfield Park District, 2500 South 11th Street, P.O. Box 5052, Springfield, Illinois 62705; 217/544-1751

48. Lincoln Memorial Garden

Trail Length: 5 miles (8.05 kilometers)

Location: This trail system is located on the southeast side of Lake Springfield in Springfield. To reach the Garden, southbound traffic should exit off Interstate 55 at Stevenson Drive (Exit 94) and proceed eastbound on East Lake Drive for six miles. Northbound traffic on Interstate 55 can exit at the Chatham Exit (Exit 88) and go eastbound on East Lake Drive for about three miles. Parking is located right in front of the Gardens off of East Lake Drive.

County: Sangamon

Illinois Highway Map Coordinates: H-5

U.S.G.S. Topographical Name and Scale: New City, 1:24,000

Hours Open: The grounds are open every day of the year. Hiking is allowed from sunrise to sunset. The nature center's hours are Monday through Saturday 10:00 a.m. to 4:00 p.m. and Sunday from 1:00 p.m. until 4:00 p.m.

History and Trail Description: Lake Springfield is the water supply for the residents of Springfield and the surrounding communities, and it also provides recreational activities, such as fishing, hiking, boating, and swimming.

In 1932, while Lake Springfield was being dammed and filled, Mrs. T. J. Knudson, a member of the Garden Club of Illinois, requested that the city set aside a portion of land to be developed as a living memorial to Abraham Lincoln. At the time, the surrounding area was farmland with barely a dozen trees. The Garden Club of Illinois began planting trees in the Garden in 1932. They used shrubs, plants, and trees which are native to Illinois. Today the Garden's hills are covered with maples, hickories, oaks,

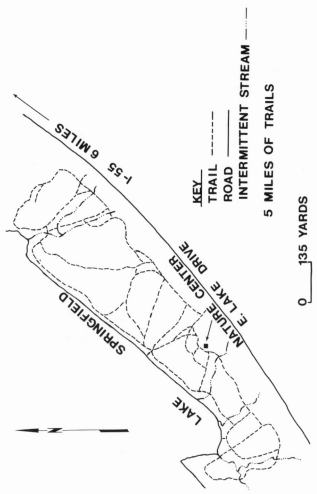

KEY

TRAIL ------

ROAD

INTERMITTENT STREAM —·—

5 MILES OF TRAILS

0   135 YARDS

I-55 6 MILES

SPRINGFIELD

E. LAKE CENTER

NATURE CENTER DRIVE

LAKE

N

48. Lincoln Memorial Garden. Redrawn from Lincoln
Memorial Garden trail map.

sweet gum, coffee tree, red bud, white dogwood, plum, shad, and silver bell. The Garden is maintained by volunteers and relies on contributions. It consists of about 80 acres.

The Garden's trail system comprises eighteen interconnecting trails which total about 5 miles. All of the trails are well defined, with signposts naming each trail. The trails are all fairly easy to walk, with the longest trail (Lake Trail) being about a half mile. The trails are all well cleared, made of dirt, and are about seven feet wide. The trails go over small wooden bridges and by Lake Springfield.

The Witch Hazel Trail has a set of stairs that have to be climbed. Some of the trails are on gently rolling hills leading down to the lake. Some spots on the trails in low areas can be quite muddy in the rainy season and have water bars to help divert the water from the trail. The trail system is also an excellent area for cross-country skiing in the winter.

Facilities: A nature center is located on the grounds. The center has maps and other general information about the Garden. The center serves groups that come for field trips, and it provides office space, areas for exhibits, Sunday family programs, and craft instruction. Water, soda machines, and restrooms are all located inside the nature center. A bicycle rack is located at the entrance to the park to lock your bikes.

Park Rules and Regulations: No picnicking, picking flowers, pets, bicycles, swimming, motorcycles, horses, snowmobiles, alcohol, or fishing are allowed on the grounds.

Mailing Address and Phone Number: Lincoln Memorial Garden, 2301 East Lake Drive, Springfield, Illinois 62707; 217/529-1111

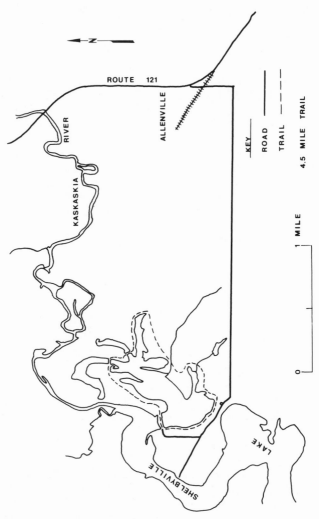

49. Fishhook Waterfowl Area

49. Fishhook Waterfowl Area

Trail Length: 4.5 miles (7.2 kilometers)

Location: Fishhook Waterfowl Area is part of the Kaskaskia Fish and Wildlife Area and is approximately ten miles southeast of Sullivan and three miles west of Allenville. To reach Fishhook Area, State Route 121 may be taken northwest out of Mattoon or east out of Sullivan. At the southern edge of Allenville, a paved road heads west. Turn west on this road, go over the railroad tracks and proceed for three miles. At about two and a half miles you will run into another road that heads north. Turn right on this gravel road and proceed to the parking area. The road is a dead end at this point.

County: Moultrie

Illinois Highway Map Coordinates: I-8

U.S.G.S. Topographical Map Name And Scale: Sullivan, 1:24,000

Hours Open: The park is open year-round.

History and Trail Description: Lake Shelbyville is an 11,000-acre impoundment between Shelbyville and Sullivan. The lands in this area are managed by the Corps of Engineers and the Department of Conservation for various recreation purposes. Lake Shelbyville is situated along the Kaskaskia and West Okaw rivers.

In the upper reaches of Lake Shelbyville are two separate wildlife units: Kaskaskia and West Okaw. The 3,700-acre Kaskaskia Unit is located along the Kaskaskia River; the 2,700-acre West Okaw Unit lies along the West Okaw River.

The trail at Fishhook starts at the parking area and boat launch. A trailboard is set up just west of the parking area. The trailboard shows the trail layout and the location of items, such as benches and bridges, that will be seen along the trail.

The trail, called the Fishhook Trail, measures 4.5 miles and is marked with wooden posts illustrated with a picture of a hiker. The trail is a mowed path about eight feet wide. At times old roads and farm roads join with the trail; therefore, hikers must keep an eye out for the trail markers to avoid getting lost. The trail goes around the water in the Fishhook Area, which is visible almost the entire length of the trail.

The trail, which goes in a counterclockwise direction, starts out by going through a small stand of woods on top of very small bluffs. From here you will see the parking lot at the entrance. Continue through this parking lot and then onto a gravel path. This path takes the hiker to an observation platform which overlooks the waterfowl area. The trail continues in a easterly direction, passing some shrub growth and farm plots on the east side of the trail.

The trail then goes west and continues into a denser forest. The hiker will go over some small wooden bridges and will follow the trail to the lake and a levee.

You will have to cross this levee and continue along the path on the other side. The trail passes close by another parking area, and from here you will have to cross another levee that goes across part of the water. This levee may be covered by water, and therefore impassable, during the wet season.

Beyond this levee the trail turns south, paralleling the Kaskaskia River. The trail continues through wooded areas and a few open fields. The trail then descends a small hill, leading to the water again. Here you will have to cross another levee. Once past this last levee, you will be at the parking area and trailhead.

Facilities: Fishhook Waterfowl Area has a trailboard, a restroom, and a boat launch. Fishing is allowed anywhere in the area with all Illinois fishing rules and regulations in effect. Hunting is also permitted in the area in accordance with statewide regulations.

Permits Required: Dog training and trapping are regulated by permit.

Park Rules and Regulations: Camping is not allowed in this area. See Appendix A.

Mailing Address and Phone Number: Site Superinten-dent, Shelbyville Fish and Wildlife Area, R.R. 1, Box 42-A, Bethany, Illinois 61914; 217/665-3112

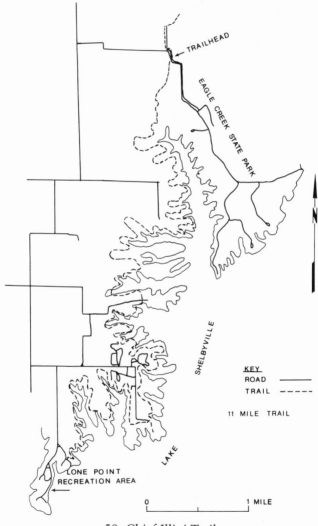

TRAILHEAD

EAGLE CREEK STATE PARK

N

SHELBYVILLE

KEY
ROAD ———
TRAIL - - - - -

11 MILE TRAIL

LAKE

LONE POINT
RECREATION AREA

0   1 MILE

50. Chief Illini Trail

50. Chief Illini Trail

Trail Length: 11 miles (17.6 kilometers)

Location: The Chief Illini Trail is located on the west shore of Lake Shelbyville. There are two main starting points for this trail. The first trailhead is located at Eagle Creek State Park, and the second is on U.S. Army Corps of Engineers' property at Lone Point Recreation Area.

To reach Eagle Creek State Park, travelers need to get on either north-south roads 128 or 32. Follow one of these roads to the Bruce Findlay Road. A sign along the road will be seen which states Eagle Creek State Park. Follow Bruce Findlay Road until a sign is seen for Eagle Creek State Park. Turn south on this road and follow the roads and signs 3 miles to the park entrance.

To get to Lone Point Recreation Area, travelers can take east-west Route 16. At the junction of Routes 16 and 128 in Shelbyville, follow Route 128 north for 4.5 miles. A sign along the road will be seen here that states Lake Shelbyville, Coon Creek A/A, Lone Point A/A. Turn east at this point and follow the road and the signs for Lone Point Recreation Area for approximately 5.5 miles.

County: Shelby

Illinois Highway Map Coordinates: I-7

Topographical Map Names and Scale: Kirksville and Middlesworth, both 1:24,000

Hours Open: The trail is open year-round. The campground at Lone Point is closed during the winter months, and Eagle Creek is closed on Thanksgiving and Christmas.

History and Trail Description: The Chief Illini Trail is part of a master plan initially developed in the 1970s by the U.S. Army Corps of Engineers. According to Al Lookofsky, in a phone conversation, November 1991, the original plans called for developing a trail from Opossum Creek Recreation Area all the way to Eagle Creek State Park, paralleling Lake Shelbyville. Due to dwindling federal funds for the project, the undertaking was pared down to the existing trail length, working in conjunction with the State of Illinois.

The trail was developed in the early 1980s and is managed both by the Illinois Department of Conservation (DOC) as well as the Corps of Engineers (Corps). The DOC manages the first 7 miles of trail south from Eagle Creek State Park, while the Corps manages the 4 miles from Lone Point Recreation Area heading north. In addition, a Boy Scout troop from Decatur helps to clear and mark the trail. In 1990, the trail was also designated a National Recreation Trail.

Hikers on this 11-mile trail may start at either Eagle Creek State Park or Lone Point Recreation Area. Since this is not a loop trail, hikers would have to either shuttle a vehicle to the other end or have someone pick them up.

The trail is marked with white diamond-shaped blazes which are painted on trees or may be found on metal posts. At times, these paint blazes may be hard to see, especially when another trail is crossed or along

Chief Illini trailboard, Chief Illini Trail

open fields. But if the hiker continues along the trail, he or she will soon see the next trail blaze.

To reach the parking area and trailhead at Eagle Creek State Park, travelers first coming into the park must follow the road into the campground. Right past the campground check-in station, a sign will be seen for backpack camping, the Chief Illini Trail, and tent camping. Turn on this gravel road and follow it until one comes to a small parking area and a trailboard for the Chief Illini Trail. Also seen here will be hiker signs with a white backpacker on brown background.

From the parking area, the trail may be walked in two directions. The trail heading north is the last one-mile segment and goes to the tent and group camping spot. This is where the trail ends. Found here are camping spots, pit toilets, tables, grills, and garbage cans.

If the hiker goes south of the parking lot, he or she will cross the main park road and then walk through and along the end of an open field for a short period of time. The trail then heads into the woods and for the most part becomes a single-lane path for most of the remaining 10 miles.

Once the hiker starts into the woods, he or she will shortly walk into a small valley where he or she will encounter scrub growth and thickets. Shortly, two wood bridges will have to be crossed over some small feeder creeks. These two bridges are just some of the many that the hiker will cross. In addition, at one point along the trail, the hiker will walk on a tree which serves as a bridge over a creek.

Eventually the trail begins to parallel the lake, and the hiker will have some great views of some of the small inlets found on the lake. If the hiker likes to fish, the many inlets provide a great fishing opportunity, as many times they are very secluded.

The trail goes up and down the small ridges along the lake, through open fields and some beautifully wooded spots. While hiking through the fields, one should keep an eye open for either painted white diamonds or hikers on metal posts.

The northern half of the trail is basically wooded with the hiker going by some abandoned roads as well as passing a very small farm and residential site.

Toward the middle half of the trail, the hiker will pass by some trailers, small subdivisions, and private campgrounds which border the DOC and Corps properties. The hiker is cautioned that some other trails may lead from these locations and he or she could start following the wrong trail segment. Keep an eye out for trail blazes. In addition, since this is private property, do not stray off the trail. The Corps property only extends 300 feet away from the lake shore.

The hiker will also notice either 4″ x 4″ or 6″ x 6″ wooden posts along the trail. The 6″ x 6″ posts signify even miles, and the 4″ x 4″ posts signify half miles.

About 3 miles away from Lone Point Recreation Area, the hiker will come to a road and then will see a sign that says End Little Chief Trail. If the hiker follows a wide dirt lane down toward the lake he or she will come to an overnight shelter. This is a three-walled shelter which can hold 8 to 10 people. A reservation is needed from the Corps to camp here. No other facilities are available.

The last three miles to Lone Point are wooded and parallel the lake. Hikers will go over two small wooden bridges and around two large inlets. Eventually hikers will make their way out to Lone Point Recreation Area.

Found here at Lone Point Recreation Area is a parking lot with a Chief Illini trailboard. Also seen is a marker signifying that this trail is a National Recreation Trail. The parking lot also is used by fishermen who put in their boats at the boat ramp.

Facilities: Lone Point Recreation Area has a campground with 94 sites, most with electricity. Also found here are showers and flush toilets, group picnicking and camping, playground equipment, and a boat launch. This campground is closed in the winter months, so check with the Corps if one desires to camp here. The parking lot for the trailhead is left open year-round.

Eagle Creek State Park has several fully developed picnic areas with grills, toilets, water, and sanitary facilities. There is a Class B campground with 160 sites, a tent camping area, and group camping. A boat-launching ramp is available here also. For the less rugged, the relatively new Eagle Creek Resort with 138 rooms, swimming pool, whirlpool, and sauna is here also. A golf course is also available.

Fishing is allowed in Lake Shelbyville with a valid fishing license.

In addition to Lone Point Recreation Area and Eagle Creek State Park, there are numerous other DOC and Corps recreation facilities found around Lake Shelbyville. For information on other recreation facilities found nearby, contact the DOC or the Corps.

Permits Required: Camping permits are required.

Park Rules and Regulations: No camping along the trail except at the designated shelter. See Appendixes A and F.

Mailing Addresses and Phone Numbers: Site Superintendent, Eagle Creek State Park, R.R. 1, Box 6, Findlay, Illinois 62534; 217/756-8260; or U.S. Army Corps of Engineers, Route 4, Box 128B, Shelbyville, Illinois 62565; 217/774-3951

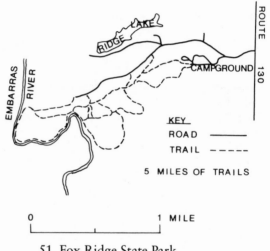

51. Fox Ridge State Park

51. Fox Ridge State Park

Trail Length: 5 miles (8 kilometers)

Location: Fox Ridge State Park is located 7 miles south of Charleston, Illinois, along Route 130. To reach the park, travelers on Interstate 57 can exit on State Route 16. Head east on Route 16 for 8 miles to the junction of Routes 16 and 130 in Charleston. Turn south on Route 130 and proceed 7 miles to the park entrance where there is a sign along the road stating Fox Ridge State Park.

County: Coles

Illinois Highway Map Coordinates: I-9

U.S.G.S. Topographical Map Name and Scale: Charleston South, 1:24,000

Hours Open: Fox Ridge State Park is open year-round, except on Christmas Day and New Year's Day. The park opens at 6:00 a.m. and closes at 10:00 p.m.

History and Trail Description: Much of the pioneer life of this area was centered around the Embarras River. The river provided a main source of transportation, fishing, trapping, and water supply. Indians such as the Piankeshaw and Illinois also inhabited the area.

In 1938 the State of Illinois took over the management and ownership of Fox Ridge. Since then, with the help of the Civilian Conservation Corps, the residence/workshop complex, the Natural History Survey laboratory, the dam and spillway, the large brick pavilion, and hiking trails were constructed.

The trail system at Fox Ridge State Park consists of 5 interconnected trails which total 5 miles in length. These trails are all found on the south side of the park road. There also are some additional trails found on the north side of the road. A 4-mile horse trail also is found at the north end of the park.

Trail overlook, Fox Ridge State Park

The paths described in this section include the Trail of Trees, Acorn Avenue, River View, No Name Trail, and Natures Corner. There are five main locations where one can get to these trails. These are: 1) the campground; 2) the first trailboard, Trail of Trees; 3) the second trailboard, Acorn Avenue; 4) the third trailboard, River Trail; and 5) the end of the park road. Since all of the trails are connected, starting at any one of these trailheads will lead to all of the other trails.

Found along the trails, usually at trail junctions, are trailboards which show the trail layout and where you are. The trails are all coded by numbers. For example, the Trail of Trees is trail 1. If the hiker begins going from trailheads 2, 3, or 4, he or she will have to climb down stairs to get to the valley below. The trails follow this

Trail sign, Fox Ridge State Park

valley and then make their way up to some trails which follow the ridges. Some wooden bridges will have to be crossed, and there are water bars set up on the trails to help stop erosion. In addition, the wooden stairs and bridges could be slippery when wet.

The No Name Trail, Natures Corner Trail, and the River View Trail are partially located in the Embarras River floodplain, and at certain times of the year, they may be inundated. Extreme caution should be exercised if hiking these trails during inclement weather conditions. The No Name Trail is found on the west end of the park and can be reached at the last parking area. There will be a picnic area here and a gravel and dirt road. This road leads the hiker down into the floodplain. The trail circles here, going through an open field and along the Embarras River. The No Name Trail then meets the River

View Trail, which leads to the other trails in the park. Up at Goblers Knob on the River Trail, hikers will come to an overlook which has a tree growing through the center of it. Natures Corner Trail takes the hiker up on a ridgetop and along a field connecting with Acorn Avenue Trail.

Acorn Avenue Trail is a very pleasant trail as it winds its way through some mature hardwoods which are very scenic. The trail also makes its way down a hill and into a creek valley where it ties in with the Trail of Trees.

The Trail of Trees also is a nice trail which winds its way up and down ridges going through some pretty wooded areas. At the east end of the trail, the hiker will walk by a park road and the campground. Found here also will be some pit toilets.

Facilities: Fox Ridge State Park has many designated picnic areas with tables and grills, shelters, restrooms, drinking water, playgrounds, and a baseball diamond. Camping is also available with a trailer camp area, a group camping area, and a Rent-A-Camp cabin. Picnic tables, cooking grills, water, toilet facilities, and a sanitary dumping station are all located in the campground.

Fishing is allowed in the Embarras River as well as Ridge Lake. Fishing is permitted in Ridge Lake only by reservation, since it is a research facility. To obtain a permit to fish in Ridge Lake, contact the Illinois Natural History Survey at 217/345-6490 or write to the park office for a permit. A fishing license is required.

Permits Required: Camping permits are required.

Park Rules and Regulations: No ground fires. No biking on trails. No swimming. See Appendix A.

Mailing Address and Phone Number: Site Superintendent, Fox Ridge State Park, R.R. 1, Charleston, Illinois 61920; 217/345-6416

52. Pere Marquette State Park

Trail Length: Various trails totaling 10 miles (16 kilometers)

Location: Pere Marquette State Park is located five miles west of Grafton on State Route 100 and twenty-five miles northwest of Alton. The park has many bluffs which overlook the Illinois River and offers many diversified forms of recreation.

County: Jersey

Illinois Highway Map Coordinates: K-3

U.S.G.S. Topographical Map Names and Scale: Grafton, Brussels, and Nutwood, all 1:24,000

Hours Open: The park is open every day of the year except Christmas Day and New Year's Day. At certain times, the park may be closed due to freezing and thawing of the roads.

History and Trail Description: This park was named in memory of Father Jacques Marquette, a French Jesuit missionary priest. In 1673, Father Marquette and explorer Louis Jolliet were the first Europeans to enter what is now Illinois at the confluence of the Mississippi and Illinois rivers. A large white cross east of the park entrance along Route 100 marks where these two men landed.

In 1932, the State acquired the 2,605-acre park and adjoining 2,574-acre conservation area. They were combined into the Pere Marquette State Park by legislative action in 1967. Later acquisitions brought the park to its present total of 8,000 acres, making it the largest state park in Illinois.

The park's trail system comprises ten interconnecting hiking/horseback riding trails that vary in length from a half mile to over 2 miles in length. Most of the

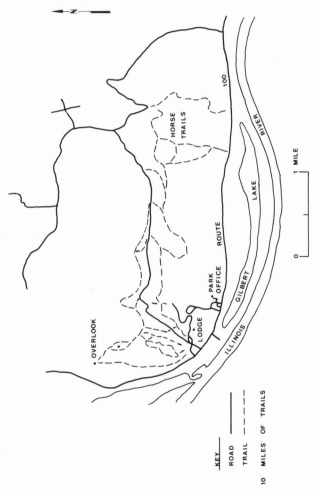

52. Pere Marquette State Park. Redrawn from park map.

trails begin at the Visitors Center parking lot. At the Visitors Center there is a trailboard which shows an outline of each of the trails. The trails are all color-coded. The trail markers consist of paint blazes on the trees. The trails are all very well marked and well traveled.

The following is a list of some of the more traveled trails and the lengths and colors: Goat Cliff Trail, 2 miles, yellow; Dogwood, .75 mile, dark blue; Ridge, .50 mile, light blue; Ravine, 1 mile, green; Oak, .75 mile, pink; and Hickory South, 1.5 miles, red with white circle.

All of the trails are wide averaging about 8 feet. Some of the trails have benches along them, and a few have some scenic overlooks of the Illinois River Valley. The Goat Cliff, Dogwood, and Ridge trails are on some ridges in the park. Beautiful views of the river and backwaters can be seen from the overlooks on these trails. Goat Cliff overlook is located on McAdam's Peak. The overlook was built in 1934 by the State of Illinois. At this point the peak is 791 feet above sea level and 372 feet above the Illinois River. A marker on this overlook describes the history of the state park and area.

To get away from the crowds, hikers may want and try walking some of the other trails in the park which get less use. These paths include Fern Hollow, Rattlesnake, and Hickory North trails. A horse trail connects with a part of the Rattlesnake Trail.

Each of the trails goes through some very pretty wooded areas and up and down the steep ridges in the park. Numerous wildlife may also be found along these paths. In addition to the main hiking trails, there also is a one-mile numbered exercise trail and a separate horse trail.

Facilities: A park office is located in the park offering maps, brochures, and other general information. The park has an amphitheater which offers campfire programs and a boat harbor. Camping for tents and trailers offers electricity, restrooms, shower facilities, and a trailer dump. There are also a lodge and cabins (reservation suggested) and picnic areas with water, playground equipment, and stables for horseback riding. A boat-launching ramp and parking area provide access to the river. Fishing is permitted on the Illinois River, contingent upon Illinois rules and regulations.

Permits Required: A camping permit is required.

Park Rules and Regulations: See Appendix A.

Mailing Address and Phone Number: Site Superintendent, Pere Marquette State Park, Route 100, Box 158, Grafton, Illinois 62037; 618/786-3323

53. Newton Lake Conservation Area

Trail Length: 15 miles (24 kilometers)

Location: Newton Lake Conservation Area is located on the west side of Newton Lake. The park is located ten miles southwest of Newton and twenty-five miles southeast of Effingham. To reach the park, take State Route 33 out of Effingham. Fifteen miles out of Effingham there is a sign to turn south on County Road 8. Proceed on this road for ten miles, following the signs to the park entrance.

County: Jasper

Illinois Highway Map Coordinates: K-8

U.S.G.S. Topographical Map Name and Scale: Sailor Springs, 1:24,000

Hours Open: The park is open every day of the year except for Christmas Day and New Year's Day. The park closes at 10:00 p.m. daily.

History and Trail Description: Newton Lake was impounded by the Central Illinois Public Service Company (CIPS) to provide water for its Newton electric power generating plant. In 1979, the Illinois Department of Conservation (IDOC) signed a twenty-five year lease with CIPS which designates the 1,755-acre Newton Lake and 540 acres of shoreland as a day use conservation area. By agreement, recreational activities in the area consist of bank and boat fishing, picnicking, hiking, and horseback riding. CIPS financed the initial recreational development of the area.

The trail system consists of a 15-mile hiking/horseback riding trail. The trail starts at a horse trail parking lot at the north access area. A trailboard there shows the trail layout along with an arrow pointing to the direction of the trailhead. The trail is well marked with metal poles

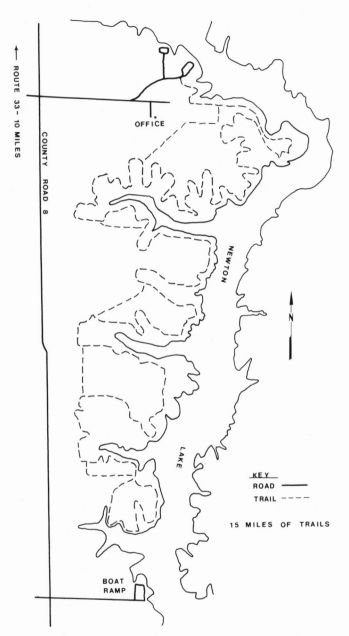

53. Newton Lake Conservation Area. Redrawn from
Newton Lake map. Map not drawn to scale.

that have arrows indicating the direction of the trail and orange ribbons hanging from trees.

The trail parallels the lake and its coves for more than ten miles. The trail also winds around grasslands and along fields. Animals, such as whitetail deer, Canada geese, mallards, blue heron, and pintails, may be observed when hiking. The trail is about six feet wide and is mowed to keep it clear. Generally on flat land, the trail does go up and down in some areas. At a few points, the trail crosses intermittent streams, which can be fairly high during the wet season. Benches are located on the trail at about 3 and 7 miles, where the trail intersects the lake. In addition, at mile 7 there is a wooden platform on the lake that can be used as a fishing pier. At about 4.5 miles the hiker will come across a junk pile scattered around the trail.

The hiker has the option of returning on different loops so that the hike can be reduced in length if desired; the six return loops are all clearly marked. The most scenic and forested areas on the trail are located on the second half of the trail. The return loops generally pass through open grasslands with little shade available.

Facilities: A site office is located in the park to provide information. Picnic facilities are located at the north and south access areas. A boat ramp is located at the south access area. Currently, there are no concessions or rental services available at the site. Water is available at the site office, and toilets are located by the parking area. There are no camping facilities at Newton Lake; primitive camping may be found at Sam Parr State Park which is sixteen miles from the lake, and there is a private campground about four miles south of the dam. Fishing is allowed in Newton Lake with all Illinois fishing rules and regulations in effect.

Park Rules and Regulations: Swimming, camping, ice fishing and hunting are prohibited. See Appendix A.

Mailing Address and Phone Number: Site Superintendent, Newton Lake Conservation Area, R.R. 4, Newton, Illinois 62448; 618/783-3478

PART IV

Hiking Trails in Southern Illinois

SOUTHERN ILLINOIS

54. Beall Woods State Park
55. Washington County Conservation Area
56. Pyramid State Park
57. Randolph County Conservation Area
58. Turkey Bluffs State Fish and Wildlife Area
59. Kinkaid Lake Trail
60. Giant City State Park
61. Cedar Lake Trail
62. Garden of the Gods Recreation Area
63. Ferne Clyffe State Park
64. Bell Smith Springs Recreation Area
65. River-to-River Trail
66. Beaver Trail
67. Trail of Tears State Forest
68. Lake Glendale Recreation Area
69. Little Black Slough Trail

Figure 4. Hiking trails in southern Illinois

54. Beall Woods State Park

Trail Length: 4.5 miles of interconnecting trails (7.2 kilometers)

Location: Beall Woods State Park is located three miles east of Keensburg and six miles south of Mt. Carmel. The southeastern edge of the park borders the Wabash River. To reach the park, take State Route 1 south out of Mt. Carmel or north out of Carmi. In Keensburg a sign points to the direction of the park. Turn east and proceed down a gravel road for three miles following the signs to the park entrance.

County: Wabash

Illinois Highway Map Coordinates: L-10

U.S.G.S. Topographical Map Name and Scale: Keensburg, 1:24,000

Hours Open: The park is open year-round except on Christmas Day and New Year's Day. At certain times, due to freezing and thawing periods, the park is closed, and access to the park is by foot only.

History and Trail Description: The state park derives its name from the Beall family who owned the land from 1861 to 1962. Beall Woods is the only sizable, near-virgin deciduous forest left in Illinois. The stand has several distinct forest sites, ranging from well-drained, rolling uplands, to low areas subject to frequent flooding and standing water. The area has over sixty-four species of trees and over one hundred different birds. Many large sycamores grow in the bottomland area, with some sycamores, shumard's oak, bur oak, and big shellbark hickory trees measuring over three feet in diameter. On one of the trails you can view the largest Shumard red oak tree in the United States. The tree is over 150 years old and measures 16.5 feet in circumference.

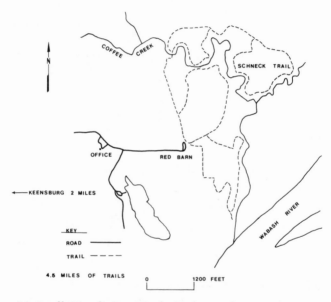

54. Beall Woods State Park. Redrawn from park map.

The state initially purchased the property for $287,000 from Mr. James Bower in 1965. Mr. Bower had threatened to clear the land of trees and farm the area. A group of conservationists then persuaded the state to buy the land and preserve it in its natural state. The Bower family did get to keep its mineral rights; some of their oil wells may be observed from the Ridgeway Trail. A coal mine extends underneath Beall Woods and the Wabash River. The coal company is mining only forty percent of the coal under the park, leaving the remaining coal columns to support the forest to lessen the chance of land subsidance.

The current acreage in the park is 635; 329 acres of this property lie within the Illinois Nature Preserve and is registered as a National Natural Landmark. The United States Register of National Landmarks lists the landmark as the Forest of the Wabash.

The trail system in Beall Woods consists of five interconnecting trails that measure 4.5 miles. Each trail has a particular name and is marked with a distinctive symbol. All trails can be started at the Red Barn Nature Center. The Schneck Trail has been closed by the park because a sizable population of pileated woodpeckers thrives there, and the state wants to protect the woodpecker from human encroachment.

A trailboard behind the Red Barn Nature Center shows the trail layout. Each trail is well marked with a wooden post which has the trail name and the trail symbol carved on it.

All the trails are about eight feet in width and well traveled. The trails are located in the nature preserve; therefore, no pets, food, or drinks are allowed on the trail. All the trails are to be hiked in the direction indicated on the map.

The White Oak Trail has an oak leaf for its symbol, the Tulip Tree Trail, a tulip, and the Sweet Gum Trail, a sweet gum leaf.

All of the trails are fairly short and easy to follow. The Tulip Tree Trail measures 1.5 miles and follows the edge of a small rock cliff with Coffee Creek in the valley. From the Tulip Tree Trail, you may join the Sweet Gum Trail by crossing Coffee Creek at Rocky Ford and climbing some stairs. During the wet season, crossing at Rocky Ford may be dangerous due to high water. The Sweet Gum Trail parallels Coffee Creek for a short distance and has some nice views of rock outcrops. This trail intersects with the Schneck Trail, currently closed, and then circles back to Rocky Ford. From here the trail can be hiked back to the Red Barn, where more trails may be reached.

The White Oak Trail begins as a loop off of the Tulip Tree Trail. This trail offers the greatest variety of vegetation and forest conditions. Many large trees may be seen in the valley floor from this trail.

Facilities: A site superintendent's office is located on the grounds to offer additional information. Picnic areas, water, park stoves, and restrooms are provided near the Red Barn and the park lake. A boat launch is located on the lake, and fishing is allowed contingent upon Illinois fishing rules and regulations. The Red Barn Nature Center has materials for the public, old pictures of the site, and displays of plants and animals that may be seen at the park.

Park Rules and Regulations: No pets, food, or drinks allowed on any of the trails. No camping allowed at the park. See Appendixes A and B.

Mailing Address and Phone Number: Site Superintendent, Beall Woods State Park, R.R. 2, Mt. Carmel, Illinois 62863; 618/298-2442

55. Washington County Conservation Area

Trail Length: 7-mile loop (11.3 kilometers)

Location: Washington County Conservation Area is located four miles south of Nashville. To reach the park, north- and southbound traffic may take State Route 127. Four miles south of Nashville a sign on Route 127 points to the park. Turn east on a gravel road and proceed for one mile to the park entrance.

County: Washington

Illinois Highway Map Coordinates: L-6

U.S.G.S. Topographical Map Name and Scale: Beaucoup, 1:24,000

Hours Open: The park is open all year except on Christmas Day and New Year's Day. At certain times, due to freezing and thawing periods, the park is closed, and access to the park is by foot only.

History and Trail Description: In 1959 the State of Illinois acquired 160 acres that is now known as Washington County Conservation Area. One year later Washington County Lake was built; it covers 248 acres, with a maximum depth of twenty-five feet and a shoreline of 13.3 miles. The area varies in its abundance of cover, with fallow fields, stands of hardwood timber, pine stands, and small cultivated fields. Current acreage in the park is now over 1,417 acres.

    The park trail, a 7-mile loop known as the Wacca Lake Trail, can be started west of the concession stand. A parking lot and boat launch area are located at the concession stand. A wooden sign south of the boat launch reads Wacca Lake Trail. The trail is marked with white wooden rectangles nailed onto trees and fences. These trail markers are very scarce during the first few miles of the trail since the trail follows the park road.

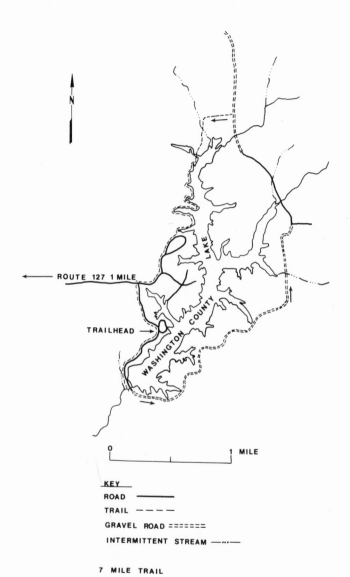

N

← ROUTE 127 1 MILE

LAKE

WASHINGTON COUNTY

TRAILHEAD →

0   1 MILE

KEY

ROAD ———————

TRAIL — — — —

GRAVEL ROAD =======

INTERMITTENT STREAM —···—

7 MILE TRAIL

55. Washington County Conservation Area

The trail goes counterclockwise around the lake following the park road for the first five miles. Shortly after starting the trail, you will walk by the dam and see the entire lake. After three and a half miles you will go past a gate and continue on a dirt road. At the northern tip of the lake the trail leaves the road and starts into the woods. At this point you will see trail markers.

The trail through the woods is a single lane and is used infrequently. The trail goes up and down small hills through the woods and crosses a few creeks. One of the creeks has a wooden pole placed across it with a steel cable for a handrail. You should be very cautious when using this pole: the cable swings very easily and could leave you in the creek.

The trail parallels the lake and offers some beautiful views. The trail eventually meanders to the Shady Rest Camping Area. At this point, the trail comes out of the forest and follows the road in the camping area back to the park entrance. From here, you can go back to the starting point following the park road.

Facilities: A park office on the grounds offers additional information. The park has several picnic sites that have tables, grills, drinking water, restrooms, and playground equipment. A concession stand is located on the lake and offers food, drinks, and fishing tackle; it also rents boats. Hunting is permitted only in restricted areas. Tent and trailer camping is available in the park, along with electricity, a trailer disposal area, and a shower building. Fishing is allowed in the lake with all Illinois fishing laws and regulations in effect.

Permits Required: A camping permit is required.

Park Rules and Regulations: No fishing off of the docks. See Appendix A.

Mailing Address and Phone Number: Site Superintendent, Washington County Conservation Area, R.R. 3, Nashville, Illinois 62263; 618/327-3137

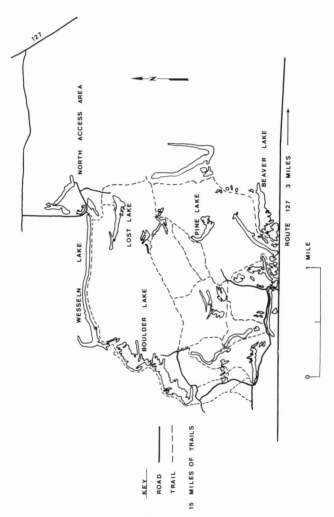

56. Pyramid State Park

56. Pyramid State Park

Trail Length: 15 miles (24.2 kilometers)

Location: Pyramid State Park is located six miles south-west of Pinckneyville. To reach the main park entrance, north and south traffic may take State Route 127. A sign for the park is located three miles south of Pinckneyville. Turn west on this road and go approximately three miles to the park entrance.

Trails may also be reached from the north access area. To reach the north access area, go two miles north of the park road on Route 127 to a gravel road. Turn west on this road, go over a set of railroad tracks, pass by a coal company building, and proceed for one and a half miles to the park entrance. There is a sign along the road which says Pyramid State Park, North Area.

County: Perry

Illinois Highway Map Coordinates: M-6

U.S.G.S. Topographical Map Name and Scale: Pinckney-ville, 1:24,000

Hours Open: The park is open all year except on Christmas Day and New Year's Day. At certain times, due to freezing and thawing periods, the park is closed, and access to the park is by foot only. The park closes at 10:00 p.m. except to campers.

History and Trail Description: Pyramid State Park gets its name from one of the major coal companies in Perry County that was strip-mining land in this area. The park was formerly used as Southern Illinois University's Research Area. In 1965, the State of Illinois acquired 1,600 acres of land and has since increased the acreage to over 2,528 acres.

The park features rough topography with multiple ridges and cuts that resulted from mining operations

Trail along one of the strip mines, Pyramid State Park

between 1930 and 1950. Numerous lakes and ponds were created by the strip-mining operation; these vary in size from .01 to 24 acres and include over 135 acres of water. The park is now heavily wooded with cottonwood, box elder, sycamore, small oak, and hickory trees.

The trail system in the park consists of an 8-mile backpack trail and 7 miles of additional trails. The park board states that the backpack trail measures 10 miles; our measurement differs. The main trailheads for the backpack trail may be started at the east end or the west end of the park, or from short connecting trails in the center of the park. At the west end the trail may be found at the first camping area as you enter the park. A trailboard is seen here and states Rugged 10-Mile Trail. The eastern part of the trail may be found by going back out of the park and going east for two blocks and parking in the area of Little Beaver Lake.

Horseback riders may also ride on parts of the backpack trail. Some of the sections of the trails are off-limits to horses and are marked accordingly.

The trail at both ends is well marked with a wooden trailboard bearing the trail name and length. The trail is about eight feet wide and generally follows mine spoil ridge tops. It offers some beautiful views of the numerous

Trail marker, Pyramid State Park

small ponds and lakes in the park. The trails in the center of the park are all well marked with wooden posts bearing the name and direction of the trail. Also seen along the trails are hiker symbols.

If you start hiking the trail from the east end, you will come across another trail that, within three miles, intersects with the east end trail. This trail, which goes west and passes by Pine Lake, is a loop trail centered in the park. From here one can hike around numerous small lakes and pick up other connecting trails to go to other areas in the park.

Shortly after the trail intersection, the trail passes Beehive Lake, which is at the north park access. A side trail off the main trail leads past Beehive Lake and to the road in the north access area.

Lost Lake is to the south, and a connecting trail

takes you to this lake. Soon you will see Wesseln Lake from the north side of the trail. The trail parallels this lake for about one and a half miles.

The trail then goes between Boulder Lake and Wesseln Lake, paralleling the west side of Boulder Lake. Close to the south end of Boulder Lake, the trail crosses the park road and goes by Pine Grove Picnic Area. A shelter, picnic tables, and restrooms are available here. Beyond Pine Grove Picnic Area, the trail passes by an open field and goes to the campground on the west side of the park.

There is no designated camping along the backpack trail, but there are numerous hike-in campsites available in the center of the park. These campsites have a picnic table, garbage can, and an area for a fire. Permits are required to camp here.

Facilities: A park office located in the park has additional information. Many picnic areas, which have tables, restrooms, and stoves, are scattered through the park. Over 100 tent and trailer campsites are in the park. Water is available at the park office. There are also boat launches on the larger lakes. Fishing is allowed on any of the lakes in the park, contingent upon all Illinois fishing rules and regulations. Horse trail parking is located west of the park office.

Restrooms, picnic tables, grills, a boat launch, and camping facilities are available at the north access area.

Permits Required: A camping permit is required.

Park Rules and Regulations: No vehicles on the trails. Horse camping area is restricted to horse campers only. No horses are allowed at the north end of the park. Horses must stay on the trails and are not permitted on or along roads, except where the trail crosses the park road. Camping is permitted only in designated areas. Ten is the maximum horsepower on the lakes. Swimming, diving, and bathing in the lakes are prohibited. No fires are permitted on the ground. See Appendix A.

Mailing Address and Phone Number: Site Superintendent, Pyramid State Park, R.R. 1, 115-A, Pinckneyville, Illinois 62274; 618/357-2574

57. Randolph County Conservation Area

Trail Length: 7 miles (11.25 kilometers)

Location: Randolph County Conservation Area is located approximately 5 miles north of Chester, Illinois. To reach the park from Chester, go three blocks east of the intersection of Stacey Street and State Street (Route 150) to Van Zant Street. A road sign points out the turn north on Van Zant Street. Additional signs direct one along Palestine Road to Baldwin Road or County Road D&D. About 4.5 miles north on County Road D&D will be a very low sign for Randolph County Conservation Area — pointing east. Turn east and follow this road into the wildlife area.

County: Randolph

Illinois Highway Map Coordinates: M-5

U.S.G.S. Topographical Map Name and Scale: Chester, 1:24,000

Hours Open: The area is open year-round. Site office hours are 8:00 a.m. to 4:00 p.m., Monday through Friday, from November 1 until May 31. From June 1 through October 31 the office is open seven days a week from 8:00 a.m. to 4:00 p.m.

History and Trail Description: The original land acquisition was in 1958 for a total of 25 acres. Completion of a dam and spillway in 1961 added a 65-acre lake. The area has rolling hills with steep slopes. The wildlife area has large stands of mature hardwood trees along with a variety of shrubs and other cover. Today there are 1,031 acres in the park.

Most of the trail system is located on the north and west side of the park, with the exception of a connecting trail from the north side of Rolling Hills Camping Area going along the east side of the lake, back down to the

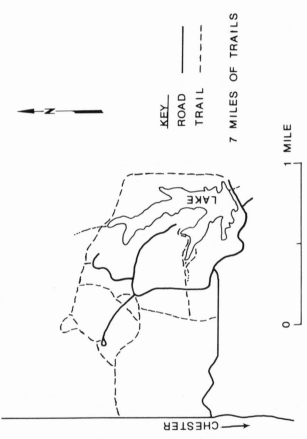

57. Randolph County Conservation Area

parking area and road at the dam. The hiking trails within the area are commonly referred to as horse trails; however, these trails are multiuse. A convenient starting point is at the parking area for the Rolling Hills Camping Area or at Shelter 4/Meadow Picnic Area. From the northwest side of Rolling Hills Camping Area, the trail begins at the gate across the firelane/trail.

Hiking north out of the Rolling Hills Camping Area one will come across a marked post with a sign Trail to County Road. Going east, this trail goes about .5 mile south and east to the Old County Road which then leads directly south another .5 mile connecting with the park-ing area at the dam. This section of trail (between Rolling Hills Camping Area and the dam) offers frequent views of the lake.

Going west from the Rolling Hills Camping Area, the trail is made up of shorter loop trails/sections which combine to make longer portions. These trail sections loop northeast and south of the Youth Group Camping Area. These trails offer diversity in topography as well as in the natural scene. Various types of timber and shrubs, along with open spaces, are scattered throughout the area. One highlight of the trail system is the waterfall accessed along the foot trail about .25 mile west of Shelter 4 and the Meadow Picnic Area. There is a short connecting trail from the boat dock launch and conces-sion area going west to the Meadow Picnic Area and continuing west to the waterfall.

Facilities: Randolph County Conservation Area has Class C (vehicle access), D (tent camping), and E (youth groups) campsites and handicap access. Also, there is a sanitary dump station, concession stand, drinking water, toilets, fishing, boating, boat rentals, launching ramp, and hunt-ing on site. All Illinois fishing rules and regulations are in effect.

Permits Required: Permits are required for camping and hunting.

Park Rules and Regulations: Hunting is restricted to areas posted as open. Groups of twenty-five or more must have permission from the site superintendent. All pets must be leashed. See Appendix A.

Mailing Address and Phone Number: Site Superinten-dent, Randolph County Conservation Area, R.R. 1, Box 345, Chester, Illinois 62233; 618/826-2706

58. Turkey Bluffs State Fish and Wildlife Area

Trail Length: 7 miles (11.2 kilometers)

Location: The entrance is 2 miles south of Chester on Illinois Highway 3.

County: Randolph

Illinois Highway Map Coordinates: N-5

U.S.G.S. Topographical Map Name and Scale: Randolph County, 1:24,000

Hours Open: The area is open year-round, and the office is open from 8:00 a.m. until 4:00 p.m., Monday through Friday, November 1 through May 31; and 8:00 a.m. until 4:00 p.m. seven days a week from June 1 through October 31.

History and Trail Description: Turkey Bluffs State Fish and Wildlife Area is 2,265 acres in extent, of which 1,700 acres are woodland and bushy area. From the access points on Pleasant Ridge Road one has a great view of the Mary's River floodplain along with the varied topography of rolling-to-steep hills, open areas, and wooded spots.

There is a trailboard at the parking area along Pleasant Ridge Road, at which is the starting point or connecting trail for the entire system. The hiking trails are made up of a 4.5-mile loop connecting with a shorter 1.5-mile loop which is combined with a .5-mile (one-way) trail from Trail Ridge Road. This trail system offers nice variety through the varied topography of this area. Different kinds of wildlife exist in the area, including wild turkey and deer. As one might expect, the longer loop offers more challenges in topography but also gives one the opportunity to experience the scenery of many

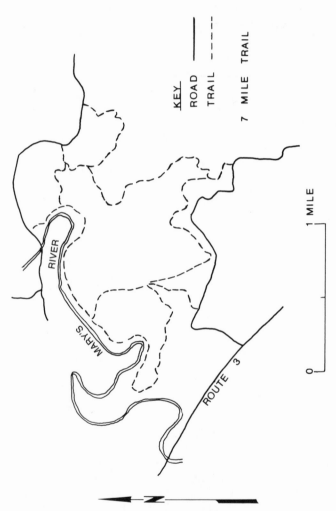

KEY

ROAD ————

TRAIL -----

7 MILE TRAIL

MARY'S RIVER

ROUTE 3

1 MILE

0

N

58. Turkey Bluffs State Fish and Wildlife Area

locations including open, bushy, and wooded areas, as well as the bluffs paralleling Mary's River.

The area is bordered by Illinois Route 3 and the Mississippi River to the south and mostly private property to the north and east. Views of the Mississippi River are available at the day use areas, overlook, and 1.75-mile loop hiking trail at the southeastern edge of the park, reached by following Pleasant Ridge Road to the end.

Facilities: Picnicking and hunting opportunities exist. There are toilets at the day use areas. It is necessary to pack in your own water. Fishing is allowed in Mary's River, with all fishing rules and regulations in effect.

Permits Required: A permit is required for hunting.

Park Rules and Regulations: No camping allowed. See Appendix A.

Mailing Address and Phone Number: Site Superintendent, Turkey Bluffs Fish and Wildlife Area, R.R. 1, Box 345, Chester, Illinois 62233; 618/826-2706

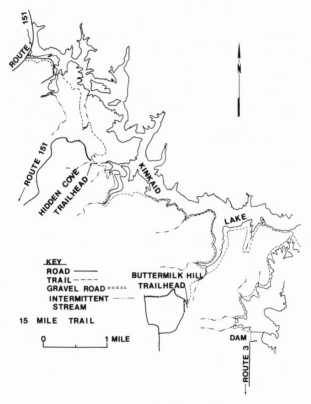

59. Kincaid Lake Trail

59. Kinkaid Lake Trail

Trail Length: 15 miles (24 kilometers)

Location: Kinkaid Lake is located west of Murphysboro. The trail may be started either at the southern end next to the dam or at Johnson Creek Recreation Area off State Route 151. To reach the dam area, take State Route 149 west out of Murphysboro for six miles. There is a turnoff to the north just beyond Kinkaid Creek. Follow this gravel road to the parking area by the dam and spillway. To reach Johnson Creek Recreation Area, continue on Route 149 to the junction of Route 3. Turn north on Route 3 and proceed to State Route 151. Turn north on Route 151 and proceed for four miles to the site entrance.

County: Jackson

Illinois Highway Map Coordinates: N-6

U.S.G.S. Topographical Map Names and Scale: Oraville and Raddle, both 1:24,000

U.S. Forest Service Quad Maps: Oraville and Raddle

Hours Open: Hiking is permitted from sunrise to 10:00 p.m. Johnson Creek Campground is open year-round. Picnicking is permitted from sunrise to 10:00 p.m. The beach is open between 10:00 a.m. and 7:00 p.m.

History and Trail Description: Johnson Creek Recreation Area is the newest campground facility opened by the U.S. Forest Service in the Shawnee National Forest. The site was opened in 1981 and offers many recreation opportunities for the public. Kinkaid Lake has a surface area of approximately 3,000 acres and a shoreline of 81 miles. The lake's main purposes are to supply water and to provide recreation. Prior to the lake being impounded, the land was primarily cropland, grasslands, and woodlands.

The main hiking trail parallels Lake Kinkaid from Johnson Creek Recreation Area all the way to the dam.

This trail, the Kinkaid Lake Trail, is marked with white diamonds painted on trees at a height of about six feet. The trail is basically a footpath, but at times it joins old roads.

If you hike the entire trail in one direction, you will have to shuttle a vehicle to the other end; or, you camp along the trail and return on the same route the following day. To reduce the length of the trail, the U.S. Forest Service set up two areas along the trail where you may leave a vehicle or arrange to be picked up. The two other trailheads are called the Hidden Cove Trailhead and the Buttermilk Hill Trailhead. To get to the Hidden Cove Trailhead parking areas, take Route 151 south out of Johnson Creek Recreation Area. Go for two miles until a hiker sign is seen. Turn east and follow the signs to the parking area. To reach the Buttermilk Hill Trail parking area, take Route 151 south to Route 3. Turn east on Route 3 and proceed for three miles until another hiker sign is seen. Turn north on a gravel road and proceed for one and a half miles to the parking area. The trail distance from Johnson Creek Recreation Area to Hidden Cove Trailhead is 3.2 miles; from Johnson Creek Recreation Area to Buttermilk Hill Trailhead is 9.2 miles.

The trailhead at Johnson Creek Recreation Area may be started at the beach area or the tent camping area. Both locations have parking areas. From the hike-in campground parking area the trail crosses a small wooden bridge over Johnson Creek. The trail goes by the eastern edge of the hike-in camping area and then into the woods.

The trail from Johnson Creek Recreation Area to Hidden Cove Trailhead goes through upland woodlands and past some open fields. The trail passes many old roads and jeep trails in this area. Caution must be used when hiking this area because it is very easy to lose the trail and start hiking an unmarked section. There is a trailboard with a map at the Hidden Cove Trailhead.

From here the trail goes to Lake Kinkaid and parallels the lake all the way to the dam. The trail goes up and down many hills and over many small creeks. Many rock formations, as well as some beautiful views of the lake, may be seen. The trail at many points goes to the lake shore and offers the hiker a nice spot to dip his hat to cool off. In addition, the hiker may wish to bring along a fishing pole. Fishing is available in the many small coves and streams.

Five and a half miles from the Hidden Cove Trailhead, you will see a wooden sign pointing to the direction of Buttermilk Hill Trailhead and Buttermilk Hill Beach. The trail can be hiked to Buttermilk Hill Beach, passing by many beautiful coves and offering some good views of the lake. Prior to reaching the beach, the trail parallels the bluffs above the lake. The trail spur becomes part of a road and goes downhill to the beach area. Beyond the beach, the trail continues along the shores of the lake a few miles to the dam and spillway. From the dam, the trail continues down the hill and finally to the parking lot below the spillway.

Facilities: Johnson Creek Recreation Area has numerous picnic facilities, a boat-launching area, a beach, restrooms, and water. There are forty-three single camping units, eleven double units, nine triple units, and twelve hike-in camping units. Fishing is allowed on Lake Kinkaid, contingent upon Illinois fishing rules and regulations.

Buttermilk Hill Beach has picnic tables, restrooms, and garbage cans. Lifeguard services are not available. No pets, food, camping, or beverages are allowed by the beach area.

Permits Required: A camping permit is required.

Park Rules and Regulations: Primitive camping is permitted anywhere on the hiking trail. All pets must be kept on a leash. See Appendix C.

Mailing Address and Phone Number: District Ranger, U.S. Forest Service, 2221 Walnut, P.O. Box 787, Murphysboro, Illinois 62966; 618/687-1731

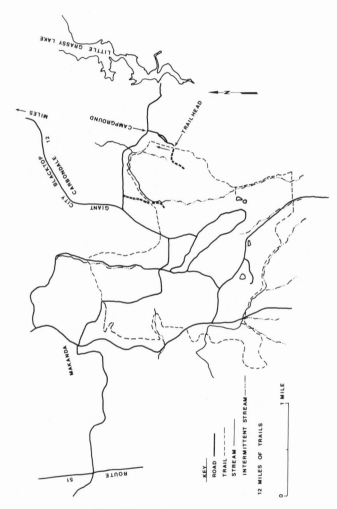

60. Giant City State Park

60. Giant City State Park

Trail Length: 12-mile loop trail (19 kilometers)

Location: Giant City State Park is located twelve miles south of Carbondale. To reach the park, take State Route 51 south out of Carbondale to Makanda. Turn east and proceed through Makanda to the park entrance. An alternative route, and a more direct one, is Giant City Blacktop Road. If you are coming from the east on Route 13, turn left (south) on Giant City Blacktop Road. Proceed for twelve miles to the park. This route goes to the entrance to the campground and to the trailhead for the hiking trail.

Counties: Jackson and Union

Illinois Highway Map Coordinates: N-6

U.S.G.S. Topographical Map Name and Scale: Makanda, 1:24,000

Hours Open: The park is open year-round except on Christmas Day and New Year's Day. The horseback campground is open May 1 through November 1. The lodge is open from mid-February through mid-December of each year.

History and Trail Description: In 1927, the State of Illinois acquired 1,162 acres of land that is now Giant City State Park. The park is part of the Shawnee National Forest and lies within the Shawnee Hills, which vary in elevation from 500 to 1,060 feet.

The name "Giant City" has been given to the park because of the groups of huge blocks of sandstone located throughout the park. Fern Rocks Nature Preserve is located at the northeastern edge of the park; all nature preserve rules must be observed. The park currently has over 3,696 acres.

Giant City State Park lies outside the glaciated area in Illinois. At one time the area was a lowland plain that slowly emerged from the sea. As the region gradually rose, a stream which had flowed over it cut the valleys deeper. Only isolated ridges and knobs are now left. Wherever the rocks are hard and resistant, they stand as steep walls along the valley; wherever they are soft, they have worn down to gentle slopes.

Some indicators of ancient man are also found in the park. A feature called Stone Fort is located at the top of an eighty-foot sandstone cliff. This fort is a great wall of loose stone that partially encloses several acres. It has been suggested that these structures might have been used as a defensive fortification, as corrals for wild or domesticated animals, as game traps, or for ceremonial purposes.

The main hiking trail in the park is a 12-mile trail known as the Red Cedar Hiking Trail. The park also has numerous nature trails, a trail built for the blind, and an extensive horse trail winding its way through the park.

The Red Cedar Trail starts and ends at the camping area located off Giant City Blacktop Road, although the trail may be started at various locations in the park. The trailhead begins by the tent camping area, where there is a parking area.

At the start of the trail a large trailboard shows the trail layout and points to the direction of the trail. The trail is marked with white bands painted on the trees. An orange spot is painted in the middle of this white band. One white band on the tree means that the trail continues ahead while two bands means that the trail changes directions. The trail is also marked with fifteen numerical markers on trees. These markers correspond to special features on the trail. These features are described in the Red Cedar Hiking Pamphlet which may be obtained from the site superintendent.

The trail begins and ends at the campground and goes in a counterclockwise direction. Starting out as a six-foot wide trail, it becomes a single-lane footpath for most of the hike. From the campground to marker number 2, the trail goes through the woods, over Indian Creek, past a closed park road, and finally to Giant City Road. The trail crosses this road and parallels an open field for a short distance until reaching the woodlands again. There is an old cemetery along the trail with a few old grave markers still visible, some dating back to 1871.

Beyond the cemetery, you cross a small stream, pass through the woods, and before reaching the park road, go around a gate. Within the next few miles you will pass under some power lines, go by numerous rock outcrops, hike a ridge top, go past waterfalls, and finally arrive at the backcountry camping area. Restrooms are available at this camping area, but there is no water. From the Red Cedar Camping Area the trail passes through open pasture, past numerous small creeks, and through woods and beautiful valleys. Two small ponds just off the trail are stocked with fish. From there the trail goes past another waterfall, over a park road, along wildlife food plots, over Indian Creek, and then finally back to the starting point.

The trail goes up and down small hills in the park and at one point goes above fifty-foot cliffs. Some areas of the trail may become difficult to hike because of the slope. The trail also passes by a few small waterfalls that are extremely beautiful during the wet season. Great caution must be used when crossing over wet rocks and rock outcrops and when hiking by the cliffs. In addition, some of the streams that must be crossed might be quite high at different times of the year and may be very difficult to cross. Water should be carried along the entire hike, and it is advisable to wear long pants since the trail goes through and by shrubs, thorns, sharp rocks, and poison ivy.

The trail also crosses the road a few times during the hike, and it is possible to hike any of the roads back to the starting point if the hiker does not want to complete the trail.

Facilities: A park office is located in the park where you may request additional park information. Numerous picnic areas, which have shelters, picnic tables, water, and pit toilets, are scattered throughout the park. A Class A campground complete with electricity, sanitary station, and showers is available for tent and trailer camping. A horse camping area, group camping area, and another tent camping area are available in the park also.

Horse stables are available for horseback riding. Fishing is allowed in the numerous streams, ponds, and at the Little Grassy Lake access area. All Illinois fishing rules and regulations apply. A lodge and cabins are also located in the park. Hunting is allowed in certain areas of the park.

Permits Required: All camping in the park requires a permit, including the backcountry camping site located along Red Cedar Hiking Trail.

Park Rules and Regulations: All plants, animals, and cultural features are protected by law. See Appendixes A, B, and F.

Mailing Address and Phone Number: Site Superintendent, Giant City State Park, P.O. Box 70, Makanda, Illinois 62958; 618/457-4836

61. Cedar Lake Trail

Trail Length: 10 miles (16 kilometers)

Location: Cedar Lake is located eleven miles south of Murphysboro off of State Route 127. To reach the trailhead, take Route 127 nine miles south of Murphysboro. Turn left (east) onto Dutch Ridge Road and follow the trail sign two miles to the trailhead. The trail may also be accessed south of Dutch Ridge Road by turning east onto Pomona Road or on the gravel road marked 300 N.

County: Jackson

Illinois Highway Map Coordinates: N-6

U.S.G.S. Topographical Map Names and Scales: Pomona and Cobden, both 1:24,000

U.S. Forest Service Quad Maps: Pomona and Cobden

Hours Open: Cedar Lake Trail may be hiked year-round (weather permitting).

History and Trail Description: Cedar Lake Reservoir was jointly sponsored by the City of Carbondale and the U.S. Forest Service. The primary purpose of the Cedar Lake Reservoir is to provide a water supply for Carbondale with secondary recreational opportunities. Construction of Cedar Lake was completed in December 1973 and reached normal lake level during the winter of 1975. The entire shoreline is in public ownership, with the City of Carbondale owning and managing the northern half and the U.S. Forest Service owning and managing the southern half.

Cedar Lake Hiking Trail parallels the western leg of Cedar Lake and becomes a loop around Little Cedar Lake.

To reach the trailhead, follow Dutch Ridge Road for two miles to a dead-end parking area. At this parking

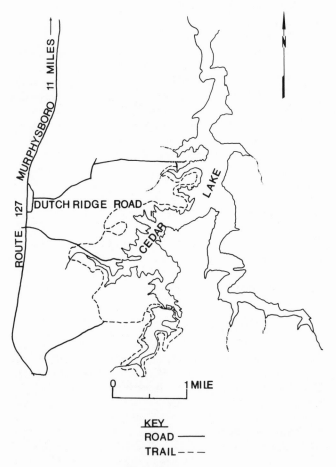

61. Cedar Lake Trail

area a trailboard is located, along with white paint blazes on wooden posts. The entire trail is marked with these white diamonds painted on trees. The trail is basically a single-lane trail for most of the length but at times runs into an old road and becomes part of it for a short distance.

The trail heads south from the parking area, following the ridge top, and then goes down to Cedar Lake, where it parallels the lake heading south.

The first three miles of the trail are probably the most beautiful. Many unique bluffs, rock formations, and cliffs are seen along this section. The trail goes up and down small winding hills and crosses a few small creeks which flow into the lake.

The trail then crosses Pomona Road, where metal hiker markers are posted. From here the trail goes through an open field for a short distance, down to a creek bed, and back into the woods. The trail continues to parallel the lake for a short distance and crosses numerous small creeks. You will soon ascend a hill and go past small rock overhangs, telephone wires, and an open field. From here continue south to the third road or access point.

At this third access point, on top of the hill, there is a small turnaround area for the cars. You will be able to

Hiker passing over the rock spillway between Cedar Lake and Little Cedar Lake

look west and see a beautiful view of the valley. The trail continues south of this little parking area and goes east atop the ridge, following it for a short distance. The trail is very wide at this point, since it is an old road bed. The trail goes by a gate and then continues downhill toward Cedar Lake.

If you follow the trail around Little Cedar Lake, you will follow the shores of this lake for almost the entire length of the trail. You will get good views of the lake from most parts of the trail. Little Cedar Lake is also referred to as Presley Lake and is managed by the U.S. Forest Service. The spillway for Little Cedar Lake is made of naturally outcropped stone, uncovered when Cedar Creek was filled in with soil. You will cross this stone spillway when passing between Little Cedar Lake and Cedar Lake.

Retracing your footsteps, you can follow the trail back to your original starting point.

Facilities: No facilities exist along the trail, and the hiker must carry his own water.

Park Rules and Regulations: 10 horsepower motor limitation on the lake. No houseboats or pontoon boats allowed. No skiing. No overnight mooring permitted on the lake. Fishing by pole and line only. No hunting on City of Carbondale land. All motor vehicles must stay on designated roadways. No cross-country travel allowed. Primitive camping is permitted anywhere along the trail. See Appendix C.

Mailing Address and Phone Number: District Ranger, Shawnee National Forest, 2221 Walnut, P.O. Box 787, Murphysboro, Illinois 62966; 618/687-1731

62. Garden of the Gods Recreation Area

Trail Length: 5 miles (8.1 kilometers)

Location: Garden of the Gods Recreation Area is located six miles northeast of Herod and fifteen miles south of Harrisburg. To reach this area, take State Route 34 south out of Herod to Karbers Ridge Blacktop. Turn left (east) on Karbers Ridge Blacktop. Go about three miles to County Blacktop 10, take a left, and follow the signs to the entrance. As an alternative to this route, take State Route 1 to Karbers Ridge Blacktop, turn right (west), and proceed to County Blacktop 10. Take a right and follow the signs north to the site.

County: Saline

Illinois Highway Map Coordinates: N-8

U.S.G.S. Topographical Map Names and Scale: Karbers Ridge and Herod, both 1:24,000

U.S. Forest Service Quad Maps: Karbers Ridge and Herod

Hours Open: The site is open year-round.

Trail Description: The trail system at Garden of the Gods consists of interconnecting trails that wind their way around the bluffs and rock formations. The hiking trails also connect with the River-to-River Trail at three different locations.

The main parking area is the easiest location from which to start hiking the trails. A large shelter here describes how the rocks and bluffs were formed over two hundred million years ago. A short paved trail, about one quarter of a mile long, leads away from the shelter and takes you past several interesting rock formations, such as Camel Rock and Devil's Smoke Stack. The trail then loops back to the parking area.

At the northern tip of the parking lot and just north of the paved trail, you will run into the main hiking trail

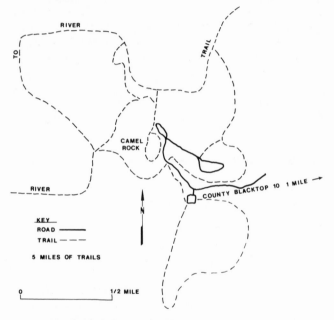

62. Garden of the Gods Recreation Area. Redrawn
from Forest Service map.

Noah's Ark rock formation, Garden of the Gods Recreation Area

system. A wooden post has a copy of the trail map on it. A small gate also marks this location. The trail heads north from this point.

Soon you will come to a trail junction. If you turn west you will reach another trail junction. A wooden sign identifies both Mushroom Rock and Noah's Ark for one trail, and another sign points to the direction of Shelter Rock. You may proceed along either trail. Both trails have beautiful rock formations.

If you take the Noah's Ark Trail, you will walk by two interesting rock formations. The trail continues north and will soon intersect the River-to-River Trail. The River-to-River Trail is blazed with blue paint. At this point you may go west or east. This area is part of the Garden of the Gods Wilderness Area.

The trail for Shelter Rock takes you past additional rock formations and finally to the River-to-River Trail. A sign will also be seen which reads Lower Trail. This trail leads you to the valley below the rock formations. From here, the trail crosses the park road and you will encounter another set of bluffs.

The trail follows the base of these bluffs for a short distance, offering beautiful views of the rock formations.

The Garden of the Gods camping area is directly above these bluffs.

The trail then circles these bluffs and comes to a trail junction. The trail to the right takes you back to the River-to-River Trail, while the branch to the left leads up the bluffs back to the picnic/camping area. A short walk along the road will take you back to the main parking area.

Facilities: Garden of the Gods has picnic facilities, with picnic tables, grills, restrooms, and water available. The campground has twelve tent or trailer units, pit toilets, and water.

Permits Required: A camping permit is required and may be obtained from the ranger or from a pay station at the entrance to the campground.

Park Rules and Regulations: See Appendixes C, D, and E.

Mailing Address and Phone Number: District Ranger, Shawnee National Forest, Elizabethtown, Illinios 62931; 618/287-2201

63. Ferne Clyffe State Park

Trail Length: 6 miles (9.6 kilometers)

Location: Ferne Clyffe State Park is located one mile south of Goreville and twelve miles south of Marion. The park can be reached by taking State Route 37 south out of Marion. Northbound travelers on Interstate 57 can exit on State Route 146 and proceed east eleven miles to Route 37. Turn north on Route 37 and proceed for eight miles to the park entrance. Southbound Interstate 57 motorists can exit on State Route 148 and proceed three miles east to Route 37. Proceed south on Route 37 seven miles to the park entrance.

County: Johnson

Illinois Highway Map Coordinates: N-7

U.S.G.S. Topographical Map Names and Scale: Goreville and Lick Creek, both 1:24,000

Hours Open: The park is open year-round except on Christmas Day and New Year's Day. At certain times, due to freezing and thawing periods, the park is closed, and access to the park is by foot only.

History and Trail Description: In the summer of 1778 George Rogers Clark and his Kentucky "Long Knives" passed through and camped close to the park en route from Fort Massac to Kaskaskia in their conquest of the Illinois country. On the site of Clark's camp is a marker erected by the Daughters of the American Revolution.

This section of the state was formerly the winter hunting grounds of the Indians. The last Indians to use it were the Cherokee, who traveled across southern Illinois in 1838–1839 and were allowed to hunt north and south of their route. The farthest north they hunted was Ferne Clyffe State Park.

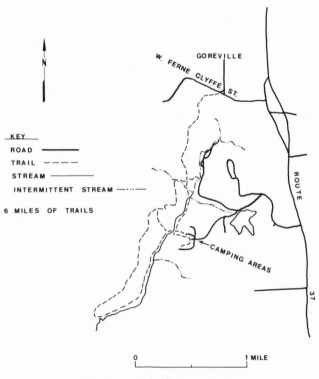

63. Ferne Clyffe State Park

The State of Illinois initially acquired about 119 acres of land here in 1949. Prior to this, Miss Emma Rebman owned most of the land for many years and had in fact operated the area as a park. Miss Rebman took pleasure in naming various points in the park, including Job's Coffin, Alligator Cave, Hawk's Cave, and Round Bluff. In 1960 a sixteen-acre fishing lake was built near the northeastern foot of Round Bluff. The maximum depth of the lake is twenty-one feet and the shoreline is about one mile. The park now has over 1,073 acres.

Ferne Clyffe State Park is a scenic area of valleys, dells, canyons, and brooks. As you enter the park, you will soon come to a place along the road where an excellent view of the valley can be had. Ferne Clyffe has a central valley with a number of gorges and canyons. In the winter, these gorges offer beautiful views of frozen waterfalls. There are several so-called caves in the park; these are not truly caves but great ledges (shelter bluffs) of rock that make an arched roof.

The trail system in the park consists of eight separate trails that total over 14 miles. These trails are scattered throughout the park and offer the hiker beautiful views of the park canyons, waterfalls, wildflowers, shelter bluffs, and unique rock formations. The main trail described here is the Happy Hollow Trail, which at six miles is the longest trail in the park. This is the only trail in the park on which horseback riders are allowed.

There are five separate trailheads for Happy Hollow Trail. You can reach the first trailhead by parking at Bluff View Picnic Area. From here go west across the park road and down the hill. You will see a wooden sign at this point showing the Happy Hollow Trail layout. The other trailheads may be reached by going to W. Ferne Clyffe Street in Goreville, the tent camping area, Turkey Ridge parking area, and the horseback camping area.

Hiking from the Bluff View Picnic Area, just past the trailboard, you will cross a small stream and come to a trail junction where there is a wooden trail sign. This sign points to the directions of the wildlife food plots and backpacking area, horse, tent, and group camping, and to the direction of Goreville.

Going toward Goreville, you will gradually climb through a sparsely wooded area. You will pass some rock outcrops and continue uphill to the top of the bluffs. At this point you will be walking northeast, paralleling the bluffs, and will start seeing some homes on the west side of the trail. When you come to a road in Goreville, you are at the end of the trail, and you will see a metal hiker marker. From here you can retrace your footsteps back to the trailboard.

Going in the other direction, toward the wildlife food plots and backpack camping area, you will hike on a wide dirt trail which passes wildlife food plots. The backpack camping area is located one-half mile away. There are five backpacking campsites here, along with pit toilets. From the camping area continue along the trail for a short distance until you reach the bluffs. At this point, the trail heads into the forest. The trail follows the top of the bluff for a distance and then turns into a footpath. The trail then descends the bluffs, reaching the valley floor close to the creek. The trail parallels the creek for a short distance. A trail marker can be seen. The trail then crosses perennial creeks a few times and heads north, paralleling a creek.

The trail follows this creek all the way back to the original trail junction. At certain times of the year, the trail along the creek may be extremely muddy and at certain times flooded. Prior to reaching the original trail junction you will see a wooden sign that points to the backpacking area. Shortly beyond this sign are two trails that head east back to the tent camping area and horseback camping area and Turkey Ridge parking area.

Facilities: The park has a site superintendent's office where one may request additional information. Several picnic areas are located throughout the park and have picnic tables, park stoves, restrooms, playground equipment, and water. There are camp sites for tents, trailers, horseback riders; also, there is a backpack camping area. Electricity, a disposal station, and a shower building are available. Fishing is allowed in the lake with all Illinois fishing rules and regulations applying.

Permits Required: All campers must secure a camping permit.

Park Rules and Regulations: Boats are not permitted in the lake. See Appendix A.

Mailing Address and Phone Number: Site Superintendent, Ferne Clyffe State Park, P.O. Box 120, Goreville, Illinois 62939; 618/995-2411

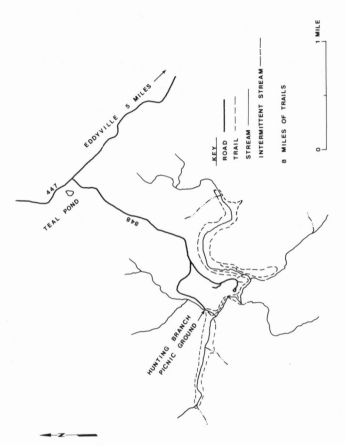

64. Bell Smith Springs Recreation Area

64. Bell Smith Springs Recreation Area

Trail Length: 8 miles (12.8 kilometers)

Location: Bell Smith Springs Recreation Area is located nineteen miles southwest of Harrisburg and seven miles northwest of Eddyville. To reach the site, southbound traffic from State Route 145 can turn right (west) onto Burden Falls Road, which is also Forest Road 402. Proceed to a T junction with Forest Road 447. Turn left (south) and proceed to Forest Road 848. Turn right on Forest Road 848 and proceed on a gravel road either to Hunting Branch Picnic Area or to the parking area past Red Bud Campground.

Northbound traffic on Route 145 can turn left onto Eddyville Road in Eddyville and proceed until it joins Forest Road 848. Proceed as described above.

County: Pope

Illinois Highway Map Coordinates: N-8

U.S.G.S. Topographical Map Name and Scale: Stonefort, 1:24,000

U.S. Forest Service Quad Map: Stonefort

Hours Open: The site is open year-round.

History and Trail Description: Bell Smith Springs Recreation Area is another recreation site built by the Civilian Conservation Corps in the late 1930s and early 1940s. The area consists primarily of deeply dissected stream valleys cut into sandstone, steep bluffs, sheer cliffs, and small waterfalls. Over 1,260 acres are part of this site.

The trail system in Bell Smith Springs Recreation Area consists of various interconnecting loop trails that wind through stream valleys and above the bluffs in the park. All of the trails are marked with color-coded diamonds painted on the trees and rocks. You can start hiking the trail system from the Hunting Branch Picnic Grounds or from the parking lot by Red Bud Campground; trail maps in a glass case are found at both locations. We recommend starting the hike at the parking lot south of Red Bud Campground because it is a central starting point.

If you start hiking the trail from Hunting Branch Picnic Grounds, you will start heading west and hike around Mill Branch Creek. The trail going around Mill Branch Creek is marked with orange diamonds painted on the rocks and trees along the trail. The trail meanders along the contours of the hill above the creek valley. As you hike this trail, beautiful views of the rock stream valley below appear. The creek bed consists of rock which has been eroded by the creek, thereby leaving numerous small waterfalls along the length of the creek, which it crosses. From here the trail ascends the hill and you will be above the creek bed again. The Mill Branch Trail then heads east along the south side of Mill Branch Creek. The trail then comes down the side of the hill, crosses the creek, and joins up with the general hiking trail which takes the hiker toward the center of the park. The trail network in the center of the park is marked with white blazes. The trail then crosses Hunting Branch Creek, parallels, and recrosses it. The hiker will hike by Devils Backbone, a beautiful cliff area with some large boulders in the clear creek. This is an excellent resting spot as well as a great place to take some photographs.

Then the hiker can follow the trails in the stream valley and wind his or her way along the creeks and bluffs above the creek bed. There are some stairs which are carved out of the rock which leads back to the parking area by Red Bud Campground. Past this point a sign will be seen that states Natural Arch.

The trail then crosses Bay Creek where yellow trail blazes are seen as well as fiberglass trail markers. The hiker can then take a lower arch trail which goes beneath the arch or another trail which goes on top of the arch. The trail going to the top of the arch starts climbing a hill and then goes on top of the bluffs.

You will soon come to a natural arch that must be crossed. Where the trail crosses it, the arch is about forty

Mill Branch Creek waterfall, Bell Smith Springs
Recreation Area

feet high and about nine feet wide. The trail goes right
over the arch, allowing a view of the opening of the arch
and the ground below. Just before the arch, there are
some metal bars wedged into the side of the cliffs which
extend to the valley below. We do not recommend climbing down these metal bars. The trails that lead to the
natural arch have yellow diamond blazes painted on the
trees.

Beyond the arch, the trail is blazed in blue starting
near the Fox Gap area. Hikers can take the trail down
from the bluffs at Fox Gap area and head back south
along the base of the bluffs, back to the lower arch area.
This trail is blazed in blue and yellow diamonds. The
bluff trail, referred to as the Sentry Bluff Trail, follows
the top of the bluffs and offers beautiful views its entire

Natural arch, Bell Smith Springs Recreation
Area

length. The trail goes past Boulder Falls and Sentry Bluff,
and then it descends a rock ledge to the stream bed. This
rock ledge is extremely slippery when wet, so you must
proceed with caution. The trail then goes back to the top
of the bluffs on the other side and toward the center of the
park. At the center of the park you can descend some
stairs to the stream valley below. From the stream bed
you can follow a myriad of trails that branch out in all
directions.

The trails at Bell Smith Springs may be hiked in any
direction, and you may vary the distances by taking
different trails.

Facilities: The Hunting Branch Picnic Grounds has seven
picnic units. The Red Bud Campground has twenty-two

tent or trailer units, and restrooms and water are available. In addition, nine tent or trailer units are available at Teal Pond Campground located on Forest Service Roads 447 and 848.

Permits Required: A camping permit is required here.

Park Rules and Regulations: No camping along the trails. See Appendix C.

Mailing Address and Phone Number: District Ranger, Shawnee National Forest, Vienna, Illinois 62995; 618/ 658-2111

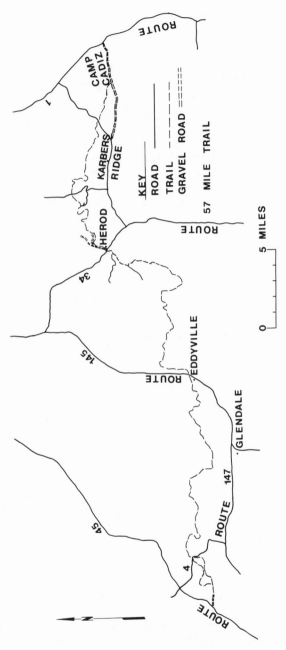

KEY
ROAD
TRAIL
GRAVEL ROAD

57 MILE TRAIL

CAMP CADIZ

ROUTE

KARBERS RIDGE

HEROD

ROUTE

34

145

ROUTE

EDDYVILLE

GLENDALE

ROUTE 147

45

4

ROUTE

0   5 MILES

65. River-to-River Trail

65. River-to-River Trail

Trail Length: 57 miles (92 kilometers)

Location: The River-to-River Trail is located in the south-eastern portion of the Shawnee National Forest. The trail may be started at either end, at Camp Cadiz or off State Route 45 north of Vienna. To reach Camp Cadiz, take State Route 13 east out of Harrisburg or west out of Shawnee-town to Route 1. Turn south on Route 1 for about twelve miles, go past Karbers Ridge Blacktop about three and a half miles to County Road 4 (a gravel road). Turn right (west) on this road and drive about three miles. Camp Cadiz is on the north side. Overnight parking at Camp Cadiz is located on the east side of the campground close to the horse corrals. Camp Cadiz may also be reached by taking State Route 34 south out of Harrisburg for fifteen miles to Karbers Ridge Blacktop. Turn left (east) and go through the town of Karbers Ridge. One mile past the town of Karbers Ridge is County Road 4. A sign for Camp Cadiz will also be seen here. Turn right on County Road 4 and proceed for five miles to Camp Cadiz.

To reach the west access of the trail, take State Route 45 north out of Vienna, Illinois, for five miles. A Forest Service sign along Route 45 (at the site of the radio tower) has the words Trigg Section written on it. Turn east on a gravel road and follow this road for one and a half miles until you see blue blazes on the trees (there are also orange letters on trees indicating the start of the River-to-River Trail [eastern section] and the Max Creek Trail going north). Vehicles can be parked off the side of the road at any point here.

Counties: Hardin, Gallatin, Saline, Pope, and Johnson

Illinois Highway Map Coordinates: N-9, N-8, and N-7

U.S.G.S. Topographical Map Names and Scale: Saline Mines, Karbers Ridge, Creal Springs, Herod, Eddyville, Waltersburg, Glendale, and Bloomfield, all 1:24,000

U.S. Forest Service Quad Maps: Saline Mines, Karbers Ridge, Creal Springs, Herod, Eddyville, Waltersburg, Glendale, and Bloomfield

Hours Open: The trail may be hiked year-round.

Trail Description: The River-to-River Trail is a 57-mile trail which may be started in Camp Cadiz and hiked west to Route 45 north of Vienna, or it may be started in Vienna and hiked east.

The trail utilizes existing hiking trails, dirt and gravel roads, and one section of state highway. The trail is marked with blue blazes in the form of the letter "i" that are visible on trees and wooden posts along the trail. The west part of the trail is marked with orange blazes and blazes that say RR. The trail is well traveled, and parts of the trail are currently being reblazed or rerouted due to logging operations.

The trail is a multipurpose trail, used by hikers as well as horseback riders. In fact, the trail goes right through two large horse campgrounds.

The trail crosses some major roads during the course of the hike, and if the hiker chooses to do so, he could plan a shorter trip.

Camping is permitted anywhere along the trail portion that lies within the Shawnee National Forest; parts of the trail go by private property, so know your location on the trail. We recommend that you carry the U.S. Forest Service Quad Maps whenever you hike this trail.

In our opinion, the River-to-River Trail is one of the most challenging and difficult trails in Illinois. The hiker will encounter a variety of terrain and vegetation, pass wildlife watering ponds, wildlife food plots and openings, cross numerous streams, go by sixty-foot cliffs, and follow many existing old farm and jeep roads.

From the east trailhead, the trail heads west away from Camp Cadiz through an open field and then goes downhill. Between Camp Cadiz and Karbers Ridge Blacktop, you will cross a small creek, climb a hill, and then come to an old road. The trail follows this road for a few miles, going past a few wildlife food plots and water holes. The trail then comes to a gravel road and follows it

north, going over Karbers Ridge Blacktop; it then heads
west along another old dirt road.

You will travel up and down many hills in this area
and will have some good views from the ridge tops.
Within two miles the trail will go by an old cemetery
located on the south side of the trail. The headstones are
so old that no writing is visible on them. Past the cemetery are two old, abandoned houses and a trail junction.
Continue hiking west past these houses until you see
some trail markers. This area may be very confusing;
therefore, the hiker must keep an eye out for the blue
blazes. The trail then connects with other trails in the
High Knob Picnic Area.

A horse ranch is located on a road beyond High
Knob Picnic Area. Follow the road north for a short
distance; the trail then goes into the woods, paralleling
the road. You will cross the road again, and then the trail
will become part of an old dirt road once more. This part
of the trail is rough in some areas because it is severely
eroded. Continue on this road for about one and a half
miles, going up a hill; at the top of a ridge, the trail will
branch off into the woods again.

The trail will head west now. This part of the trail is
very pretty, with pine trees and other conifers all along
the trail. You will cross a new logging road. Some of the
trees were cut down, so you must look closely for the
trail here. Next you will come to a paved road that leads
to the Garden of the Gods Recreation Area. A sign at this
point says River-to-River Trail. This area is part of the
Garden of the Gods Wilderness Area.

Cross this road and continue off into the woods
again. At this point, you have entered the Garden of the
Gods Recreation Area. After climbing a large hill, you
will reach another trail which goes south. This trail leads
to the Garden of the Gods area and is marked with white
diamonds blazed on the trees. If you choose to do so, you
may hike to the Garden of the Gods area and hike some
of the trails there (see Garden of the Gods Trail Map).

The River-to-River Trail makes a half-loop around
the Garden of the Gods area and then continues as a wide
path going west. It follows the ridge tops of the hills, goes
up and down stream valleys, and then comes to a gate and

a gravel road. This is Forest Service Road 114. This is the west end of the Wilderness Area. Take this road west for about one mile until it joins another gravel road. Turn south on this gravel road and follow it for about one mile to the town of Herod at Route 34.

Turn right on Route 34 (north) and go 300 feet to Forest Road 404. Follow this gravel road for a half mile to where it intersects with County Road 146. Proceed on County Road 146 for one and a half miles until you cross a concrete dip over a creek. Shortly past this dip, the trail turns south into the woods. Then you will see blue blazes.

The trail then crosses a small creek, heads uphill, and in about a half mile runs into Forest Road 186, a gravel road. Follow Forest Road 186 south toward the One Horse Gap Area. Once near the One Horse Gap Area, the hiker will see numerous other trails heading into this area. Continue following the gravel road west of One Horse Gap.

Forest Road 186 then joins Forest Road 1476. Turn on Forest Road 1476 and go north. This road follows a ridge and goes by a few wildlife food plots. The trail then passes a small cemetery and follows a gravel road west. The hiker then crosses Route 146, and the trail becomes part of an old road again. The trail goes over the East Fork of Little Lusk Creek and proceeds uphill. The trail then starts heading south, as you are on a ridge top.

The trail heads into the woods again for a short time and then connects with another dirt road. Follow this road for a few miles, heading downhill toward Lusk Creek. This area is part of the Lusk Creek Wilderness Area. During periods of high water this creek may be impassable.

Lusk Creek offers the hiker a good spot to rest and enjoy the beautiful scenery in the area. From here the trail goes uphill to another trail on top of the ridge. The trail then heads west where it comes to a road. As you cross the road the trail starts heading south, paralleling the road for about one mile.

The trail crosses the road again. At this point, follow this gravel road for about one and a half miles to Route 145 in Eddyville. Cross Route 145 and follow Pope

County Road in Eddyville to Eddyville Road. One block
south of the Eddyville Post Office is a signpost indicating
the horse trail. Follow that road (it becomes a gravel
road) west until it turns south, passing through woods
again.

The section west of Eddyville all the way to Little
Bay Creek (parallel with the Illinois Central Railroad) is
extremely difficult to follow as there are several primitive
roads, hunters' trails, and other unmarked trail intersections. By following the U.S. Forest Service Quad Maps,
the true River-to-River Trail is more easily determined.

Continuing westward, the trail meanders through
dense forest land, up and down ridges, and across perennial streams. The trail west of Bay Creek becomes single-
lane for a stretch and then joins up with old roads. A mile
east of the East Branch of Cedar Creek, the hiker will run
across another trail. By having the appropriate Quad
Map, the hiker can go up the hill here to reach the Trigg
Lookout Tower. From the Trigg Tower great views of the
Shawnee Forest will be had.

Near the East Branch of Cedar Creek, the hiker will
run across an old pioneer cemetery. One headstone has the
following words inscribed: "William Simpson Pioneer
first Settler of Johnson Co. Came in 1805 Died 1826."
Also on the north side of the cemetery is a horse camp.

The trail then goes over the East Branch of Cedar
Creek and comes to a road. The hiker goes over the
bridge and then follows an old road on the north side of
the road. Shortly some rock outcrops will be seen from
the trail. The trail then heads uphill where the hiker will
pass by some wildlife food plots.

At the top of the hill, the trail will meet another path
at a Y. Turn right and begin descending a hill toward
Cedar Creek. The trail then follows Cedar Creek going
by some very scenic and beautiful bluffs. The trail then
goes uphill and reaches an old rocky road that heads
west. This road meets up with a gravel road which turns
south for a half mile where it meets with Tunnel Hill
Road (Route 4) and turns west to McCormick's Cedar
Lake Campground, or south along Route 4.

The trail heading west along Route 4 goes to McCormick's Cedar Lake Horse Campground. A trail comes out

of here known as the Cedar Lake Trail and heads south to the River-to-River Trail. To stay on the actual River-to-River Trail, go south on Route 4 for about a quarter mile. Turn south on an asphalt road (look for the blue blazes). In about a mile the River-to-River trail goes into the woods as a single-lane trail.

The River-to-River Trail then will come to a junction with the Cedar Lake Trail and a loop trail known as the Max Creek Trail. The Max Creek Trail does a half loop next to Max Creek and then joins up with the River-to-River Trail again. You have the option of following the Max Creek Trail, which meanders up and down the valley of Max Creek while crossing the creek six times, or you can follow the original River-to-River Trail, which passes through several open areas, moves on top of ridges, and passes through many areas altered by logging operations, then west to the trailhead at the Trigg Section. Either section of the loop back to the Trigg Section trailhead is approximately two miles long.

Facilities: Camping is allowed anywhere along the River-to-River Trail so long as it is within the Shawnee Forest. Camping is also allowed at Garden of the Gods, at Camp Cadiz, and at McCormick's Cedar Lake Campground. Camp Cadiz has eleven campsites, horse campsites, a water pump, toilets, and group campsites.

Trail Rules and Regulations: See Appendixes C, D, and E.

Mailing Addresses and Phone Numbers: District Ranger, Shawnee National Forest, Elizabethtown, Illinois 62931; 618/287-2201; and District Ranger, Shawnee National Forest, Vienna, Illinois 62995; 618/658-2111

66. Beaver Trail

Trail Length: 7.5 miles (12 kilometers)

Location: The Beaver Trail trailhead is located at Camp Cadiz camping area in the Shawnee National Forest. The River-to-River Trail also starts at the same campground. To reach Camp Cadiz, southbound traffic may take State Route 1 twelve miles south of State Route 13. Go past Karbers Ridge Blacktop about three and a half miles to County Gravel Road 4. Turn right (west) and go for about three miles to Camp Cadiz. As an alternative to this route, take Route 34 south out of Harrisburg for about fifteen miles to Karbers Ridge Blacktop. Turn left (east) on Karbers Ridge Blacktop and proceed for six miles. One mile past the town of Karbers Ridge you will reach County Gravel Road 4. Turn east and follow the road for about five miles to Camp Cadiz. Camp Cadiz is located on the north side of the road and is identified with a sign.

County: Hardin

Illinois Highway Map Coordinates: N-9

U.S.G.S. Topographical Map Name and Scale: Saline Mines, 1:24,000

U.S. Forest Service Quad Map: Saline Mines

Hours Open: Camp Cadiz is open year-round.

History and Trail Description: Beaver Trail is a 7.5-mile trail which has its trailhead at Camp Cadiz. The trail may also be started at the trail end at Rim Rock National Trail. The trail is marked with white painted diamonds blazed on trees along the trail.

Parking is available at Camp Cadiz on the east side of the camping area, close to the horse area. From here, go northwest to a gravel road. This gravel road is the start of the Beaver Trail.

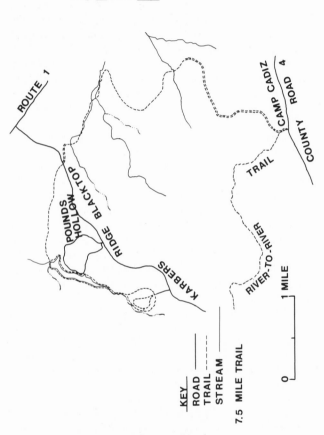

66. Beaver Trail

Follow this gravel road for about one and a half miles. The trail branches off into the forest. The trail then proceeds to go up and down the stream valleys and crosses Beaver Creek, the trail's namesake.

You will reach an old road that runs through the forest. This road proceeds first in a northeasterly direction and then in a northwesterly direction. You will intersect many other old roads while following this section of the trail, and you must be careful to keep an eye out for the white paint blazes on the trees.

You will then come across Karbers Ridge Blacktop. From here, the trail heads back into the forest and becomes a single-lane path to its end.

Between Karbers Ridge Blacktop and Pounds Hollow Lake, the trail goes up and down difficult hills, over creeks, and by rock outcrops. This section of the trail probably offers the hiker the most pleasant scenery along the trail. The trail goes downhill to the lake by the earthen dam.

The trail crosses this dam and follows the northern shore of Pounds Hollow Lake. The trail parallels the entire lake shore and offers the hiker some good views of the lake. At the end of the lake the trail goes up the stream valley, paralleling the lake's feeder creek. Crossing this creek, the trail heads south toward Rim Rock. The trail goes completely around Rim Rock and then back toward Pounds Hollow Lake.

On top of Rim Rock is a National Recreation Trail, a short nature trail paved its entire length. Views of the lake can be seen from the top of Rim Rock, and you can take the stairs down to the base of the rock. While hiking down these stairs, you will pass between some large rock formations.

Facilities: Camp Cadiz has eleven tent campsites, with additional sites for horseback riders. Restrooms, water, grills, and a horse area are all located at Camp Cadiz. Pounds Hollow Recreation Area has seventy-six campsites, picnic areas, water, restrooms, and a beach house. Rim Rock Recreation Area is a day use area with no camping allowed. Water is available at Rim Rock.

Permits Required: A camping permit is required at both Camp Cadiz and Pounds Hollow.

Park Rules and Regulations: See Appendix C.

Mailing Address and Phone Number: District Ranger, Shawnee National Forest, Elizabethtown, Illinois 62931; 618/287-2201

67. Trail of Tears State Forest

Trail Length: 45 miles (72 kilometers)

Location: Trail of Tears State Forest is located 22 miles south of Murphysboro and 5 miles northwest of Jonesboro, Illinois. Travelers can get to the park by taking either Route 127 on the east side or Route 3 on the west side. Travelers on Route 127 turn onto Union Forest Road and travel west approximately 2 miles to the park, while travelers on Route 3 go east on Union Forest Road for 6 miles to the park.

County: Union

Illinois Highway Map Coordinates: O-6

U.S.G.S. Topographical Map Names and Scale: Jonesboro and Cobden, 1:24,000

Hours Open: The park is open every day of the year except on Christmas Day and New Year's Day.

History and Trail Description: Between mid-December 1838 and early March 1839, 10,000 Cherokee Indians were forced to move 800 miles from the Great Smokies area to present-day Oklahoma. The exiled Cherokees had to stop in southern Illinois just south of what is now Trail of Tears State Forest because of ice floating in the Mississippi River. Because of poor shelters and a severe winter, many Indians died, thus the name Trail of Tears.

The Forest was originally established to demonstrate and encourage proper forest management for the private forest landowner, to protect the watershed, and to provide for multiple use of various forest recreation opportunities. The trail system at Trail of Tears State Forest consists of a network of fire trails and horse trails which total over 45 miles in length. These trails are used for hiking, backpacking, and horseback riding, as well as for providing access to hunters.

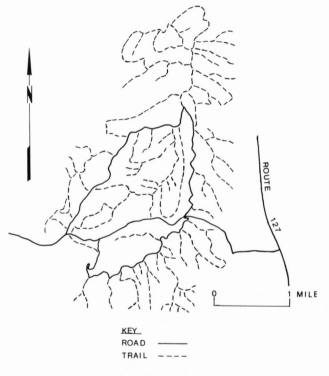

KEY
ROAD ——————
TRAIL – – – –

45 MILES OF TRAILS

67. Trail of Tears State Forest. Redrawn from park
map.

Union Forest Road divides the park in two, with the majority of the park on the north side. The trails are located on both the north and south sides of the road with most of the trails on the north. All of the trails are marked with wooden trail posts which state Fire Trail along with the number of the trail. Each fire trail has a unique number assigned to it.

The terrain is very rugged here with long, narrow ridges approximately 150 to 200 feet in height falling away sharply on either side. The slopes are very steep and the valleys very narrow. Approximately 90 percent of the area is mature hardwood forest.

The hiker can get to the trails at numerous locations along Union Forest Road or along the two dirt roads which loop on the north and south sides of the park. The hiker can park his or her vehicle near any of the trail junctions and begin hiking. There are numerous trails (40 plus) which the hiker can walk, so we will not describe these in detail other than to state that you need to be in good shape to go up and down the steep terrain here.

Facilities: There are two main picnic areas with shelters, tables, fireplaces, pit toilets, and water. A ball diamond also is available. Four shelters in remote areas of the park also provide unique picnicking opportunities. Camping also is available at four locations. Hunting is available with all relevant rules and regulations in effect.

Permits Required: A camping permit is required.

Park Rules and Regulations: See Appendix A.

Mailing Address and Phone Number: Site Superintendent, Trail of Tears State Forest, R.R. 1, Box 1331, Jonesboro, Illinois 62952; 618/833-4910

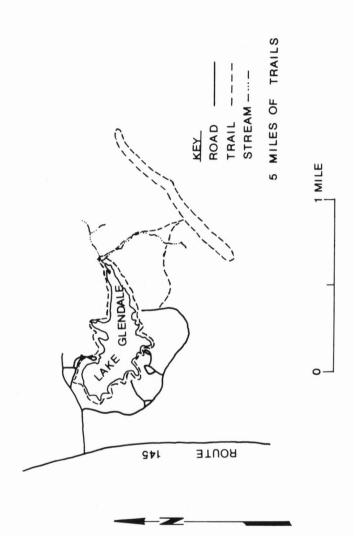

68. Lake Glendale Recreation Area

68. Lake Glendale Recreation Area

Trail Length: 5 miles (8 kilometers)

Location: Lake Glendale Recreation Area is 26 miles southwest of Harrisburg, Illinois, and is located off of Route 145. To reach this site, travelers can take Route 145 south out of Harrisburg for 26 miles, until they see a sign on the road that states Lake Glendale Recreation Area. The site is also 2 miles north of the intersections of State Routes 146 and 145.

County: Pope

Illinois Highway Map Coordinates: O-8

U.S.G.S. Topographical Map Name and Scale: Glendale, 1:24,000

U.S. Forest Service Quad Map: Glendale

Hours Open: The site is open year-round.

Trail Description: Lake Glendale Trail consists of two connected trails which total 5 miles in length. One part of the trail goes around the entire lake offering some beautiful views, while the second part, known as the Signal Point spur, is southeast of the lake.

The Lake Trail has many beginnings or trailheads. Hikers can get on the trail at Duck Bay, Goose Bay, or Pine Point Picnic Areas, the beach house, the boat area, or at Oak Point Campground. The trail around Lake Glendale is a very easy path to follow. It consists of gravel which parallels the entire lakeshore. Trail markers consist of trail signs which state Hiker Trail or some have a backpacker sign. While on this trail segment, numerous wooden bridges are crossed. The Lake Trail is especially scenic on the east end where it is wooded and away from the picnic areas and roads. Numerous waterfowl are also found here, and there seem to be some nice fishing holes for the angler.

The second part of the trail, the Signal Point spur, begins just south of Duck Bay Picnic Area on the east side of the road. The hiker will see a Forest Service trailboard which states Shawnee National Forest Trail, Signal Point, U.S. Department of Agriculture. The Signal Point Trail starts heading southeast through some woods and by some fallow fields. The trail starts out marked with yellow blazes. The trail goes up and down some small valleys and over a small creek. The trail then goes up a hill and continues until one gets close to a set of cliffs. The trail markers are now pink.

From here, the hiker can follow the base of the cliffs in either direction and eventually make his or her way up to the top of the cliff. The trail then follows the ridgetop of the cliff and then descends to ground level where the hiker follows the base of the cliff back to the beginning. Another spur trail is found which goes in a northwest direction and meets up with the Lake Trail, near the concrete spillway for the creek going into the lake. At times, especially when the trees have their full foliage, the Signal Point Trail spur can be hard to follow.

Facilities: There are 72 tent or trailer camping units at Oak Point Campground with showers, water, picnic tables, and grills. There is a swimming area with a bathhouse, concession stand, and boat rentals which are open during the summer months. Picnic units with drinking water are found around the lake, and a boat ramp is found at Cardinal Bay. A fishing license is required to fish Lake Glendale.

Permits Required: A camping permit is required.

Park Rules and Regulations: No gasoline motors on the lake. Group camping by reservation only at Bailey Place. See Appendix C.

Mailing Address and Phone Number: District Ranger, Shawnee National Forest, Vienna, Illinois 62995; 618/ 658-2111

69. Little Black Slough Trail

Trail Length: 6.5 miles (10.5 kilometers)

Location: Little Black Slough Trail is in part of the Cache River State Natural Area. To reach this trail, northbound or southbound traffic may take either Interstate 24 or Interstate 57 and exit onto State Route 146. Three and a half miles west of Vienna or about two miles east of Route 37, there is a sign on Route 146 for Wildcat Bluff. Turn south on this gravel road and proceed six miles to a dead-end road. There is a wooden trailboard here. Immediately to the south of the parking area is a fifty-foot drop to the valley below. This bluff is known as Wildcat Bluff.

County: Johnson

Illinois Highway Map Coordinates: O-7

U.S.G.S. Topographical Map Names and Scale: Karnak and Vienna, 1:24,000

Hours Open: The sites are open every day of the year.

History and Trail Description: Heron Pond—Little Black Slough was acquired by the Illinois Department of Conservation to preserve one of the finest remaining cypress swamps in the state. The nature preserve is part of a diverse landscape and harbors hundreds of different plant species. In addition, a variety of environments—such as floodplain forest, moist and dry slope forest, barren sandstone ledges, dry limestone glades, and prairie—may be found here.

   The Cache River State Natural Area consists of 8,214 acres and has two separate areas: Little Black Slough and the Lower Cache. Little Black Slough contains two Illinois nature preserves: Heron Pond Wildcat Bluff Preserve and the Little Black Slough Preserve. The Section 8 Woods Nature Preserve is located in the Lower

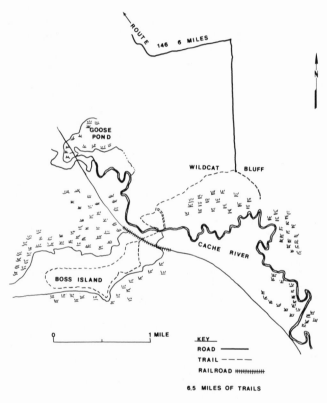

ROUTE 146 6 MILES

N

GOOSE POND

WILDCAT BLUFF

CACHE RIVER

BOSS ISLAND

0   1 MILE

KEY
ROAD ————
TRAIL – – – –
RAILROAD +++++++++++

6.5 MILES OF TRAILS

69. Little Black Slough Trail

Cache Area. These areas are significant because they contain southern swamps at the northern portion of their range.

The Little Black Slough Trail measures 6.5 miles. From the parking area at Wildcat Bluff, the trail goes both east and west. If you head east, the trail goes along an old road on top of the bluffs for about a half mile. This part of the trail takes you to an area on the edge of the bluff looking out at the Cache River floodplain.

Heading west from the parking area, you will follow an old abandoned road. This trail follows the bluff for a short distance; from the bluffs you will see many beautiful views of the valley below. In a mile there is a rock along the trail with a metal marker etched with the following words: "Little Black Slough. The Illinois Department of Conservation acquired this land in 1975 with the help of the Illinois Chapter of the Nature Conservancy and the Westvaco Corporation." Shortly you will come to a Y in the trail. Proceed to the right and follow the trail down toward the valley.

Proceeding along the Little Black Slough Trail, you will reach the Cache River. At this point you must cross the river, going over a rock ford. During the wet season, the river may be impassable; therefore, the trail cannot be followed past this point. Shortly after crossing the river, you will see an old, abandoned house. This house is a reminder of earlier settlements in this area. From here, the trail crosses a set of railroad tracks and heads toward Boss Island. This section of the trail becomes a loop. You will pass by sections of pine and sycamore trees. The trail along this branch is marked with blue rectangles on the trees.

After completing the loop, retrace your steps to the trailhead.

Facilities: There are no facilities here, although the Heron Pond parking area has restrooms and a trailboard set up.

Park Rules and Regulations: This area is protected under the Illinois Nature Preserves. Camping, horses, pets, vehicles, and firearms are prohibited. Plants, animals, and other natural features of this area are protected by law. See Appendix B.

Mailing Address and Phone Number: Site Superintendent, Cache River State Natural Area, Route 2, Box 2, Belknap, Illinois 62908; 618/634-9678

Appendixes

Selected Bibliography

Appendix A

Public Use of State Parks and Other Properties of the Department of Conservation — Illinois Administrative Code, Title 17, Chapter I, Subchapter a, Part 110

Section

Authority: Implementing and authorized by Section 8 of "AN ACT in relation to State forests, operation of forest tree nurseries, and providing penalties in connection therewith" (Ill. Rev. Stat. 1987, ch. 96 1/2, par. 5911); and by Sections 1, 4, and 6 and of "AN ACT in relation to the acquisition, control, maintenance, improvement and protection of State parks and nature preserves," approved June 26, 1925, as amended (Ill. Rev. Stat. 1987, ch. 105, pars. 465, 465a, 466, 468, 468b, and 468k); and by Sections 63a, 6311, 63a15, 63a18, and 63a28 of the Civil Administrative Code of Illinois (Ill. Rev. Stat. 1987, ch. 127, pars. 63a, 63a11, 63a15, 63a18, and 63a28).

(Source: Adopted at 4 Ill. Reg. 11, p. 59, effective March 4, 1980; emergency amendment at 5 Ill. Reg. 8933, effective August 25, 1981, for a maximum of 150 days; codified at 5 Ill. Reg. 10621, amended at 6 Ill. Reg. 7401, effective June 11, 1982; amended at 8 Ill. Reg. 9967, effective June 19, 1984; amended at 10 Ill. Reg. 9797, effective May 21, 1986; amended at 10 Ill. Reg. 13256, effective July 25, 1986; amended at 13 Ill. Reg. 3785, effective March 13, 1989.)

Section 110.5   Unlawful Activities
It shall be unlawful (Sections 110.10 through 110.170):

Section 110.20   Alcoholic Beverages — Possession, Consumption, Influence
For any person to possess or consume intoxicating beverages, including beer or wine in any Department-controlled property which is posted with signs indicating that such possession or consumption is unlawful.

(Source: Amended at 6 Ill. Reg. 7401, effective June 11, 1982.)

Section 110.30   Animals — Pets, Dogs, Cats — Noisy, Vicious, Dangerous Animals — Horses — Livestock — Animal Waste
a) For any person to allow an unleashed dog, cat, or other domesticated animal on any area and further for any person to allow any dog, cat or other domesticated animal in any area, on a leash longer than 10 feet, except that:

   1) unleashed hunting dogs are allowed during the hunting season for waterfowl and upland game including squirrel and dove on any Department areas open to hunting and so posted;

   2) at field trials unleashed dogs are allowed at sites designated by the Department in accordance with 17 Ill. Adm. Code 910; and

   3) unleashed hunting dogs are allowed by individual permit for dog training at sites designated by the Department in accordance with 17 Ill. Adm. Code 950.

b) For any leashed animal to be left unattended and not under the specific physical control of the owner or person designated by the owner. The owner or person designated by the owner for dogs or other animals must have proof that their animal has a current rabies inoculation certificate or a valid license.

c) For any person to keep a noisy, or vicious, or dangerous dog or animal, or one which is disturbing to other persons, on Department of Conservation controlled properties, and to remain therein after being asked by the Site Superintendent or assigned employee to leave.

d) For any person to ride or lead any horse in any area, other than designated bridle paths or equestrian areas, except that horses are permitted in any designated area at field trials, special events, and horse drawn conveyances authorized by permit by the Department of Conservation. The decision to grant or deny a permit will be based upon the impact upon the site and the public. Horse patrols of the Department in the performance of their duties are not excluded from any area under the control of the department.

e) For any person to allow livestock to roam or graze on any Department-controlled lands except when authorized by proper lease, license or written agreement approved by the Illinois Department of Conservation in accordance with 17 Ill. Adm. Code 150.

f) For any person responsible for an animal in a campground or day use area not to dispose of his animal's waste excrement directly into a Department garbage container with a tight fitting lid or have the excrement put into a closed water tight bag or water tight container with the lid closed and placed into a Department trash container.

g) For any person to allow a dog, cat, or other domesticated animal on any area designated as "NO PETS." Such designation will be reserved for beach areas, concession areas, and certain areas within campgrounds and picnic areas where there are concentrations of large numbers of people or the presence of food or children.

(Source: Amended at 13 Ill. Reg. 3785, effective March 13, 1989.)

Section 110.40   Boats and Other Watercraft
a) For any person to operate any sailboat, rowboat, houseboat, pontoon boat, or boat propelled by machinery or other watercraft in any pond, lake, river, canal, or other body of water where posting clearly indicates that certain specific boating usage is prohibited. However, Department of Conservation employees operating watercraft in carrying out official duties and personnel of cooperating agents or agencies operating watercraft as authorized by the Department of Conservation are exempt from boating regulations in this Section 110.40 or in specific site rules as determined by Department of Conserva-

tion supervisory managers in order to provide management actions for enhancing or saving the resource base or the safety and welfare of the using public.

b) For any person to use a motor driven boat on any body of water under the jurisdiction of the Department that has less than 60 surface acres. However, this does not exclude the use of electric trolling motors on these bodies of waters,

c) For any person to use a motor driven boat with a motor of a size larger than 10 H.P. on any body of water under the jurisdiction of the Department that has 60 or more surface acres of water area except departmentally supervised waters of over 500 acres and portions of canals having specific regulations posted on boat motor size and boat use allowed.

d) For any person to allow his boat or other watercraft to remain on any of the public recreational and fishing areas under the jurisdiction of the Department beyond the date of December 1st of each year.

(Source: Amended at 6 Ill. Reg. 7401, effective June 11, 1982.)

Section 110.45   Abandoned Watercraft
It shall be unlawful for any person to abandon a watercraft on property owned, leased or managed by the Illinois Department of Conservation.

a) Abandoned watercraft is defined as a watercraft left unattended for a single period longer than six hours on Department-managed land or water at an area which is not authorized for boat docking.

b) The Department shall have the power to remove any abandoned watercraft and store said watercraft until claimed by their owner and fees of $15.00 for removal and $5.00 for each day's storage are paid. The fees paid for removal and storage are separate from any criminal penalty and do not affect criminal prosecution.

(Source: Amended at 13 Ill. Reg. 3785, effective March 13, 1989.)

Section 110.50   Capacity of Areas — Usage Limitation
a) For any person to violate the rules and regulations pertaining to posted usage capacity of campgrounds, picnic grounds,

or other areas where limited facilities make it necessary to control use by persons and/or motor vehicles. Site Superintendents and Law Enforcement Officers of the Department of Conservation are authorized to close such facilities to additional persons until such time as the number of users falls below the capacity posted within the area.

b) For any person to violate the posted closing period for any site except as permitted in 17 Ill. Adm. Code 130.90(a).

(Source: Amended at 10 Ill. Reg. 9797, effective May 21, 1986.)

Section 110.60   Camping—Campfires
a) For any person to use a tent or trailer, or any other type of camping device except in designated camping areas, and persons camping in such designated areas shall obtain a camping authorization slip from authorized site personnel as provided by 17 Ill. Adm. Code 130.

b) For any person to build any fire in any area except in campstoves provided by the Department of Conservation or in charcoal or other types of metal grills which are furnished by the visitor at a specific campfire site designated or where bans on open fires are posted by the Department of Conservation.

c) For any person to possess or discharge any type of fireworks or other explosive devices including but not limited to model rockets or aerial displays without a written permit issued by the Department. The decision to grant or deny a permit will be based upon public safety and legal considerations, and the impact on public use/enjoyment of parks.

(Source: Amended at 13 Ill. Reg. 3785, effective March 13, 1989.)

Section 110.70   Destruction of Property—Flora—Fauna— Man-Made and Inanimate Natural Objects—Collection of Artifacts
a) For any person to injure or remove any animal, plant or part thereof, or attempt to disturb any agricultural crop, except as otherwise provided by permit, law, regulation, or by Department program activity under the direct supervision of an authorized employee.

b) For any person to remove, take, mutilate, deface or destroy any natural or man-made property, equipment, improvement, sign or building, except as otherwise provided by permit, law, regulation, or by Department program activity under the direct supervision of an authorized employee.

c) For any person to collect or take artifacts and/or mutilate, destroy, deface or excavate any archaeological site except as provided by permit according to 17 Ill. Adm. Code 370.

d) For any person to withdraw or pump water from any Department controlled lake, canal, wetland, river or stream except as authorized by Department permit. The decision to grant or deny a permit will be based upon a balancing between the need of the permittee and the protected water level or flow.

(Source: Amended at 13 Ill. Reg. 3785, effective March 13, 1989.)

Section 110.90   Group Activity
For groups of more than 25 persons to use Department of Conservation facilities unless written permission is obtained in advance from the Site Superintendent. Further, for groups of persons under the age of 18, it is required that at least one adult accompany no more than 15 of these minor individuals.

(Source: Amended at 13 Ill. Reg. 3785, effective March 13, 1989.)

Section 110.100   Littering
a) For any person using Department of Conservation facilities to discard, abandon, place, or deposit on Department of Conservation properties, except in containers provided, any wire, cans, bottles, glass, paper trash, rubbish, garbage, cardboard, wood boxes or other insoluble animal, vegetable, metal, or mineral materials.

b) For any person to bring into Department of Conservation property any of the items listed in Section 110.100(a) above, with the express purpose of disposing, abandoning, or leaving any of these types of materials on Department property, whether they are left or placed in proper containers or not.

c) For food to be consumed on swimming beaches or the discarding of cans, bottles, glass, paper, trash, or insoluble materials on the designated beach area.

(Source: Amended at 10 Ill. Reg. 9797, effective May 21, 1986.)

Section 110.110   Prohibited Fishing Areas — Cleaning of Fish
For any person to take fish from the waters of any Department controlled area contrary to the rules and regulations of the Department in accordance with 17 Ill. Adm. Code Part 810, and further, any fish or parts of fish remaining from cleaning must be placed in a proper refuse container with a tight fitting lid or removed from the area in a proper refuse container with a tight fitting lid or removed from the area upon leaving.

(Source: Amended at 8 Ill. Reg. 9967, effective June 19, 1984.)

Section 110.120   Restricted Areas — Metal Detection Devices
a) For any person to enter or remain in any area when such area has, in whole or in part, been closed to use by visitors. Site Superintendents and Law Enforcement Officers of the Department of Conservation, as well as other peace officers, are authorized to prohibit the use of such closed areas, and it shall be unlawful for any person to disobey the rules and regulations posted relative to such closed area.

b) For any person to enter or remain on any portion of a dedicated nature preserve area where posted rules and regulations prohibit such entry to protect the natural fauna or flora within such area.

c) For any person to operate a metal or mineral detection device, except that person may use hand carried devices on Department of Conservation properties that are not classified or zoned as State Historical, Archaeological, or Nature Preserve sites. In addition, persons must obtain a permit from the Department through the Site Superintendent, in advance, indicating the location where these devices shall be used. Further, only a small pen knife, ice-pick or screwdriver shall be used by permittee to recover any find in the area designated. After completing detection activity, the permittee must return the work area to its original state. No shovels, picks or entrenching devices of any size shall be used.

d) For any person to collect firewood or operate a chain saw or sound amplification system which would draw on the site's electrical system in any area which has been closed or posted to prohibit such use. Site Superintendents of the Department of Conservation shall prohibit such use in any area that does not allow the collecting of firewood, has experienced illegal cutting of timber or at which the noise will disturb other site users.

e) For any person to use electronic or electrical speakers at a volume which emits sound beyond the immediate camp or picnic site except as authorized by Department permit. The decision to grant or deny a permit will be based upon the reason for the request and the time, date and type of activity, balanced against public enjoyment of the park.

(Source: Amended at 13 Ill. Reg. 3785, effective March 13, 1989.)

Section 110.140   Soliciting/Advertising/Renting/Selling
a) For any person to place signs or distribute advertising of any type on Department owned or managed property except as provided in Section 110.140 (b) below.

b) For any person to make sales or rentals of any kind or solicit sales or rentals of any kind including placing signs, distributing advertisements in connection with these sales and/or rentals on Department owned property without first obtaining a Department permit, lease and/or license in writing in accordance with 17 Ill. Adm. Code 150 or in the case of lands managed by the Department without first obtaining a permit, lease, and/or license from the owner of the property and the approval of the Department.

(Source: Amended at 6 Ill. Reg. 7401, effective June 11, 1982.)

Section 110.150   Swimming/Wading/Diving
For any person to swim, wade or bodily enter into the water at any location. The exceptions to this rule include only the following:

a) areas designated by posting as allowing swimming. Where lifeguards are not posted, no person under 17 years of age may swim or be on the beach without supervision of a parent, guardian, or responsible adult present, or

b) areas where a Department employed lifeguard is on duty, or

c) areas posted for other uses such as waterfowl hunters, water skiers, wading anglers, or scuba divers.

d) areas authorized for Scuba diving. Scuba divers must have in their possession valid permits issued by the Department. Permits are issued to keep track of name and location of divers, to ensure that divers are certified by a recognized entity and to minimize conflicts.

(Source: Amended at 13 Ill. Reg. 3785, effective March 13, 1989.)

Section 110.160 Vehicles—Operation on Roadway—Speed—Parking—Weight Limit

a) For any person to operate any motor vehicle other than on roadways specifically posted as trafficways by the Department of Conservation, except that Site Superintendents shall, if it is to the Department's benefit, grant written permission to individuals or contractors to operate vehicles on other than roadways specifically posted as trafficways. These exceptions will include, but not be limited to access by lessees to leased property or adjacent private property; access by contractors to the contract work site(s); access by volunteers to project or program areas which assist the site.

    1) For any person to operate a snowmobile in any area other than on posted trails as provided in 17 Ill. Adm. Code 2090 except that Site Superintendents shall, if it is to the Department's benefit, grant written permission to individuals to operate snowmobiles on other than posted trails. These exceptions will include, but not be limited to, access by lessees to leased property or adjacent private property; access by contractors to the contract work site(s); access by volunteers to project or program areas which assist the site.

    2) For any person to operate any motor driven bicycle, mini-bike, motorcycle or off-road vehicle unless it is on a roadway designated for vehicular use or on a designated area established by the Department for off-road vehicular use, except that Site Superintendents shall, if it is to the Department's benefit, grant written permission to individuals to operate such vehicles on areas other than those designated for off-road vehicular use. These exceptions will include, but not be limited to, access by lessees to leased property or adjacent private property; access by contractors to the contract work site(s); access by volunteers to project or program areas which assist the site.

b) To exceed a speed of 20 M.P.H. unless it is otherwise posted by sign on any paved, concrete, asphalt or other all-weather roadway, or to exceed 10 M.P.H. unless otherwise posted by sign on any unpaved, gravel or dirt roadway or in any parking area.

c) For any person to park a motor vehicle in any prohibited area which is posted with signs, or to park a vehicle in any area for the purpose of repair, except those immediate repairs necessary to remove the vehicle from the area immediately.

d) To exceed a combined vehicle and content weight limit of 20,000 lbs. (10 tons) unless it is otherwise posted by sign on any Department roadway except that Site Superintendents shall, if it is to the Department's benefit, grant written permission to individuals or contractors to operate such vehicles on posted roadways. These exceptions will include, but not be limited to, access by lessees utilizing farm equipment to get to leased property or adjacent private property; access by contractors to the contract work site(s); access by vendors delivering materials.

e) It is unlawful for any person to operate a snowmobile in any portion of a park or recreation area with less than four inches of snow cover.

(Source: Amended at 10 Ill. Reg. 9797, effective May 21, 1986.)

Section 110.170   Weapons and Firearms—Display and Use
For any person, other than authorized peace officers, to display or use on Department-controlled lands, except as authorized by the Department on hunting (reference 17 Ill. Adm. Code 510, 530, 550, 570, 590, 650, 670, 690, 710, 730, and 740), field trials (reference 17 Ill. Adm. Code 910), target or special event areas, any gun including shotgun, rifle, pistol, revolver, air or BB gun, sling shot, bow and arrow, switchblade knife with spring-loaded blade, throwing knife, tomahawk or throwing axe, or martial arts devices.

(Source: Amended at 10 Ill. Reg. 9797, effective May 21, 1986.)

Section 110.180   Violation of Rule
a) Any person who violates any provision of this rule (Section 110.20 through Section 110.170) shall be guilty of a Class B Misdemeanor.

b) Any person who violates any provision of this rule (Section 110.10 through Section 110.170) shall be subject to arrest and/or removal from the premises under applicable statutes including Section 21–5 of the Criminal Code of 1961 (Ill. Rev. Stat. 1987, ch. 38, par. 21–5), Criminal Trespass to State Supported Land.

(Source: Amended at 13 Ill. Reg. 3785, effective March 13, 1989.)

Appendix B

Regulation of Public Use of Illinois Dedicated Nature Preserves — Article 64

It is Unlawful:

1. For any person to enter any dedicated nature preserve or portion thereof if such area has been closed to visitors by notice posted by the Department of Conservation or a duly authorized agent thereof.

2. For any person to possess or consume or be under the influence of intoxicating beverages, including beer, or dangerous or narcotic drugs in any dedicated nature preserve.

3. For any person to camp or place a tent or trailer or any type of camping device in a dedicated nature preserve.

4. For any person to cut, break, injure, destroy, take or remove any tree, shrub, timber, flower, plant, or other natural object including rocks, soil, or water from a dedicated nature preserve; except that small quantities of such materials may be collected and removed for scientific or educational purposes by written permit from the owner, the Department of Conservation and the Illinois Nature Preserves Commission, and except for management under direct supervision of a designated agent.

5. For any person to kill, cause to be killed, harass, pursue, or take any animal, whether mammal, bird, fish, reptile amphibian, or invertebrate on its nest or habitat in a dedicated nature preserve; except that small quantities of such materials may be collected and removed for scientific or educational purposes by written permit from the owner, the Department of Conservation and the Illinois Nature Preserves Commission, and except for management purposes under the direct supervision of a designated agent with the approval of the Illinois Nature Preserves Commission and the Department of Conservation.

6. For any person to conduct scientific research in a dedicated nature preserve without a written permit from the owner, the Department of Conservation and the Illinois Nature Preserves Commission.

7. For any person to possess a firearm, airgun, slingshot, bow and arrow, or any other weapon within the boundaries of any designated nature preserve, except authorized peace officers and as authorized for management and control measures

for wildlife population control under the supervision of a designated agent with the approval of the Illinois Nature Preserves Commission and the Department of Conservation.

8. For any person to take, mutilate, deface, move, or destroy any structure, improvement, work, or sign, or any stone, soil, or other natural object or material in any dedicated nature preserve, except for management under the direct supervision of a designated agent.

9. For any person to operate a motor vehicle in any dedicated nature preserve other than on designated roadways or parking areas or to park a motor vehicle except in designated parking areas, except for maintenance and management vehicles operated by designated agents.

10. For any person to operate a motor vehicle in a reckless manner, or to exceed posted speed limits on roadways within any dedicated nature preserve.

11. For any person to build or light any fire or willfully or carelessly permit any fire which has ignited or been caused to ignite or which is under his charge and care to spread or extend to or burn any part of a dedicated nature preserve, except for prescribed burning for vegetation management under the direct supervision of a designated agent.

12. For any person to discard rubbish of any kind in any dedicated nature preserve except in designated containers provided by the Department of Conservation or a duly authorized agent thereof.

13. For any person to bring or allow to enter into a dedicated nature preserve any dog, cat, horse, or other animal or pet, except that horses may be brought into areas where bridle trails are designated and posted.

14. For any person to engage in disorderly conduct within any dedicated nature preserve.

15. For any person to engage in any sporting or athletic activity, including swimming, within the boundaries of any dedicated nature preserve.

16. For admittance to be granted to groups of 25 or more persons to any nature preserve unless written permission from the Department of Conservation or other owner has been secured in advance. Groups of 25 or more will be granted permission to visit preserves if the groups do not exceed the capacity of the facility. The Site Superintendent of the affected facility shall grant permits, in advance, to groups wanting to use the facility.

17. For any group of minors to enter any dedicated nature preserve without adequate supervision. At least one responsible adult shall accompany each group of not more than 15 minors.

18. For any person to plant or disperse any native or non-native plant species or their parts into any dedicated Illinois Nature Preserve without the written approval of the Illinois Department of Conservation and the Illinois Nature Preserves Commission.

19. For any person to release or disperse any native or non-native animal species into any dedicated Illinois Nature Preserve without the written approval of the Illinois Department of Conservation and the Illinois Nature Preserves Commission.

Criteria that will be used to evaluate requests under parts 18 and 19 include:

a. Is there evidence that the species formerly occurred on the preserve or that the habitat was suitable and was probably occupied by the species.

b. Are the habitat and other ecological conditions presently suitable and adequate to support the species.

c. What is the source of origin and genotype of the proposed introductions and is it the same as that was originally occurring on the preserve.

d. Will the introduction threaten the population for which it is being taken.

e. Will the introduction threaten any species or communities presently considered desirable on the preserve.

(*Source: "A Directory of Illinois Nature Preserves; Illinois Department of Conservation and Illinois Nature Preserves Commission, 1982."*)

Appendix C

Parks, Forests, and Public Property — Title 36, Part 261, Prohibitions, Subpart A, General Prohibitions [in the National Forest System]

. . . .

Authority: 16 U.S.C. 551; U.S.C. 472; 7 U.S.C. 1011(f); U.S.C. 1246(i); 16 U.S.C. 1133(c)–(d)(1).

(Source: 42 FR 2957, Jan. 14, 1977, unless otherwise noted.)

261.1   Scope.
  (a) The prohibitions in this part apply, except as otherwise provided, when:
            (1) An act or omission occurs in the National Forest System or on a Forest development road or trail.

(2) An act or omission affects, threatens, or endangers property of the United States administered by the Forest Service.

(3) An act or omission affects, threatens, or endangers a person using, or engaged in the protection, improvement or administration of the National Forest System or a Forest development road or trail.

(4) An act or omission occurs within the designated boundaries of a component of the national Wild and Scenic Rivers System.

(b) Nothing in this part shall preclude activities as authorized by the Wilderness Act of 1964 or the U.S. Mining Laws Act of 1872 as amended.

[42 FR 35958, July 13, 1977, as amended at 43 FR 32136, July 25, 1978; 46 FR 33519, June 30, 1981]

261.1a Special use authorizations, contracts, and operating plans.
The Chief, each Regional Forester, each Forest Supervisor, and each District Ranger or equivalent officer may issue special-use authorizations, award contracts, or approve operating plans authorizing the occupancy or use of a road, trail, area, river, lake, or other part of the National Forest System in accordance with authority which is delegated elsewhere in this chapter or the Forest Service manual. These Forest Officers may permit in the authorizing document or approved plan an act or omission that would otherwise be a violation of a subpart A or subpart C regulation or a subpart B order. In authorizing such uses, the Forest Officer may place such conditions on the authorization as that officer considers necessary for the protection or administration of the National Forest System, or for the promotion of public health, safety, or welfare.

[49 FR 25450, June 21, 1984]

261.1b Penalty.
Any violation of the prohibitions of this part (261) shall be punished by a fine of not more than $500 or imprisonment for not more than six months or both pursuant to title 16 U.S.C., section 551, unless otherwise provided.

[46 FR 33519, June 30, 1981]

261.2   Definitions.

The following definitions apply to this part:

Archaeological resource means any material remains of prehistoric or historic human life or activities which are of archaeological interest and are at least 50 years of age, and the physical site, location, or context in which they are found.

Campfire means a fire, not within any building, mobile home or living accommodation mounted on a motor vehicle, which is used for cooking, personal warmth, lighting, ceremonial, or esthetic purposes. Fire includes campfire.

Camping means the temporary use of National Forest System lands for the purpose of overnight occupancy without a permanently-fixed structure.

Camping equipment means the personal property used in or suitable for camping, and includes any vehicle used for transportation and all equipment in possession of a person camping. Food and beverage are not considered camping equipment.

Damaging means to injure, mutilate, deface, destroy, cut, chop, girdle, dig, excavate, kill or in any way harm or disturb.

Developed recreation site means an area which has been improved or developed for recreation.

Forest development road means a road wholly or partly within or adjacent to and serving a part of the National Forest System and which has been included in the Forest Development Road System Plan.

Forest development trail means a trail wholly or partly within or adjacent to and serving a part of the National Forest System and which has been included in the Forest Development Trail System Plan.

Forest officer means an employee of the Forest Service.

Historical resource means any structural, architectural, archaeological, artifactual or other material remains of past human life or activities which are of historical interest and are at least 50 years of age, and the physical site, location, or context in which they are found.

Motorized equipment means any machine activated by a nonliving power source except small battery-powered handcarried devices such as flashlights, shavers, Geiger counters, and cameras.

Motor vehicle means any vehicle which is self-propelled or any vehicle which is propelled by electric power obtained from batteries, but not operated on rails.

National Forest System includes all national forest lands and waters reserved or withdrawn from the public domain of the United States, national forest lands and waters acquired through purchase, exchange, donation, or other means, national grasslands and land utilization projects and waters administered under title III of the Bankhead-Jones Farm Tenant Act (50 Stat. 525, 7 U.S.C. 1010–1012), and other lands, waters, or interests therein acquired under the Wild and Scenic River Act (16 U.S.C. 1271–1287) or National Trails System Act (16 U.S.C. 1241–1249).

National Forest wilderness means those parts of the National Forest System which were designated units of the National Wilderness Preservation System by the Wilderness Act of September 3, 1964, and such other areas of the National Forest System as are added to the wilderness system by act of Congress.

Operating plan means a plan of operations as provided for in 36 CFR part 228, subpart A, and a surface use plan of operations as provided for in 36 CFR part 228, subpart E.

Paleontological resource means any evidence of fossilized remains of multi-cellular invertebrate and vertebrate animals and multicellular plants, including imprints thereof. Organic remains primarily collected for use as fuel such as coal and oil are Paleontological Resources, but are excluded from the prohibitions under the rule.

Person means natural person, corporation, company partnership, trust, firm or association of persons.

Permission means oral authorization by a Forest Officer.

Permit means authorization in writing by a Forest Officer.

Prehistoric resource means any structural, architectural, archaeological remains of past human life or activity generally prior to the advent of written records and of anthropological interest, and the physical site, location, or context in which they are found.

Primitive areas are those areas within the National Forest System classified as Primitive on the effective date of the Wilderness Act, September 3, 1964.

Publicly nude means nude in any place where a person may be observed by another person. Any person is nude if the person has failed to cover the rectal area, pubic area or genitals. A female person is also nude if she has failed to cover both breasts below a point immediately above the top of the areola. Each such covering must be fully opaque. No person under the age of 10 years shall be considered publicly nude.

Special-use authorization means a permit, term permit, lease or easement which allows occupancy, or use of rights or privileges of National Forest System land.

State means any State, the Commonwealth of Puerto Rico, and the District of Columbia.

State law means the law of any State in whose exterior boundaries an act or omission occurs regardless of whether State law is otherwise applicable.

Stove fire means a campfire built inside an enclosed stove or grill, a portable brazier, or a pressurized liquid or gas stove, including a space-heating device.

Unauthorized livestock means any cattle, sheep, goat, hog, or equine not defined as a wild free-roaming horse or burro by 222.20(b)(13), which is not authorized by permit to be upon the land on which the livestock is located and which is not related to use authorized by a grazing permit; provided, that noncommercial pack and saddle stock used by recreationists, travelers, other Forest visitors for occasional trips, as well as livestock to be trailed over an established driveway when there is no overnight stop on Forest Service administered land do not fall under this definition.

Vehicle means any device in, upon, or by which any person or property is or may be transported, including any frame, chassis, or body of any motor vehicle, except devices used exclusively upon stationary rails or tracks.

Volunteer or hosted enrollee means any person, not a Forest Service employee, officially participating in a Forest Service human resource program as authorized by an act of Congress and identified to accomplish one or more of the following objectives: provide skill training; education; useful work; develop understanding of ecological systems and conservation of natural resources; build cultural and communication bridges between various socioeconomic groups; and further the administration, development, and management of National Forest resources, forest research, and State and Private Forest activities.

Wild free-roaming horses and burros means all unbranded and unclaimed horses and burros and their progeny that have used lands of the National Forest System on or after December 15, 1971, or do hereafter use these lands as all or part of their habitat, but does not include any horse or burro introduced onto National Forest System lands on or after December 15, 1971, by accident, negligence or willful disregard of private ownership. Unbranded, claimed horses and burros, where the claim is found to be erroneous, are also considered as wild and free-roaming if they meet the criteria above.

[42 FR 2957, Jan. 14, 1977, as amended at 42 FR 35959, July 13, 1977; 46 FR 33519, June 30, 1981; 47 FR 29230, July 6, 1982; 49 FR 25450, June 24, 1984; 51 FR 1250, Jan. 10, 1986; 55 FR 10452, Mar. 21, 1990]

261.3   Interfering with a Forest Officer, volunteer, or human resource program enrollee or giving false report to a Forest Officer.
The following are prohibited:

(a) Threatening, resisting, intimidating, or interfering with any Forest Officer engaged in or on account of the performance of his official duties in the protection, improvement, or administration of the National Forest System is prohibited.

(b) Giving any false, fictitious or fraudulent report or other information to any Forest Officer engaged in or on account of the performance of his official duties knowing that such report or other information contains false, fictitious or fraudulent statement or entry.

(c) Threatening, intimidating, or intentionally interfering with any Forest Officer, volunteer, or human resource program enrollee while engaged in, or on account of, the performance of duties for the protection, improvement, or administration of the National Forest System or other duties assigned by the Forest Service.

[42 FR 2957, Jan 14, 1977, as amended at 46 FR 33520, June 30, 1981; 49 FR 25450, June 21, 1984]

261.4   Disorderly conduct.
The following are prohibited:

(a) Engaging in fighting.

(b) Addressing any offensive, derisive, or annoying communication to any other person who is lawfully present when such communication has a direct tendency to cause acts of violence by the person to whom, individually, the remark is addressed.

(c) Make statements or other actions directed toward inciting or producing imminent lawless action and likely to incite or produce such action.

(d) Causing public inconvenience, annoyance, or alarm by making unreasonably loud noise.

[46 FR 33520, June 30, 1981]

261.5   Fire.
The following are prohibited:

(a) Carelessly or negligently throwing or placing any ignited substance or other substance that may cause a fire.

(b) Firing any tracer bullet or incendiary ammunition.

(c) Causing timber, trees, slash, brush or grass to burn except as authorized by permit.

(d) Leaving a fire without completely extinguishing it.

(e) Allowing a fire to escape from control.

(f) Building, attending, maintaining, or using a campfire without removing all flammable material from around the campfire adequate to prevent its escape.

[42 FR 2957, Jan. 14, 1977, as amended at 40 FR 33520, June 30, 1981]

261.6   Timber and other forest products.
The following are prohibited:

(a) Cutting or otherwise damaging any timber, tree, or other forest product, except as authorized by a special-use authorization, timber sale contract, or Federal law or regulation.

(b) Cutting any standing tree, under permit or timber sale contract, before a Forest Officer has marked it or has otherwise designated it for cutting.

(c) Removing any timber or other forest product cut under permit or timber sale contract, except to a place designated for scaling, or removing it from that place before it is scaled, measured, counted, or otherwise accounted for by a Forest Officer.

(d) Stamping, marking with paint, or otherwise identifying any tree or other forest product in a manner similar to that employed by Forest Officers to mark or designate a tree or any other forest product for cutting or removal.

(e) Loading, removing or hauling timber or other forest product acquired under any permit or timber sale contract unless such product is identified as required in such permit or contract.

(f) Selling or exchanging any timber or other forest product obtained under free use pursuant to 223.5 through 223.11.

(g) Violating any timber export or substitution restriction in 223.160 through 223.164.

(h) Removing any timber, tree or other forest product, except as authorized by a special-use authorization, timber sale contract, or Federal law or regulation.

[42 FR 2957, Jan. 14, 1977; 42 FR 24739, May 16, 1977, as amended at 49 FR 25450, June 21, 1984; 51 FR 1250, Jan. 10, 1986]

261.7   Livestock.
The following are prohibited:

(a) Placing or allowing unauthorized livestock to enter or be in the National Forest System or other lands under Forest Service control.

(b) Not removing unauthorized livestock from the National Forest System or other lands under Forest Service control when requested by a Forest Officer.

(c) Failing to reclose any gate or other entry.

(d) Molesting, injuring, removing, or releasing any livestock impounded under 262.10 while in the custody of the Forest Service or its authorized agents.

[42 FR 35959, July 13, 1977, as amended at 51 FR 1251, Jan. 10, 1986]

261.8   Fish and wildlife.
The following are prohibited to the extent Federal or State law is violated:

(a) Hunting, trapping, fishing, catching, molesting, killing or having in possession any kind of wild animal, bird, or fish, or taking the eggs of any such bird.

(b) Possessing a firearm or other implement designed to discharge a missile capable of destroying animal life.

(c) Possessing equipment which could be used for hunting, fishing, or trapping.

(d) Possessing a dog not on a leash or otherwise confined.

[42 FR 2957, Jan. 14, 1977, as amended at 46 FR 33520, June 30, 1981]

261.9   Property.
The following are prohibited:

(a) Damaging any natural feature or other property of the United States.

(b) Removing any natural feature or other property of the United States.

(c) Damaging any plant that is classified as a threatened, endangered, sensitive, rare, or unique species.

(d) Removing any plant that is classified as a threatened, endangered, sensitive, rare or unique species.

(e) Entering any building, structure, or enclosed area owned or controlled by the United States when such building, structure, or enclosed area is not open to the public.

(f) Using any pesticide except for personal use as an insect repellent or as provided by special-use authorization for other minor uses.

(g) Digging, excavating, disturbing, injuring, destroying, or in any way damaging any prehistoric, historic, or archaeological resource, structure, site, artifact, or property.

(h) Removing any prehistoric, historic, or archaeological

resource, structure, site, artifact, property.

(i) Excavating, damaging, or removing any vertebrate fossil or removing any paleontological resource for commercial purposes without a special use authorization.

[46 FR 33520, June 30, 1981, as amended at 49 FR 25450, June 21, 1984; 51 FR 30356, Aug. 26, 1986]

261.10 Occupancy and use.
The following are prohibited:

(a) Constructing, placing, or maintaining any kind of road, trail, structure, fence, enclosure, communication equipment, or other improvement on National Forest System land or facilities without a special-use authorization, contract, or approved operating plan.

(b) Taking possession of, occupying, or otherwise using National Forest System lands for residential purposes without a special-use authorization, or as otherwise authorized by Federal law or regulation.

(c) Selling or offering for sale any merchandise or conducting any kind of work activity or service unless authorized by Federal law, regulation, or special-use authorization.

(d) Discharging a firearm or any other implement capable of taking human life, causing injury, or damaging property:

    (1) In or within 150 yards of a residence, building, campsite, developed recreation site or occupied area, or

    (2) Across or on a Forest Development road or a body of water adjacent thereto, or in any manner or place whereby any person or property is exposed to injury or damage as a result in such discharge.

(e) Abandoning any personal property.

(f) Placing a vehicle or other object in such a manner that it is an impediment or hazard to the safety or convenience of any person.

(g) Disseminating, posting, placing, or erecting any paper, notice, advertising material, sign, handbill, petition, or similar written and/or graphic matter without a special use authorization.

(h) Operating or using in or near a campsite, developed recreation site, or over an adjacent body of water without a permit, any device which produces noise, such as a radio, television, musical instrument, motor or engine in such a manner and at such a time so as to unreasonably disturb any person.

(i) Operating or using a public address system, whether fixed, portable or vehicle mounted, in or near a campsite or developed recreation site or over an adjacent body of water without a special-use authorization.

(j) Use or occupancy of National Forest System land or facilities without special-use authorization when such authorization is required.

(k) Violating any term or condition of a special-use authorization, contract or approved operating plan.

(l) Failing to stop a vehicle when directed to do so by a Forest Officer.

(m) Failing to pay any special use fee or other charges as required.

[42 FR 2957, Jan. 14, 1977, as amended at 46 FR 33520, June 30, 1981; 49 FR 25450, June 21, 1984; 53 Fr 16550, May 10, 1988]

261.11   Sanitation.
The following are prohibited:

(a) Depositing in any toilet, toilet vault, or plumbing fixture any substance which could damage or interfere with the operation or maintenance of the fixture.

(b) Possessing or leaving refuse, debris, or litter in an exposed or unsanitary condition.

(c) Placing in or near a stream, lake, or other water any substance which does or may pollute a stream, lake, or other water.

(d) Failing to dispose of all garbage, including any paper, can, bottle, sewage, waste water material, or rubbish either by removal from the site or area, or by depositing it into receptacles or at places provided for such purposes.

(e) Dumping of any refuse, debris, trash or litter brought as such from private property or from land occupied under permit, except, where a container, dump or similar facility has been provided and is identified as such, to receive trash generated from private lands or lands occupied under permit.

[42 FR 2957, Jan. 14, 1977, as amended at 46 FR 33520, June 30, 1981]

261.12   Forest development roads and trails.
The following are prohibited:

(a) Violating the load, weight, height, length, or width limitations prescribed by State law except by special-use authorization or written agreement or by order issued under 261.54 of this chapter.

(b) Failing to have a vehicle weighed at a Forest Service weighing station, if required by a sign.

(c) Damaging and leaving in a damaged condition any such road, trail, or segment thereof.

(d) Blocking, restricting, or otherwise interfering with the use of a road, trail, or gate.

[42 FR 2957, Jan. 14, 1977, as amended at 46 FR 33520, June 30, 1981; 49 FR 25450, June 21, 1984; 55 FR 25832, June 25, 1990]

261.13   Use of vehicles off roads.
It is prohibited to operate any vehicle off Forest Development, State or County roads:

(a) Without a valid license as required by State law.

(b) Without an operable braking system.

(c) From one-half hour after sunset to one-half hour before sunrise unless equipped with working head and tail lights.

(d) In violation of any applicable noise emission standard established by any Federal or State agency.

(e) While under the influence of alcohol or other drugs.

(f) Creating excessive or unusual smoke.

(g) Carelessly, recklessly, or without regard for the safety of any person, or in a manner that endangers, or is likely to endanger, any person or property.

(h) In a manner which damages or unreasonably disturbs the land, wildlife, or vegetative resources.

(i) In violation of State law established for vehicles used off roads.

[42 FR 2957, Jan. 14, 1977, as amended at 42 FR 35959, July 13, 1977]

261.14   Developed recreation sites.
The following are prohibited:

(a) Occupying any portion of the site for other than recreation purposes.

(b) Building, attending, maintaining, or using a fire outside of a fire ring provided by the Forest Service for such purpose or outside of a stove, grill or fireplace.

(c) Cleaning or washing any personal property, fish, animal, or food, or bathing, or washing, at a hydrant or water faucet not provided for that purpose.

(d) Discharging or igniting a firecracker, rocket, or other firework, or explosive.

(e) Occupying between 10 p.m. and 6 a.m. a place designated for day use only.

(f) Failing to remove all camping equipment or personal property when vacating the area or site.

(g) Placing, maintaining, or using camping equipment except in a place specifically designated or provided for such equipment.

(h) Without permission, failing to have at least one person occupy a camping area during the first night after camping equipment has been set up.

(i) Leaving camping equipment unattended for more than 24 hours without permission.

(j) Bringing in or possessing in a swimming area an animal except as authorized by posted instructions.

(k) Bringing in or possessing in a swimming area an animal, other than a Seeing Eye dog.

(l) Bringing in or possesing a saddle, pack, or draft animal except as authorized by posted instructions.

(m) Operating or parking a motor vehicle or trailer except in places developed or designated for this purpose.

(n) Operating a bicycle, motorbike, or motorcycle on a trail unless designated for this use.

(o) Operating a motorbike, motorcycle, or other motor vehicle for any purpose other than entering or leaving the site.

(p) Disturbing any handbill, circular, paper or notice without a special-use authorization.

(q) Depositing any body waste except into receptacles provided for that purpose.

[42 FR 2957, Jan. 14, 1977, as amended at 46 FR 33520, June 30, 1981; 49 FR 25450, June 21, 1984]

261.15   Admission, recreation use and special recreation permit fees.
Failing to pay any fee established for admission or entrance to or use of a site, facility, equipment or service furnished by the United States is prohibited. The maximum fine shall not exceed $100.

(Sec. 2, 78 Stat. 897, as amended; 16 U.S.C. 4601–6[e])

[46 FR 33520, June 30, 1981]

261.16   National Forest Wilderness.
The following are prohibited in a National Forest Wilderness:

(a) Possessing or using a motor vehicle, motorboat or motorized equipment except as authorized by Federal law or regulation.

(b) Possessing or using a hang glider or bicycle.

(c) Landing of aircraft, or dropping or picking up of any

material, supplies, or person by means of aircraft, including a
helicopter.

*[42 FR 2957, Jan 14, 1977, as amended at 42 FR 35959, July 13,
1977; 50 FR 16231, Apr. 25, 1985]*

Appendix D

Illinois Wilderness Act of 1990—Public Law 101-633, November 28, 1990, 101st Congress

An Act

To designate certain public lands in the State of Illinois as wilderness, and for other purposes.

Be it enacted by the Senate and House of Representatives of the United States of America in Congress assembled,

Sec. 1. Short Title.
This Act may be cited as the "Illinois Wilderness Act of 1990."

Sec. 2. Findings.
In designating wilderness areas in the Shawnee National Forest pursuant to this Act, the Congress finds, as provided in the Wilderness Act, that such areas—

(1) generally appear to have been affected primarily by the forces of nature, with the imprint of man's work substantially unnoticeable;

(2) have outstanding opportunities for solitude or a primitive and unconfined type of recreation; and

(3) contain ecological, geological, and other features of scientific, educational, and scenic value.

Sec. 3. Designation of Wilderness Areas.
In furtherance of the purposes of the Wilderness Act (16 U.S.C. 1131 et seq.), the following lands in the Shawnee National Forest in the State of Illinois are hereby designated as wilderness and therefore as components of the National Wilderness Preservation System—

(1) certain lands comprising approximately 5,918 acres, as generally depicted on a map entitled "Bald Knob Wilderness—Proposed," dated July 1990, and which shall be known as the Bald Knob Wilderness;

(2) certain lands comprising approximately 2,866 acres, as generally depicted on a map entitled "Bay Creek Wilderness—Proposed," dated July 1990, and which shall be known as the Bay Creek Wilderness;

(3) certain lands comprising approximately 3,723 acres, as generally depicted on a map entitled "Burden Falls Wilderness — Proposed," dated July 1990, and which shall be known as Burden Falls Wilderness;

(4) certain lands comprising approximately 4,730 acres, as generally depicted on a map entitled "Clear Springs Wilderness — Proposed," dated July 1990, and which shall be known as the Clear Springs Wilderness;

(5) certain lands comprising approximately 3,293 acres, as generally depicted on a map entitled "Garden of the Gods Wilderness — Proposed," dated July 1990, and which shall be known as the Garden of the Gods Wilderness;

(6) certain lands comprising approximately 4,796 acres, as generally depicted on a map entitled "Lusk Creek Wilderness — Proposed," dated July 1990, and which shall be known as the Lusk Creek Wilderness; and

(7) certain lands comprising approximately 940 acres, as generally depicted on a map entitled "Panther Den Wilderness — Proposed," dated July 1990, and which shall be known as Panther Den Wilderness.

Sec. 4. Description and Maps.

As soon as practicable after the enactment of this Act, the Secretary of Agriculture (hereafter in this Act referred to as the "Secretary") shall file maps and legal descriptions of each wilderness area designated by this Act with the Committee on Agriculture, Nutrition, and Forestry of the Senate, and the Committees on Agriculture and Interior and Insular Affairs of the House of Representatives. Each such map and legal description shall have the same force and effect as if included in this Act, except that correction of clerical and typographical errors in such legal descriptions and maps may be made. Each such map and legal description shall be on file and available for public inspection in the office of the Chief of the Forest Service, Department of Agriculture.

Sec. 5. Administration of Wilderness Areas.

Subject to valid existing rights, each wilderness area designated by this Act shall be administered by the Secretary in accordance with the provisions of the Wilderness Act, except that any reference in such provisions to the effective date of the Wilderness Act shall be deemed to be a reference to the effective date of this Act.

Sec. 6. Adjacent Areas.

Congress does not intend that designation of wilderness areas in the State of Illinois lead to the creation of protective perimeters or buffer zones around each wilderness area. The fact that nonwilderness activities or uses can be seen or heard from areas within the wilderness shall not, of itself, preclude such activities or uses up to the boundary of the wilderness areas.

Sec. 7. Hunting, Fishing, and Disease Control.
As provided in section 4(d)(7) of the Wilderness Act, nothing in this Act shall be construed as affecting the jurisdiction or responsibilities of the State of Illinois with respect to wildlife and fish in the national forests in Illinois.

Sec. 8. Fire, Insects, and Disease Control.
As provided in section 4(d)(1) of the Wilderness Act, the Secretary may take such measures as may be necessary to control fire, insects, and diseases within any area designated by this Act.

Sec. 9. Cemetery Access.
The Secretary shall permit relatives and descendants of those interred in cemeteries located within the wilderness areas designated by this Act, and those accompanying such relatives and descendants, to access and maintain such cemeteries. The Secretary shall regulate such appropriate access and maintenance to minimize any detrimental effects on the wilderness resource or any uses incompatible with the provisions of the Wilderness Act.

Sec. 10. Designation of Special Management Areas.
   (a) Area Designations—(1) Mining and prospecting for fluorspar and associated minerals shall be permitted in the lands in the Shawnee National Forest described in paragraph (2) in accordance with this section and other applicable law. These lands shall also be managed, to the extent practicable, to preserve their potential for future inclusion in the National Wilderness Preservation System.
   (2) The lands Described in this paragraph are—
      (A) certain lands comprising approximately 2,042 acres as generally depicted on a map entitled "East Fork Area—Proposed," dated July 1990, and which shall be known as the East Fork Area; and
      (B) certain lands comprising approximately 722 acres as generally depicted on a map entitled "Eagle Creek Area—Proposed," dated July 1990, and which shall be known as the Eagle Creek Area.
   (b) Time Limitation—Prospecting for fluorspar and associated minerals in the lands described in subsection (a)(2) may be allowed for a period of not more than 8 years beginning on

the date of enactment of this Act. If significant deposits of fluorspar and associated minerals are found to exist in parts or all of such lands, then mining for those minerals may be allowed for a 20-year period beginning on the date of enactment of this Act.

   (c) Mineral Rights—Nothing in this section shall be construed to change in any way the process by which mining and prospecting permits and rights are granted on National Forest System lands.

   (d) Cessation of Certain Uses—Twenty years following the date of enactment of this Act (or 8 years following enactment if no prospecting for fluorspar and associated minerals has been done, as determined by the Secretary), such lands described in subsection (a)(2) shall be designated as wilderness and components of the National Wilderness Preservation System, in furtherance of the purposes of the Wilderness Act (16 U.S.C. 1131 et seq.).

Approved November 28, 1990.

Appendix E

National Wilderness Preservation System—United States
Code, Chapter 23, Title 16, Conservation

Sec.
1131. **National Wilderness Preservation System.**
   (a) Establishment; Congressional declaration of poli-
       cy; wilderness areas; administration for public use
       and enjoyment, protection, preservation, and gath-
       ering and dissemination of information; provisions
       for designation as wilderness areas.
   (b) Management of area included in System; appro-
       priations.
   (c) "Wilderness" defined.

1132. **Extent of System.**
   (a) Designation of wilderness areas; filing of maps and
       descriptions with Congressional committees; cor-
       rection of errors; public records; availability of
       records in regional offices.
   (b) Review by Secretary of Agriculture of classifica-
       tions as primitive areas; Presidential recommenda-
       tions to Congress; approval of Congress; size of
       primitive areas; Gore Range–Eagles Nest Primitive
       Area, Colorado.
   (c) Review by Secretary of the Interior of roadless
       areas of national park system and national wildlife
       refuges and game ranges and suitability of areas for
       preservation as wilderness; authority of Secretary
       of the Interior to maintain roadless areas in nation-
       al park system unaffected.
   (d) Conditions precedent to administrative recommen-
       dations of suitability of areas for preservation as
       wilderness; publication in Federal Register; public
       hearings; views of State, county, and Federal offi-
       cials; submission of views to Congress.
   (e) Modification or adjustment of boundaries; public
       notice and hearings; administrative and executive
       recommendations to Congress; approval of Con-
       gress.

1133. Use of Wilderness Areas.
  (a) Purposes of national forests, national park system, and national wildlife refuge system; other provisions applicable to national forests, Superior National Forest, and national park system.
  (b) Agency responsibility for preservation and administration to preserve wilderness character; public purposes of wilderness areas.
  (c) Prohibition provisions: commercial enterprise, permanent or temporary roads, mechanical transports, and structures or installations; exceptions: area administration and personal health and safety emergencies.
  (d) Special provisions.

....

Chapter Referred to in Other Sections

1131. National Wilderness Preservation System.
(a) Establishment; Congressional declaration of policy; wilderness areas; administration for public use and enjoyment, protection, preservation, and gathering and dissemination of information; provisions for designation as wilderness areas.
   In order to assure that an increasing population, accompanied by expanding settlement and growing mechanization, does not occupy and modify all areas within the United States and its possessions, leaving no lands designated for preservation and protection in their natural condition, it is hereby declared to be the policy of the Congress to secure for the American people of present and future generations the benefits of an enduring resource of wilderness. For this purpose there is hereby established a National Wilderness Preservation System to be composed of federally owned areas designated by Congress as "wilderness areas," and these shall be administered for the use and enjoyment of the American people in such manner as will leave them unimpaired for future use and enjoyment as wilderness, and so as to provide for the protection of these areas, the preservation of their wilderness character, and for the gathering and dissemination of information regarding their use and enjoyment as wilderness: and no Federal lands shall be

designated as "wilderness areas" except as provided for in this chapter or by a subsequent Act.

(b) Management of area included in System; appropriations.
The inclusion of an area in the National Wilderness Preservation System notwithstanding, the area shall continue to be managed by the Department and agency having jurisdiction thereover immediately before its inclusion in the National Wilderness Preservation System unless otherwise provided by Act of Congress. No appropriation shall be available for the payment of expenses or salaries for the administration of the National Wilderness Preservation System as a separate unit nor shall any appropriations be available for additional personnel as being required solely for the purpose of managing or administering areas solely because they are included within the National Wilderness Preservation System.

(c) "Wilderness" defined.
A wilderness, in contrast with those areas where man and his works dominate the landscape, is hereby recognized as an area where the earth and its community of life are untrammeled by man, where man himself is a visitor who does not remain. An area of wilderness is further defined to mean in this chapter an area of underdeveloped Federal land retaining its primeval character and influence, without permanent improvements or human habitation, which is protected and managed so as to preserve its natural conditions and which (1) generally appears to have been affected primarily by the forces by nature, with the imprint of man's work substantially unnoticeable; (2) has outstanding opportunities for solitude or a primitive and unconfined type of recreation; (3) has at least five thousand acres of land or is of sufficient size as to make practicable its preservation and use in an unimpaired condition; and (4) may also contain ecological, geological, or other features of scientific, educational, scenic, or historical value.

(Pub. L. 88-577, 2, Sept. 3, 1964, 78 Stat. 890.)

Short Title

Section 1 of Pub. L. 88-577 provided that: "This Act [enacting this chapter] may be cited as the 'Wilderness Act.'"

Section Referred to in Other Sections

This section is referred to in title 43 section 1702.

1132. Extent of System.

(a) Designation of wilderness areas; filing of maps and descriptions with Congressional committees; correction of errors; public records; availability of records in regional offices.

All areas within the national forests classified at least 30 days before September 3, 1964, by the Secretary of Agriculture or the Chief of the Forest Service as "wilderness," "wild," or "canoe" are hereby designated as wilderness areas. The Secretary of Agriculture shall—

(1) Within one year after September 3, 1964, file a map and legal description of each wilderness area with the Interior and Insular Affairs Committees of the United States Senate and the House of Representatives, and such descriptions shall have the same force and effect as if included in this chapter; provided, however, that correction of clerical and typographical errors in such legal descriptions and maps may be made.

(2) Maintain, available to the public, records pertaining to said wilderness, including maps and legal descriptions, copies of regulations governing them, copies of public notices of, and reports submitted to Congress regarding pending additions, eliminations, or modifications. Maps, legal descriptions, and regulations pertaining to wilderness areas within their respective jurisdictions also shall be available to the public in the offices of regional foresters, national forest supervisors, and forest rangers.

(b) Review by Secretary of Agriculture of classifications as primitive areas; Presidential recommendations to Congress; approval of Congress; size of primitive areas; Gore Range– Eagles Nest Primitive Area, Colorado.

The Secretary of Agriculture shall, within ten years after September 3, 1964, review, as to its suitability or nonsuitability for preservation as wilderness, each area in the national forests classified on September 3, 1964, by the Secretary of Agriculture or the Chief of the Forest Service as "primitive" and report his findings to the President. The President shall advise the United States Senate and House of Representatives of his recommendations with respect to the designation as "wilderness" or other reclassification of each area on which review has been completed, together with maps and a definition of boundaries. Such advice shall be given with respect to not less than one-third of all the areas now classified as "primitive" within three years after September 3, 1964, not less than two-thirds within seven years after September 3, 1964, and the reamining areas within ten years after September 3, 1964. Each recommendation of the

President for designation as "wilderness" shall become effective only if so provided by an Act of Congress. Areas classified as "primitive" on September 3, 1964, shall continue to be administered under the rules and regulations affecting such areas on September 3, 1964, until Congress has determined otherwise. Any such area may be increased in size by the President at the time he submits his recommendations to the Congress by not more than five thousand acres with no more than one thousand two hundred and eighty acres of such increase in any one compact unit; if it is proposed to increase the size of any such area by more than five thousand acres or by more than one thousand two hundred and eighty acres in any one compact unit the increase in size shall not become effective until acted upon by Congress. Nothing herein contained shall limit the President in proposing, as part of his recommendations to Congress, the alteration of existing boundaries of primitive areas or recommending the addition of any contiguous area of national forest lands predominantly of wilderness value. Notwithstanding any other provisions of this chapter, the Secretary of Agriculture may complete his review and delete such area as may be necessary, but not to exceed seven thousand acres, from the southern tip of the Gore Range–Eagles Nest Primitive Area, Colorado, if the Secretary determines that such action is in the public interest.

(c) *Review by Secretary of the Interior of roadless areas of national park system and national wildlife refuges and game ranges and suitability of areas for preservation as wilderness; authority of Secretary of the Interior to maintain roadless areas in national park system unaffected.*

Within ten years after September 3, 1964, the Secretary of the Interior shall review every roadless area of five thousand contiguous acres or more in the national parks, monuments and other units of the national park system and every such area of, and every roadless island within the national wildlife refuges and game ranges, under his jurisdiction on September 3, 1964, and shall report to the President his recommendations as to the suitability or nonsuitability of each such area or island for preservation for wilderness. The President shall advise the President of the Senate and the Speaker of the House of Representatives of his recommendations with respect to the designation as wilderness of each such area or island on which review has been completed, together with a map thereof and a definition of its boundaries. Such advice shall be given with respect to not less than one-third of the areas and islands to be reviewed under this subsection within three years after September 3,

1964, not less than two-thirds within seven years of September 3, 1964, and the remainder within ten years of September 3, 1964. A recommendation of the President for designation as wilderness shall become effective only if so provided by an Act of Congress. Nothing contained herein shall, by implication or otherwise, be construed to lessen the present statutory authority of the Secretary of the Interior with respect to the maintenance of roadless areas within units of the national park system.

(d) Conditions precedent to administrative recommendations of suitability of areas for preservation as wilderness; publication in Federal Register; public hearings; views of State, county, and Federal officials; submission of views to Congress.

(1) The Secretary of Agriculture and the Secretary of the Interior shall, prior to submitting any recommendations to the president with respect to the suitability of any area for preservation as wilderness—

(A) give such public notice of the proposed action as they deem appropriate, including publication in the Federal Register and in a newspaper having general circulation in the area or areas in the vicinity of the affected land;

(B) hold a public hearing or hearings at a location or locations convenient to the area affected. The hearings shall be announced through such means as the respective Secretaries involved deem appropriate, including notices in the Federal Register and in newspapers of general circulation in the area: provided, that if the lands involved are located in more than one State, at least one hearing shall be held in each State in which a portion of the land lies;

(C) at least thirty days before the date of a hearing advise the Governor of each State and the governing board of each county, or in Alaska the borough, in which the lands are located, and Federal departments and agencies concerned, and invite such officials and Federal agencies to submit their views on the proposed action at the hearing or by no later than thirty days following the date of the hearing.

(2) Any views submitted to the appropriate Secretary under the provisions of (1) of this subsection with respect to any area shall be included with any recommendations to the President and to Congress with respect to such area.

(e) Modification or adjustment of boundaries; public notice and hearings; administrative and executive recommendations to Congress; approval of Congress.

Any modification or adjustment of boundaries of any wilderness area shall be recommended by the appropriate Secretary after public notice of such proposal and public hearing or hearings as provided in subsection (d) of this section. The proposed modification or adjustment shall then be recommended with map and description thereof to the President. The President shall advise the United States Senate and the House of Representatives of his recommendations with respect to such modification or adjustment and such recommendations shall become effective only in the same manner as provided for in subsections (b) and (c) of this section.

(Pub. L. 88-577, 3, Sept. 3, 1964, 78 Stat. 891.)

1133. Use of Wilderness Areas.
(a) Purposes of national forests, national park system, and national wildlife refuge system; other provisions applicable to national forests, Superior National Forest, and national park system.

The purposes of this chapter are hereby declared to be within and supplemental to the purposes for which national forests and units of the national park and national wildlife refuge systems are established and administered and—

(1) Nothing in this chapter shall be deemed to be in interference with the purpose for which national forests are established as set forth in the Act of June 4, 1897 (30 Stat. 11), and the Multi-Use Sustained-Yield Act of June 12, 1960 (74 Stat. 215) [16 U.S.C. 528–531].

(2) Nothing in this chapter shall modify the restrictions and provisions of the Shipstead-Nolan Act (Public Law 539, Seventy-first Congress, July 10, 1930; 46 Stat. 1020), the Thye-Blatnik Act (Public Law 733, Eightieth Congress, June 22, 1948; 62 Stat. 568), and the Humphrey-Thye-Blatnik-Anderson Act (Public Law 607, Eighty-Fourth Congress, June 22, 1956; 70 Stat. 326), as applying to the Superior National Forest or the regulations of the Secretary of Agriculture.

(3) Nothing in this chapter shall modify the statutory authority under which units of the national park system are created. Further, the designation of any area of any park, monument, or other unit of the national park system as a wilderness area pursuant to this chapter shall in no manner lower the standards evolved for the use and preservation of such park, monument, or other unit of the national park system in

accordance with sections 1 and 2 to 4 of this title, the statutory authority under which the area was created, or any other Act of Congress which might pertain to or affect such area, including, but not limited to, the Act of June 8, 1906 (34 Stat. 225; 16 U.S.C. 432 et seq.); section 3(2) of the Federal Power Act (16 U.S.C. 796[2]); and the Act of August 21, 1935 (49 Stat. 666; 16 U.S.C. 461 et seq.).

(b) Agency responsibility for preservation and administration to preserve wilderness character; public purposes of wilderness areas.

Except as otherwise provided in this chapter, each agency administering any area designated as wilderness shall be responsible for preserving the wilderness character of the area and shall so administer such area for such other purposes for which it may have been established as also to preserve its wilderness character. Except as otherwise provided in this chapter, wilderness areas shall be devoted to the public purposes of recreational, scenic, scientific, educational, conservation, and historical use.

(c) Prohibition provisions: commercial enterprise, permanent or temporary roads, mechanical transports, and structures or installations; exceptions: area administration and personal health and safety emergencies.

Except as specifically provided for in this chapter, and subject to existing private rights, there shall be no commercial enterprise and no permanent road within any wilderness area designated by this chapter and, except as necessary to meet minimum requirements for the administration of the area for the purpose of this chapter (including measures required in emergencies involving the health and safety of persons within the area), there shall be no temporary road, no use of motorized equipment or motorboats, no landing of aircraft, no other form of mechanical transport, and no structure or installation within any such area.

(d) Special provisions.

The following special provisions are hereby made:

(1) Aircraft or motorboats; fire, insects, and diseases.

Within wilderness areas designated by this chapter the use of aircraft or motorboats, where these uses have already become established, may be permitted to continue subject to such restrictions as the Secretary of Agriculture deems desirable. In addition, such measures may be taken as may be necessary in

the control of fire, insects, and diseases, subject to such conditions as the Secretary deems desirable.

(2) Mineral activities, surveys for mineral value.

Nothing in this chapter shall prevent within national forest
wilderness areas any activity, including prospecting, for the
purpose of gathering information about mineral or other resources, if such activity is carried on in a manner compatible
with the preservation of the wilderness environment. Furthermore, in accordance with such program as the Secretary of the
Interior shall develop and conduct in consultation with the
Secretary of Agriculture, such areas shall be surveyed on a
planned, recurring basis consistent with the concept of wilderness preservation by the Geological Survey and the Bureau of
Mines to determine the mineral values, if any, that may be
present; and the results of such surveys shall be made available
to the public and submitted to the President and Congress.

(3) Mining and mineral leasing laws; leases, permits, and
licenses; withdrawal of minerals from appropriation and
disposition.

Notwithstanding any other provisions of this chapter, until
midnight December 31, 1983, the United States mining laws and
all laws pertaining to mineral leasing shall, to the same extent as
applicable prior to September 3, 1964, extend to those national
forest lands designated by this chapter as "wilderness areas";
subject, however, to such reasonable regulations governing
ingress and egress as may be prescribed by the Secretary of
Agriculture consistent with the use of the land for mineral
location and development and exploration, drilling, and production, and use of land for transmission lines, waterlines,
telephone lines, or facilities necessary in exploring, drilling,
producing, mining, and processing operations, including where
essential the use of mechanized ground or air equipment and
restoration as near as practicable of the surface of the land
disturbed in performing prospecting, location, and, in oil and
gas leasing, discovery work, exploration, drilling, and production, as soon as they have served their purpose. Mining locations lying within the boundaries of said wilderness areas shall
be held and used solely for mining or processing operations and
uses reasonably incident thereto; and hereafter, subject to valid
existing rights, all patents issued under the mining laws of the
United States affecting national forest lands designated by this
chapter as wilderness areas shall convey title to the mineral
deposits within the claim, together with the right to cut and use
so much of the mature timber therefrom as may be needed in the

extraction, removal, and beneficiation of the mineral deposits, if needed timber is not otherwise reasonably available, and if the timber is cut under sound principles of forest management as defined by the national forest rules and regulations, but each such patent shall reserve to the United States all title in or to the surface of the lands and products thereof, and no use of the surface of the claim or the resources therefrom not reasonably required for carrying on mining or prospecting shall be allowed except as otherwise expressly provided in this chapter: provided, that, unless hereafter specifically authorized, no patent within wilderness areas designated by this chapter shall issue after December 31, 1983, except for the valid claims existing on or before December 31, 1983. Mining claims located after September 3, 1964, within the boundaries of wilderness areas designated by this chapter shall create no rights in excess of those rights which may be patented under the provisions of this subsection. Mineral leases, permits, and licenses covering lands within national forest wilderness areas designated by this chapter shall contain such reasonable stipulations as may be prescribed by the Secretary of Agriculture for the protection of the wilderness character of the land consistent with the use of the land for the purposes for which they are leased, permitted, or licensed. Subject to valid rights then existing, effective January 1, 1984, the minerals in lands designated by this chapter as wilderness areas are withdrawn from all forms of appropriation under the mining laws and from disposition under all laws pertaining to mineral leasing and all amendments thereto.

(4) Water resources, reservoirs, and other facilities; grazing.

Within wilderness areas in the national forests designated by this chapter, (1) the President may, within a specific area and in accordance with such regulations as he may deem desirable, authorize prospecting for water resources, the establishment and maintenance of reservoirs, water-conservation works, power projects, transmission lines, and other facilities needed in the public interest, including the road construction and maintenance essential to development and use thereof, upon his determination that such use or uses in the specific area will better serve the interests of the United States and the people thereof than will its denial; and (2) the grazing of livestock, where established prior to continue subject to such reasonable regulations as are deemed necessary by the Secretary of Agriculture.

(5) Commercial services.

Commercial services may be performed within the wilderness areas designated by this chapter to the extent necessary for activities which are proper for realizing the recreational or other wilderness purposes of the areas.

(6) State water laws exemption.

Nothing in this chapter shall constitute an express or implied claim or denial on the part of the Federal Government as to exemption from State water laws.

(7) State jurisdiction of wildlife and fish in national forests.

Nothing in this chapter shall be construed as affecting the jurisdiction or responsibilities of the several States with respect to wildlife and fish in the national forests.

(Pub. L. 88-577, 4, Sept. 3, 1964, 78 Stat. 893; Pub. L. 95-495, 4(b), Oct. 21, 1978, 92 Stat. 1650.)

Appendix F

The National Trails System Act and the National Recreation Trails in Illinois

The National Trails System Act (Public Law 90–543, as amended) was passed in 1968 and established a nationwide network of trails consisting of four categories: National Scenic Trails, National Historic Trails, National Recreation Trails (NRT), and connecting trails. National Recreation Trails provide a variety of outdoor recreation uses in or reasonably accessible to urban areas. National Scenic Trails are extended trails so located to provide for maximum outdoor recreation potential and for the conservation and enjoyment of the nationally significant scenic, historic, natural or cultural qualities of the areas through which such trails pass. National Historic Trails are extended trails which follow as closely as possible and practicable the original trails or routes of travel of national historical significance. Connecting or side trails also make up the National Trails System. Connecting trails provide additional points of public access to national recreation, national scenic, or national historic trails, or which will provide connections between such trails.

The bulk of the system consist of NRTs which generally are in or near urban areas and provide for a wide variety of trail experiences. In Illinois there are fourteen trails designated as NRTs, totaling 132 miles. In addition, the eastern end of the Mormon Pioneer National Historic Trail is located in Nauvoo, Illinois; the beginning point for the Lewis and Clark National Historic Trail is at Wood River, Illinois; and the Trail of Tears Historic Trail passes through southern Illinois.

The most recent update to the National Trails System Act is on the Illinois Trail. In September 1991, the Secretary of the Interior submitted a letter to Congress on the feasibility of including the Illinois Trail as a national historic trail as part of the National Trails System. The Secretary of Interior submitted a finding to Congress that the Illinois Trail should be designated a National Historic Trail.

Following is a list of the National Recreation Trails that are located in Illinois as of December 1991.

1. The Illinois Prairie Path
2. Rim Rock Trail
3. Inspiration Point Trail
4. Greenbelt Bikeway
5. Virgil L. Gilman Nature Trail
6. Starved Rock State Park Trail System
7. Red Cedar Hiking Trail
8. Camp Camfield Nature Trail
9. Roby Recreation Trail
10. Eberley Park Fit-Trail
11. Lake Forest Bike Trail
12. Shag Bark Nature Preserve Trail
13. Great Western Trail
14. Chief Illini Trail

For additional information on this program contact: National Park Service, Midwest Regional office, 1709 Jackson Street, Omaha, Nebraska 68102.

(Source: Modified from National Park Service, "Directory of Sources of Trails Information.")

Appendix G

Where to Order Maps for Illinois

The U.S.G.S. publishes a series of standard topographical (topo) maps for Illinois. The unit of survey is a quadrangle bounded by parallels of latitude and meridians of longitude. U.S.G.S. topo maps may be ordered from:

> U.S. Geological Survey
> Earth Science Information Center
> 1400 Independence Rd.
> Rolla, Missouri 65401

> or:

> U.S. Geological Survey, Map Sales
> Box 25286, Federal Center
> Denver, Colorado 80225

Topo maps for Illinois may also be ordered from the Illinois State Geological Survey at:

> Illinois State Geological Survey
> Natural Resources Building
> 615 East Peabody Drive
> Champaign, Illinois 61820

Topo maps may also be purchased at selected sporting or camping goods stores throughout the state.

The Illinois Department of Transportation (IDOT) prepares and publishes various special-purpose state, county, township and city maps that are available for sale to the general public. A description of the maps available for Illinois and their prices may be obtained from IDOT at the following address:

> Map Sales
> Illinois Department of Transportation
> 2300 Dirksen Parkway
> Springfield, Illinois 62764

The Quad Maps for the Shawnee National Forest may be obtained by contacting one of the following Forest Service offices:

Forest Supervisor
Shawnee National Forest
901 South Commercial
Harrisburg, Illinois 62946

District Ranger
Shawnee National Forest
Elizabethtown, Illinois 62931

District Ranger
Shawnee National Forest
Jonesboro, Illinois 62952

District Ranger
Shawnee National Forest
Murphysboro, Illinois 62966

District Ranger
Shawnee National Forest
Vienna, Illinois 62995

Appendix H

Illinois Map Reference Libraries

Many libraries maintain reference files of the published maps of the United States Geological Survey (U.S.G.S.). In Illinois, U.S.G.S. topo maps are deposited and may be viewed in the libraries listed below:

Aurora: Aurora Public Library
Carbondale: Morris Library, Southern Illinois University
Charleston: Library, Eastern Illinois University
Chicago: Chicago Public Library
Library, Loyola University of Chicago
Library, University of Chicago
Library, University of Illinois at Chicago
The John Crerar Library, Illinois Institute of Technology in Chicago
De Kalb: Northern Illinois University Library
Edwardsville: Library, Southern Illinois University
Elgin: Gail Borden Public Library
Evanston: Northwestern University Library
Galesburg: Knox College Library
Kankakee: Library, Olivet Nazarene College
Macomb: Map Library, Western Illinois University
Monmouth: Library, Monmouth College
Normal: Illinois State University Library
Peoria: Peoria Public Library
Rock Island: Augustana College Library
Springfield: Illinois State Library
Urbana: University of Illinois Library

(Source: "U.S.G.S. Illinois Map Index, 1979")

Appendix I

Telephone Numbers for Weather Forecasts for Selected Areas in Illinois

The following phone numbers may be used by hikers to find out the weather conditions and forecasts for certain areas in Illinois.

Chicagoland forecast—708/298-1413
Moline—Quad Cities and surrounding area—
   309/799-8164
Peoria area forecast—309/697-8620
Rockford area forecast—815/963-8518
St. Louis and area forecast—314/928-1198
Springfield area forecast—217/492-4949

Appendix J

Other Hiking Trails in Illinois

The following list of hiking trails and distances was compiled by the authors by writing to the park or organization or by telephone. The appendix is divided into three sections: northern, central, and southern Illinois. Each trail has either the park or trail name, trail owner/administrator, and the trail length. These trails include Boy Scout and Girl Scout trails, state parks, forests, conservation areas and nature preserves, forest preserves, county and city parks, not-for-profit parks, and conservation districts. (Note: Short trails were not measured, but were listed or described as less than 4 miles in length.)

Northern Illinois

Chicago Lake Front Path, Chicago Park District, 20-mile trail

Oxpojke Trail, Bishop Hill Heritage Ass., 11-mile trail

Boone County Bicentennial Heritage Trail, Boone County Bicentennial Commission, 30-mile trail

Sac–Fox Trail, Boy Scouts, 15-mile trail

Black Hawk Trail, Boy Scouts, 20-mile trail

Kishawaukee–Barb/Wire, Boy Scouts, 10-mile trail

Chief Chicagou Trail, Boy Scouts, 14-mile trail

Mitigwaki Trail, Boy Scouts, 13-mile trail

Veteran Acres, Crystal Lake Park District, short trail

Sannauk, De Kalb Park District (DPD), short trail

Chief Shabbona, DPD, short trail

Russell, DPD, short trail

P.A. Nehring, DPD, short trail

Afton, DPD, short trail

Randall Oaks, DPD, short trail

Crabtree Nature Center, Forest Preserve District of Cook County (FPDCC), 3-mile trail

River Trail Nature Center, FPDCC, 2.5-mile trail

Little Red School House Nature Center, FPDCC, 3-mile trail

Sand Ridge Nature Center, FPDCC, 3.5-mile trail

Arie Crown Forest Preserve, FPDCC, 3.2-mile trail

Fullersburg Forest Preserve, Forest Preserve District of Du Page County (FPDDC), 1.5-mile trail

Nelson Lake, Forest Preserve District of Kane County (FPDKC), short trail

Burnidge Forest Preserve, FPDKC, short trail

Tyler Creek Forest Preserve, FPDKC, short trail

Campton Forest Preserve, FPDKC, short trail

Lone Grove Forest Preserve, FPDKC, short trail

Oakhurst Forest Preserve, FPDKC, short trail

Trail of the Old Oakes, Forest Preserve District of Will County (FPDWC), short trail

Heritage Trail, FPDWC, short trail

Goodenon Grove Forest Preserve, FPDWC, short trail

Plum Creek Nature Center, FPDWC, short trail

Nettle Creek Nature Trail, Illinois Department of Conservation (IDOC), short trail

Johnson Sauk Trail State Park, IDOC, 4-mile trail

Apple River State Park, IDOC, 5 trails, 1 mile each

Lowden State Park, IDOC, 2 trails, 1.5 mile each

White Pines State Forest, IDOC, 4 miles of trails

Morrison Rockwood State Park, IDOC, 3.5 miles of trails

Silver Spring State Park, IDOC, 3.5-mile trail

Chain of Lakes State Park, IDOC, 2 trails, 4 miles of trails

Black Hawk State Park, IDOC, short trail

Volo Bog State Park, IDOC, 3-mile trail

Franklin Creek State Preserve Area, IDOC, 3 trails, 1 mile each

Illini State Park, IDOC, 3-mile trail

Old School Forest Preserve, Lake County Forest Preserve District (LCFPD), 5.5-mile trail

Greenbelt Forest Preserve, LCFPD, 4-mile trail

Spring Bluff Preserve, LCFPD, 2.5-mile trail

Old School Preserve, LCFPD, 3-mile trail

Van Patten Woods, LCFPD, 3-mile trail

Harrison–Benwell, McHenry County Conservation District (MCCD), 2-mile trail

Burrow's Woods, MCCD, 3-mile trail

Marengo Ridge, MCCD, 3.5-mile trail

Queen Anne Prairie, MCCD, short trail

Deep Cut Marsh, MCCD, short

Rush Creek Conservation Area, MCCD, 3-mile trail

Northwoods Park, Morton Park District, 3 miles of trails

Nature Center Area, Park District of Highland Park, 3 miles of trails

Loud Thunder Forest Preserve, Rock Island County Forest Preserve District, 2-mile trail

Aldeon Nature Trail, Rockford Park District, 1.5-mile trail

Hammel Woods, Will County Forest Preserve District (WCFPD), 3 miles of trails

Messenger Woods, WCFPD, 1-mile trail

Runyon Preserve, WCFPD, short trail

Thorn Creek Woods, WCFPD, 2 miles of trails

Hononegah, Winnebago County Forest Preserve District (WCFPD-2), 1-mile trail

Kieselburg, WCFPD-2, 1-mile trail

Espenscheid, WCFPD-2, short trail

Blackhawk Springs, WCFPD-2, 7.5 miles of trails

Kishwaukee River, WCFPD-2, 1.5-mile trail

Kilbuck Bluffs, WCFPD-2, 1.5-mile trail

Fuller Memorial, WCFPD-2, 3 miles of trails

Severson Dells, WCFPD-2, 3 miles of trails

Seward Bluffs, WCFPD-2, 3 miles of trails

Four Lakes, WCFPD-2, 1-mile trail

Pecatonica River, WCFPD-2, 3 miles of trails

Colored Sands, WCFPD-2, 3 miles of trails

Central Illinois

Rapatuck Trail, Boy Scouts, 16-mile trail

Carl Sandburg Trail, Boy Scouts, 16-mile trail

Lincoln Circuit Trail, Boy Scouts, 16-mile trail

Court House Trail, Boy Scouts, 11-mile trail

Cedar Creek Trail, Boy Scouts, 10-mile trail

Lincoln Trail Hike, Boy Scouts, 16-mile trail

Lake Bloomington, Bloomington Park District, 3-mile trail

Lake of the Woods County Park, Champaign County Park District, short trail

Scovill Gardens, Decatur Park District (DPD), short trail

Wildwood Park, DPD, short trail

Baker Woods, DPD, short trail

Big Creek Riding Center, DPD, short trail

Fairview Park, DPD, short trail

Friends Creek Regional Park, DPD, 2.5 miles of trails

Garman Park, DPD, short trail

Hidden Springs State Forest, IDOC, 5 miles of hiking trails, 17 miles of fire lanes

Peoria and Galena Trail and Coachhead, Girl Scouts, 10-mile trail

Spring Lake Conservation Area, IDOC, 1.8-mile trail

Crawford County Conservation Area, IDOC, 1-mile trail

Turkey Bluffs Fish and Wildlife area, IDOC, 5 miles of trails

Piney Creek Nature Preserve, IDOC, 2 miles of trails
Big River State Forest, IDOC, 4.2 miles of trails, various
    lengths of horse trails
Nauvoo State Park, IDOC, 1.5-mile trail
Beaver Dam State Park, IDOC, 7 miles of trails
Sangchris Lake State Park, IDOC, 3-mile trail
Spittler Woods State Park, IDOC, 3 short trails
Ramsey Lake State Park, IDOC, 2-mile trail
Lincoln Trail State Park, IDOC, short trail
Moraine View State Park, IDOC, 3 miles of trails
Delabar State Park, IDOC, 2 miles of trails
Walnut Point State Park, IDOC, 2.5-mile trail
Sam Parr State Park, IDOC, 2-mile trail
Weldon Springs State Park, IDOC, 4.5 miles of trails
Wolf Creek State Park, IDOC, 9 miles of trails
Henderson County Conservation Area, IDOC, 2 miles of
    trails
Marshall County Conservation Area, IDOC, 3.5 miles of
    trails
Kankakee River State Park, IDOC, 3-mile trail
Iroquis County Conservation Area, IDOC, 2-mile trail
Mascoutin Hiking Trail, IDOC, 3.5-mile trail
Fall Creek Rest Area, IDOC, two 1-mile trails
Coffeen State Fish & Wildlife Area, IDOC, short trail
Weinberg–King State Park, IDOC, 2-mile trail
Kinsbury Nature Trail, Kingsburg Park District, 2.5-mile
    trail
Spring Lake Park, Macomb Park District, 3.5-mile trail
Fort Daniel Conservation Area, Macon County
    Conservation District (MCCD), 1.5-mile trail
Griswold Conservation Area, MCCD, short trail
Detweiller Park, PPD, short trail
Robinson Park, PDD, short trail
Natural Lands Area, Putnam County Conservation
    District (PCCD), 1.5-mile trail
Fox Run Conservation Area, PCCD, 1.5-mile trail
Miller–Anderson Woods, PCCD, 1-mile trail
Sangamon State University Nature Trail, Sangamon State
    University, short trail
Wildlife Sanctuary Park, City of Springfield, 1.5-mile
    trail
Gurgens Park, Springfield Park District (SPD), short trail
Lincoln Park, SPD, short trail
Timberbrooke Park, SPD, short trail
Walnut Valley Park, SPD, short trail
Washington Park, SPD, short trail

Spoon River Trail, Spoon River Drive Ass., 55-mile trail
Greenbelt Bikeway, Urbana Park District, 2.5-mile trail
Kennekuk Cove County Park, Vermilion Conservation
    District, 6 short trails

Southern Illinois
    Gordon F. Moore Community Park, Alton Park and
        Recreation Commission, short trail
    South Marcum Recreation Area, Army Corps of
        Engineers, .75-mile trail
    Eagle Trail, Boy Scouts, 10-mile trail
    Lewis and Clark Trail, Boy Scouts, 13-mile trail
    Grafton–Marquette Trail, Boy Scouts, 10-mile trail
    Crab Orchard National Wildlife Refuge, Department of
        the Interior, 1-mile trail
    Sam Dale Lake Conservation Area, IDOC, 3.5-mile trail
    Lusk Creek Canyon Nature Preserve, IDOC, short trail
    Saline County Conservation Area, IDOC, 7 miles of
        trails
    Cave-in-Rock State Park, IDOC, 2 miles of trails
    Fort Massac State Park, IDOC, 4.5 miles of trails
    Fort De Charles Historic Site, IDOC, 3 miles of trails
    Dixon Springs State Park, IDOC, 2 miles of trails
    Eldon Hazlet State Park, IDOC, 3 miles of trails
    Pounds Hollow Recreation Area, U.S. Forest Service,
        3-mile trail
    Stephen Forbes State Park, IDOC, 4.25 miles of trails
    Red Hills State Park, IDOC, 5.5 miles of trails
    Lake Murphysboro State Park, IDOC, 3.5-mile trail
    Wayne Fitzgerrell State Park, IDOC, 1.5-mile trail
    Hamilton County Conservation Area, IDOC, 1-mile trail
    Sam Parr State Park, IDOC, 2 miles of trails
    Kaskaskia River State Fish & Wildlife Area, IDOC,
        12-mile trail
    SIUC Campus Lake Trail, Southern Illinois University at
        Carbondale, short trail
    SIUE Nature Trail, Southern Illinois University at
        Edwardsville, short trail
    Wood River Massacre Historical Trail, Trails
        Incorporated, 10-mile trail

Appendix K

Illinois and National Hiking Organizations

Many of the trails listed in this book are located at parks (both public and private), forest preserve districts, Shawnee National Forest, and other not-for-profit lands. Some of these parks have rangers or park interpreters who offer guided nature trail walks. Other times, various hiking groups or organizations offer hiking outings. Many times the hiker might be interested in joining a local or national hiking club or organization to participate in hiking outings or to help in developing a new trail. This appendix was written for the hiker who wishes to find hiking organizations in Illinois and nationally which offer hiking outings or support other trail activities.

The following list shows the organizations which are involved in sponsoring hiking outings or which support trail-related activities.

A. Illinois Hiking Organizations

Sierra Club, Illinois Chapter, 506 South Wabash, Suite 505, Chicago, Illinois 60605. The Sierra Chapter in Illinois has its headquarters in Chicago and is called the Illinois Chapter. The Illinois Chapter has twenty-three thousand members statewide and offers many hiking outings by the various regional groups. The chapter has fourteen regional groups in Illinois. The following list shows the names of the local groups and the towns where they have their meetings. For additional information on each of these groups contact the chapter office in Chicago.

Regional Group	Town
Blackhawk	Rockford
Chicago	Chicago
Eagle Bluff	Moline
Heart of Illinois	Peoria
Kaskaskia	Belleville
North Suburban	Lake County
Northwest Suburban	Northwestern Suburbs
Piasa Palisades	Alton

Prairie	Champaign-Urbana
River Prairie	Wheaton
Sangamon Valley	Springfield
Sauk–Calumet	Park Forest
Shawnee	Carbondale
Valley of the Fox	Aurora

American Youth Hostels, Inc., 3712 North Clark Street, Chicago, Illinois 60613. The American Youth Hostels is a non-profit volunteer organization which sponsors many recreational activities, including hiking trips.

The Prairie Club, 10 S. Wabash Ave., Chicago, Illinois 60603. The Prairie Club is a not-for-profit organization set up to promote outdoor recreation in the form of walks, outings, camping, and canoeing. In addition, the Club also pursues the preservation of suitable areas in which outdoor recreation may be increased, such as the establishment and maintenance of camps.

Illinois Department of Conservation, Division of Land Management, 600 N. Grand Ave., Springfield, Illinois 62702. Each spring the Department offers spring volk walks at their state parks. These walks are family oriented and provide all age groups an inexpensive way to enjoy some of the state parks in Illinois. For more information on the state parks which are participating in this program, contact the Department.

Rails-to-Trails Conservancy, Illinois Chapter, 319 West Cook Street, Springfield, Illinois 62704. The Rails-to-Trails Conservancy (RTC) is committed to the conversion of abandoned railroad rights-of-way into linear parks and the preservation of open space. The Illinois chapter of the RTC works with individuals as well as governmental agencies to achieve its goal. With 5,000 members in Illinois, various activities are planned during the year on rail-trails.

In addition, many local colleges and universities in Illinois have recreation clubs or groups that sponsor organized hiking outings. These colleges and universities may be contacted directly to receive information on their outings.

A source of hiking outings for families with children is through their local scout troops. Both the Boy and Girl Scout troops in Illinois sponsor many hiking outings in the state, as well as on many of the trails which are listed in this book.

B. National Hiking Organizations
    Sierra Club Headquarters, 730 Polk Street, San Francisco, California 94109

American Hiking Society, 1015 31st St., N.W., Washington, D.C. 20007

C. Illinois and National Organizations That Either Support,
    Protect, or Expand Trail Activities
The following groups or organizations are involved in many areas of trail support or activities. These include:

American Trails, 1400 Sixteenth Street NW, Washington, DC 20036

Friends of the Rock Island Trail, P.O. Box 272, Peoria, Illinois 61650

Friends of the Constitution Trail, P.O. Box 4494, Bloomington, Illinois 61702

Friends of the Illinois and Michigan Canal National Heritage Corridor, P.O. Box 867, Ottawa, Illinois 61350

Great River Trail Council, P.O. Box 384, Rapid City, Illinois 61278

Gateway Trailnet, 7185 Manchester Road, St. Louis, Missouri 63143

Illinois Department of Conservation, c/o Trail Specialist, 525 S. Second, Room 310, Springfield, Illinois 62701-1787

Illinois Prairie Path, P.O. Box 1086, 616 Delles Road, Wheaton, Illinois 60187

Illinois Parks and Recreation Association, 500 S. Plum Grove Road, Palatine, Illinois 60067

National Campers and Hikers Association, Inc., 4808 Transit Road, Depew, New York 14043

National Park Service, Midwest Regional Office, 1709 Jackson Street, Omaha, Nebraska 68102

The organizations listed in sections A and B also support trail activities, in addition to offering hiking outings.

Selected Bibliography

This reading list is not meant to be exhaustive; rather, it contains works related to the subject and the trail areas which the hiker might find useful.

Bohlen, H. D. *An Annotated Checklist of the Birds of Illinois.* Volume 9. Springfield: Illinois State Museum, 1978.

Bretz, J. H., and S. E. Harris. *Caves of Illinois.* Report of Investigation 215. Urbana: Illinois State Geological Survey, 1961.

Calder, Jean. *Walking. A Guide to Beautiful Walks and Trails in America.* New York: William Morrow and Company, 1977.

Carra, Andrew J. *The Complete Guide to Hiking and Backpacking.* New York: Winchester Press, 1977.

Changnon, Stanley A. *Illinois Weather and Climate Information. Where to Find It.* Circular 123. Urbana: Illinois State Water Survey, 1975.

Changnon, Stanley A., and David Changnon. *Record Winter Storms in Illinois, 1977–1978.* Urbana: Illinois State Water Survey, 1978.

Changnon, Stanley A., and Floyd A. Huff. *Review of Illinois Summer Precipitation Conditions.* Urbana: Illinois State Water Survey, 1980.

Condit, Carlton. *Fossils of Illinois.* Springfield: Illinois State Museum, 1954.

Cote, William E., et al. *Guide to the Use of Illinois Topographic Maps.* Urbana: Illinois State Geological Survey, 1972, revised 1978.

DeLorme Mapping. *Illinois Atlas and Gazetteer.* Freeport, Maine: DeLorme Mapping, 1991.

Dubberdt, Walter F. *Weather for Outdoorsmen.* New York: Charles Scribner's Sons, 1981.

Dunlop, Richard. *Rand McNally Backpacking and Outdoor Guide.* Chicago: Rand McNally, 1981.

Evers, Robert A., and Lawrence M. Page. *Some Unusual Natural Areas in Illinois.* Urbana: Illinois Natural History Survey, 1977.

Fritz, Arnold W. *Lake Shelbyville Fishing Guide.* Springfield: Illinois Department of Conservation, 1971.

George, Jean C. *The American Walk Book. Major Historic and Natural Walking Trails from New England to the Pacific*

Coast. New York: Dutton Publishers, 1978.

Harris, Stanley E., Jr., William C. Horrell, and Daniel Irwin. *Exploring the Land and Rocks of Southern Illinois, A Geological Guide*. Carbondale: Southern Illinois University Press, 1977.

Hoffmeister, Donald F., and Carl O. Mohr. *Fieldbook of Illinois Mammals*. New York: Dover Publications, Inc., 1972.

Howe, Walter A. *Documentary History of the Illinois and Michigan Canal, Legislation, Litigation, and Titles*. Springfield: Illinois Department of Public Works and Buildings, 1956.

Illinois Department of Conservation. *A Directory of Illinois Nature Preserves*. Springfield: Illinois Department of Conservation, 1991.

Illinois Natural History Survey. *The Natural Resources of Illinois*. Special Publication 6. Champaign: Illinois Natural History Survey, 1987.

Illinois State Geological Survey. *Guide to Rocks and Minerals of Illinois*. Sixth Printing. Urbana: Illinois State Geological Survey, 1976.

Irwin, Roderick R., and John C. Downey. *Annotated Checklist of Butterflies of Illinois*. Biological Notes 81. Urbana: Illinois Natural History Survey, 1973.

Jones, Douglas M., et al. *Causes for Precipitation Increase in the Hills of Southern Illinois*. Report of Investigation 75. Urbana: Illinois State Water Survey, 1974.

Jones, G. Almut, and David T. Bell. *Guide to Common Woody Plants of Robert Allerton Park*. Champaign: Stipes Publishing Company, 1976.

Kjellstrom, Bjorn. *Be an Expert with Map and Compass, the Orienteering Handbook*. New York: Charles Scribner's Sons, 1975.

Learn, C. R., and Mike O'Neal. *Backpacker's Digest*. Northfield: DBI Books, Inc., Northfield, Illinois, 1976.

May, George W. *Down Illinois Rivers*. Ann Arbor: Edmund Brothers, Inc., 1981.

Meves, Eric. *Guide to Backpacking in the U.S. Where to Go and How to Get There*. New York: Collier Books, 1979.

Mohlenbrock, Robert H. *Spring Woodland Wildflowers of Illinois*. Springfield: Illinois Department of Conservation, 1980.

———. *Giant City State Park, An Illustrated Handbook*. Springfield: Illinois Department of Conservation, 1981.

———. *The Field Guide to U.S. Natural Forests*. New York: Congdon & Weed, Inc., 1984.

Nixon, Charles M., et al. *Distribution of the Gray Squirrel in Illinois*. Biological Notes 105. Urbana: Illinois Natural History Survey, 1978.

Parmalee, Paul W. *Amphibians of Illinois*. Springfield: Illinois State Museum, 1954.

———. *Reptiles of Illinois*. Springfield: Illinois State Museum, 1955.

Proudman, Robert D., and Reuben Rajala. *AMC Field Guide to Trail Building and Maintenance*. 2nd edition. Appalachian Mountain Club, 1981.

Rockford Map Publishers. *Illinois State Atlas*. Rockford Map Publishers, 1980.

Roos, Herbert H. *A Synopsis of the Mosquitoes of Illinois*. Biological Notes 52. Urbana: Illinois Natural History Survey, 1965.

Roseboom, Donald P., Ralph L. Evans, and Thomas E. Hill. *Effect of Agriculture on Cedar Lake Water Quality*. Urbana: Illinois State Water Survey, 1979.

Runkel, Sylvan T., and Bill F. Alvin. *Wildflowers of Illinois' Woodlands*. Wallace Homestead Book Company, 1979.

Schiffman, Ted, and Susan Lariviere. *Amphoto Guide to Backpacking Photography*. New York: American Photographic Book Publishing, 1981.

Schreiber, Lee. *Backpacking: A Complete Guide to Why, How and Where for Hikers and Backpackers*. New York: Briarcliff Manor, Stein and Day, 1978.

Smith, P. W. *The Fishes of Illinois*. Urbana: University of Illinois Press, 1978.

Tacoma Mountain Rescue Unit. *Outdoor Living: Problems, Solutions, Guidelines*. Tacoma, Washington: Mountain Rescue Unit.

Thomas, Lowell J. *First Aid for Backpackers and Campers: A Practical Guide to Outdoor Emergencies*. New York: Rinehart and Winston, 1978.

Voigt, John W., and Robert H. Mohlenbrock. *Prairie Plants of Illinois*. Springfield, Illinois.

Voss, John, and Virginia S. Eifert. *Illinois Wild Flowers*. Springfield: Illinois State Museum, 1951.

William, H. B. *Geology Along the Illinois Waterway—A Basis for Environmental Planning*. Circular 478. Urbana: Illinois State Geological Survey, 1973.

Wilson, John W., and A. Stanley Changnon. *Illinois Tornadoes*. Circular 103. Urbana: Illinois State Water Survey, 1971.

Winterringer, Glen S. *Poison Ivy and Poison Sumac*. Springfield: Illinois State Museum, 1963.

Winterringer, Glen S., and Alvin C. Opinot. *Aquatic Plants of Illinois*. Springfield: Illinois State Museum, 1966.

Wright, A. G. *Common Illinois Insects and Why They Are Interesting*. Springfield: Illinois State Museum, 1955.

Walter G. Zyznieuski is supervisor of environmental programs for City Water, Light and Power, a municipal utility of Springfield, Illinois, and a board member of Rails-to-Trails Conservancy of Illinois. He has written a number of environmental research reports while employed by the State of Illinois and has had articles published in periodicals. He has a B.S. degree in environmental planning from Southern Illinois University at Carbondale and has completed course work for an M.A. degree in environmental administration from Sangamon State University.

George S. Zyznieuski is a sales engineer for Hunter Douglas, Inc., Window Fashions Division, in Broomfield, Colorado. He has a B.S. degree in industrial technology from Illinois State University.